# This Was San Francisco

BOOKS BY OSCAR LEWIS

*The Big Four*
*Silver Kings*
*Bonanza Inn (with Carroll D. Hall)*
*Sea Routes to the Gold Fields*
*High Sierra Country*
*California Heritage*
*Bayside Bohemia*
*Sagebrush Casinos*
*Here Lived the Californians*
*The Autobiography of the West*
*George Davidson: Pioneer West Coast Scientist*
*Fabulous San Simeon*
*The War in the Far West, 1861–1865*
*I Remember Christine* (novel)
*The Uncertain Journey* (novel)
*The Lost Years* (fantasy)
*Hawaii: Gem of the Pacific* (juvenile)
*The Story of California* (juvenile)
*The Story of Oregon* (juvenile)
*This Was San Francisco*

# This Was San Francisco

BEING FIRST-HAND ACCOUNTS OF THE EVOLUTION
OF ONE OF AMERICA'S FAVORITE CITIES

Compiled and Edited by

OSCAR LEWIS

DAVID McKAY COMPANY, INC.

NEW YORK

THIS WAS SAN FRANCISCO

COPYRIGHT © 1962 BY OSCAR LEWIS

PUBLISHED SIMULTANEOUSLY IN THE DOMINION OF CANADA

FIRST EDITION

LIBRARY OF CONGRESS CATALOG CARD NUMBER: 61–18348

MANUFACTURED IN THE UNITED STATES OF AMERICA

# Foreword

ONE WHO undertakes to compile an anthology of writings pertaining to San Francisco faces a difficult assignment. For from its beginnings the city has been something of a maverick; at almost no stage of its evolution has it been content to follow conventional patterns. Thus the anthologist who hopes to make clear those elements that have given the city its unique flavor must select his material with care.

There is a great deal of material from which to choose. During its brief history (not until 1835 was the first house put up on Yerba Buena Cove) hundreds of writers have found the city a tempting subject, and have written about it, always with enthusiasm and usually at length. The result is that for well over a century books, pamphlets, newspaper and magazine articles have been flowing from the presses in such number as to constitute an embarrassment of riches.

Out of this mass of material how is one to choose that which makes clear the qualities that have been characteristic of the city from its beginnings? On what basis must the selections be made?

The aim here has been to emphasize those phases that have long set San Francisco apart from other cities. Many things have combined to give it the individuality and charm it possesses today—climate, the beauty of its site, its heritage from Spanish-Mexican days, the mighty influx of gold

v

hunters that transformed it overnight into a city of tents and board shacks, the spectacular advances of the post-gold rush period, the no less spectacular extravagancies of the Comstock era, the profuse flowering of artistic and literary talent in the nineties and early 1900's; finally, the cat-astrophic visitation of April 18, 1906, which marked the end of the old city and the beginning of the new.

Several other matters have influenced the choice of material. First, it has been decided to quote sparingly from those writings that are already well known to many San Franciscans. The omission of those has permitted the in-clusion of certain works that have long been buried in the pages of little-known books or in the files of local dailies and weeklies, and which well deserve to be remembered.

It should be emphasized, too, that with few exceptions the material here reprinted is by men or women who wrote from firsthand knowledge—who were present either as observers or as participants at the events they described. It is felt that such narratives, set down while the happenings were fresh in their minds—and frequently while they were still in progress—serve to re-create the past much more vividly than those of later commentators.

Mention also should be made of the length of the passages quoted. These have been kept brief; rarely do they run more than half a dozen pages. This has permitted the inclusion of a greater variety of material and made it possible to cover certain little-known but significant aspects of the com-munity life that would otherwise have had to be omitted. Also in the interest of brevity, the compiler has not hesitated to exclude from quoted material passages of doubtful perti-nency, or those that are fully covered elsewhere on these pages.

Two final points. So far as possible the material has been

arranged in chronological order, with items dealing with like phases of the city's evolution grouped under common headings. Finally, because to bring the story down to date would have made the book overlong, no attempt has been made to describe events of the past half century; the narrative ends with the destruction of the old town by the earthquake and fire of 1906.

A list of sources, and acknowledgments to institutions and individuals, will be found at the end of the volume.

OSCAR LEWIS

*San Francisco*

# Contents

# Illustrations

*(between pages 148 and 149)*

Map of early California missions
Yerba Buena (now San Francisco) in spring, 1837
San Francisco celebrates California's admission to the Union
Lincoln obsequies, 1865
San Franciscans watch the doomed city
Early-day fire-fighting apparatus
The Mission Dolores, founded in 1776
The Tivoli Theater
Fort Gunnybags, 1856
Medal worn by the Vigilantes
View of the city in 1856
Montgomery Street in 1856
The Palace Hotel
The Montgomery Block
Early-day cable car
Henry Casebolt's "Baloon Car"

# Illustrations

# Part One

# Farthest Frontier
# 1776–1847

i

T HE DISCOVERY of San Francisco Bay was curiously
delayed. For, although the ships of pioneer explorers
had been plying the waters of the North Pacific since the
middle of the sixteenth century, well over two hundred
years passed before the first white man laid eyes on this,
one of the world's most magnificent harbors.

The fact that the early-day navigators—Cabrillo in
1542, Drake in 1579, Cermeño in 1595, and Vizcaíno six
years later—failed to discover the bay was mainly due
to two circumstances: first, because the high hills on
both sides of the Golden Gate all but completely shut off
the view of the bay from the seaward side and, second,
because at most seasons of the year the narrow channel
is often so obscured by fog as to be invisible from ships
passing at any distance offshore.

It was not until well past the middle of the eighteenth
century—by which time the British colonies on the far
side of the continent were already preparing to throw
off the yoke of the mother country—that the discovery
was made. Meanwhile, in 1769, on orders of the Marquis
de Croix, the Viceroy of New Spain, an expedition was
dispatched from Mexico charged with establishing permanent settlements in what is now California. This first

party of colonists reached San Diego on April 29 of that year. Two months later Father Junípero Serra founded the mission of San Diego de Acalá, the first of twenty-one such establishments that presently extended north-ward as far as Sonoma.

In charge of the expedition—which had for its purpose the founding not only of missions but of military posts, or presidios—was Gaspar de Portolá, a captain in the Spanish army, and it was while carrying out his assign-ment that Portolá, in the fall of 1769, led his party north to the vicinity of the bay. He was in search of a harbor where, in 1595, Cermeño's ship, the *San Augustín,* had been lost—the spot now known as Drake's Bay, which lies some twenty-five miles north of the Golden Gate.

During their long march up the coast, Portolá's party—which included, besides himself, two Franciscan priests, several officers, and twenty-seven soldiers, muleteers, and Christianized Indians—missed (or failed to recog-nize) Monterey Bay, and pushed on in quest of the spot described by Cermeño. On this leg of their journey the group was beset by many difficulties. Not only was the terrain rugged in the extreme, but fall rains and an acute shortage of food added to their discomfort. At the begin-ning of November camp was made at a spot somewhere to the north of Half Moon Bay while a party of scouts, under Sergeant José Francisco Ortega, was sent to explore the country ahead.

During the absence of Ortega and his scouts, a party of hunters set off in search of game for their half-starved companions, and it was this group that made the momen-tous discovery. For on reaching the crest of a ridge of

hills to the north of the main camp, they looked down on
what Fray Juan Crespi, the historian of the expedition,
described as "a very large and fine harbor, such as not
only all the navy of our most Catholic Majesty but those
of all Europe could take shelter in it." Portolá, however,
seems to have regarded the great bay only as an obstacle
that would prevent his further progress. Accordingly,
when Ortega returned and reported his failure to find a
feasible route to Cermeño's landing place, the leader
ordered his expedition to turn about and return to San
Diego.

The presence of the great, landlocked bay having been
made known to the authorities in the south, preparations
presently got under way to occupy the spot and to establish a mission and a presidio on its shores. Consequently,
in the summer of 1776, a second expedition headed
northward. In the party, commanded by Lieutenant
José Moraga, were a sergeant, two corporals, and ten
soldiers (some of the latter with their wives and families), together with seven families of settlers, and two
priests. One of the latter, Father Francisco Palou, kept a
journal of the expedition, and it is from it that the following is quoted:

On the 27th day of June the expedition arrived in the
neighborhood of the harbor, and the commander ordered
the party halted on the bank of a lagoon called "Nuestra
Señora de los Dolores," which is in sight of the bay of Los
Llorones and the beach of the bay or arm of the sea which
runs to the southeast, with the intention of waiting here for
the bark [which had earlier been dispatched from Monterey]
in order to select the spot for the founding of the fort and

presidio, and in the meantime to explore the land. On the following day he ordered a shelter of branches built to serve as a chapel in which to celebrate the holy sacrifice of the Mass. . . .

As soon as the expedition halted, the heathen of the neighboring villages came to the camp, attracted by the novelty of seeing such neighbors in their country. They came to visit us frequently, bringing their rude gifts of mussels and wild seeds, which were always reciprocated with beads and some of our food, to which they soon took a liking, except the milk, which they did not wish to taste.

These natives are well formed, many of them being bearded, bald, and rather ugly, for they have a habit of pulling out the hair of their eyebrows by the roots, which makes them ugly. They are poor, and have no houses except little fences made of branches to shelter them somewhat from the heavy winds which prevail. . . . The men go totally naked, though here and there one covers his shoulders with a sort of little cape of beaver skins and pelican feathers. The women cover themselves only with plaited tules, for very few skins of animals are seen among them.

For an entire month the expedition remained in that camp, which was composed of field tents, waiting for the *San Carlos*. Meanwhile soldiers, citizens, and servants employed themselves in cutting logs in order to have this much done when the vessel should arrive. The lieutenant busied himself in exploring the land in the vicinity, where he found some springs of water, lagoons, pastures, and good sites for all kinds of stock. Near the white cliff he found two springs of water sufficient for the use of the presidio, and not far from them he found a good plain which was in sight of the harbor and entrance, and also of its interior. As soon as he saw the spot the lieutenant decided that it was suitable for the presidio, but he delayed moving the people there, as he was waiting day by day for the packet.

On her trip up the coast the *San Carlos* encountered contrary winds, and it was not until the middle of August that she dropped anchor inside the harbor.

As soon as the bark was made fast [Father Palou's narrative continues], the commander, pilots, and Father Necodal went ashore. When they saw the site of the camp they were all of the opinion that it was a very suitable place for the fort and presidio, and they thought the same of the site of the Laguna de los Dolores for the mission. In view of the opinion of the captain of the bark and the pilots, work was begun on the building of the houses and the presidio. A square measuring ninety-two *varas* each way was marked out for it, and divisions for church, royal offices, warehouses, guardhouse, and houses for soldiers and settlers, a map of the plan being formed and drawn by the first pilot. . . .

The work on the presidio being now under way, Captain Don Fernando Quiros came to the site of the mission, accompanied by the chaplain, a pilot, the surgeon, and six sailors, to aid in building a church or chapel in which to celebrate Mass and a room to live in. With this assistance the buildings were begun, and everything progressed so well that by the middle of September the soldiers had their houses already made of logs, all with flat roofs; the lieutenant had his govenment house; and the warehouse was finished of the same material, large enough to store all the provisions brought by the bark.

It was then decided that the formal act of possession should take place, the day appointed being that on which our Mother Church celebrates the impression of the stig-

mata of Our Seraphic Father San Francisco, that is, the
17th of September, a most appropriate day, since he is the
patron of the harbor, the new presidio, and the mission. And
for taking formal possession of the mission, the 4th of October
was designated, which is the day dedicated to Our Seraphic
Father San Francisco. The commander of the packet, his
two pilots, and the greater part of the crew were present at
the ceremony of taking formal possession, only those who
were absolutely necessary remaining on board; and with
the people from the presidio, troops as well as citizens, they
made up a goodly number.

## ii

THE FIRST capital of Spanish California was Monterey,
more than a hundred miles to the south of San Francisco's new mission and presidio, and it was at Monterey
and at the older stations farther south that the life of
the province centered. The consequence was that for the
first several decades after their founding the local establishments remained remote and unimportant outposts.
The garrison at the presidio rarely numbered more than
a squad or two of soldiers. The mission, too, failed to
grow and prosper. A lack of arable land in the area
caused the original group of settlers to move to the fertile Santa Clara Valley, where the pueblo of San José
Guadalupe was established in 1777.

A revealing picture of the deplorable condition into
which the local mission and presidio had been allowed
to fall is to be found in the report of Count Nikolai Reza-

nov, agent for the Russian czar, who brought his ship, the *Juno*, into the bay in the spring of 1806. One purpose of Rezanov's visit was to buy provisions for the Russian fur trading post at Sitka, Alaska, the inhabitants of which were then in desperate straits for lack of food. In this errand he was successful—mainly, it was said, because the dashing Rezanov succeeded in winning the love of Doña Concepción, fifteen-year-old daughter of the commandant of the local presidio, José Dario Arguello—a romantic episode of early California that has long been celebrated in verse and fiction.

Of the *Juno's* arrival in the bay, Rezanov wrote:

Embracing at once the opportunity offered by a favoring wind and tide to enter the port of San Francisco the following morning (April 6), and the suspicious nature of the Spanish government being known to me, I thought it best to go straight through the gate and by the fort.

As we neared the fort a great commotion was observed among the soldiers, and when abreast of it one of them asked, through a speaking trumpet, "What ship is that?" "Russian," we replied. They shouted to us several times to anchor, but we merely replied, "Sí, Señor!" and simulated an active effort to comply with their demands, but in the meantime we had passed the fort and were running up the *puerto*. At a cannon shot's distance we complied.

Some twenty horsemen, among whom were the *comandante* and one *misionero*, soon after demanded the surrender of the ship, but we were not alarmed as their cavalry was within reach of our grapeshot. I dispatched Lt. Davidov to inform them that I was the Russian officer of whose coming I hoped they had been notified; that I should have proceeded to Monterey had not my ship been damaged by storms,

which compelled me to seek shelter in the first port; that I
should leave as soon as the repairs were made.

The answer came back that orders had been received
from the Spanish sovereign to render us all necessary
assistance, and that the *comandante* invited me to dine with
him at the Presidio. I thereupon went ashore and was met
by Don Luis Arguello, son of the *comandante,* temporarily
in command in the absence of his father.

Don Luis informed me with marked courtesy and tact
that he must send a courier to the *gobernador* at Monterey,
the capital, to advise him of my arrival. By this same courier
I also sent a letter in which I thanked the *gobernador* for
his gracious manifestations of hospitality, and informed him
that as soon as the vessel was repaired I should leave for
Monterey. His reply was framed in the most courteous
terms. He would not permit me to go to so much trouble;
he would undertake the journey himself the following day,
and he stated that he had sent orders that I should be
assisted in everything.

Having reported these polite exchanges, the Russian
commented:

Thereupon I recognized the suspicious nature of the
Spanish government, which at every point prevents foreign
visitors from gaining a knowledge of the interior of their
country, and from observing the weakness of their military
defenses.

Of the beginnings of his romance with the charming
Doña Concepción, Rezanov wrote:

While awaiting the arrival of the *gobernador* we made
visits daily to the residence of the hospitable Arguellos, and
soon became on intimate terms with them. Loveliest of the

lovely sisters of Don Luis, the *comandante temporal*, the Doña Concepción is the universally recognized beauty of Nueva California, and your excellency will concur with me that our past sufferings were thus delightfully requited, and our time was passed very joyously. (Pardon me, gracious sir, that in such a serious report I mingle something of the romantic—but I must be very sincere.)

Pleasant as was this romantic interlude, the visitor did not permit it to interfere with the missions that had brought him to California; namely to promote trade between the Spanish province and the Russian settlement to the north—and incidentally to learn what he could of how strong were its military defenses. Accordingly, on the arrival of Governor Arrillago some ten days after the *Juno's* appearance in the bay, Rezanov at once sought an interview.

When I had disclosed myself personally to him [he reported], I proceeded to tell him that my presence in Nueva California had for its primary object the welfare of the American possessions of both Russia and Spain, and, entering at once into the matter, I impressed upon his mind the wants of Nueva California, as well as those of the Russian colonies, which could be supplied by mutual commercial intercourse; that only in that way could lasting bonds of comity be established between the courts of both countries; that the American colonies of both would flourish, and that our coasts would form a bond between us which would always be equally protected by both powers, and that nobody would dare to settle in the unoccupied territory between us. . . .
I frankly tell you we need breadstuffs. These we can

procure at Canton, but Nueva California being nearer to us, and having a surplus that it cannot sell, I came here to negotiate with you with a view to purchase. Assuredly we can agree upon the preliminary conditions, and send them to our respective courts for examination and approval. That is the true motive of my voyage, and I respectfully ask you to decide speedily in the matter, so that I shall not lose valuable time.

The upshot was that the persuasive Russian gained his major objective; that is, he was allowed to purchase a full cargo of grain and other foodstuffs to carry back to his hungry countrymen at Sitka. He was able to accomplish this—notwithstanding the fact that the Spanish authorities were under strict orders not to trade with foreigners—mainly because of the influence of the Arguello family and in particular of the fair Concepción. Of this charming ally Rezanov wrote:

Associating daily with and paying my addresses to the beautiful Spanish señorita, I could not fail to perceive her active, venturesome disposition and character, her unlimited and overweening desire for rank and honors, which, with her age of fifteen years, made her, alone among her family, dissatisfied with the land of her birth. She always referred to it jokingly; thus, as "a beautiful country, a warm climate, an abundance of grain and cattle—and nothing else."

I described Russia to her as a colder country, but still abounding in everything, and she was willing to live there, and at length I imperceptibly created in her an impatient desire to hear something more explicit from me, and when I proffered my hand she accepted.

My proposal was a shock to her parents, whose religious

upbringing was fanatical. The difference in religion, besides the prospective separation from their daughter, was, in contemplation, a dreadful blow to them.

They sought the counsel of the *misioneros,* who did not know what to do. The parents forced their daughter to church and had her confessed. They urged her to refuse me, but her brave front finally quieted them all. The holy padres decided to leave the final decision to the throne of Rome.

Thus when Rezanov sailed away to the north it was with the understanding that he would presently return and claim the hand of his inamorata. From Sitka he crossed to Kamchatka and began the long journey to St. Petersburg to report on the success of his expedition and presumedly to ask the czar's permission to the marriage. But while crossing Siberia he sickened and died, and Doña Concepción, after years of waiting for his return, eventually abandoned hope. Thereupon she became a nun and, in the best romantic tradition, is said to have devoted her remaining years to easing the lot of the friendless and poor.

### iii

MUCH OF what we know today of life on the peninsula during the first half century after the founding of the mission and the presidio is due to the ships of foreign nations that from time to time dropped anchor in the bay. For in nearly every case some sort of record was kept, either day-by-day entries in the ship's log or the more detailed accounts of captain, supercargo, crew member, or passenger.

One such narrative—which has recently come to light —is the journal of a sailor on the British sloop-of-war *Racoon,* which during the War of 1812 was dispatched to the West Coast under orders to seize John Jacob Astor's fur trading post at the mouth of the Columbia River. The ship reached Astoria late in 1813, only to learn that the post had been sold to the Canadian Fur Company. On leaving that port to prey on United States shipping in the Pacific, the *Racoon* was damaged while crossing the Columbia River bar and put in at San Francisco Bay for repairs. There the visitors were hospitably received at both presidio and mission, and during their weeks-long stay made the most of such amusements as the place afforded.

The author (whose name is unknown) evidently served as captain's clerk. For all its crudities, his journal—which is quoted verbatim—throws interesting light on certain phases of the life of the period. The entry for March 16, 1813, reads:

We went every day on Shore, the Officers to ride, as there were plenty of horses, and the men also, on Sundays, and that was quite enough for them, for the fatigue which Jack endured with his horse for that day was more than he now suffered the whole week. It certainly was truly laughable to see us all mounted, as we called it, on a field day, which was always Sundays. . . .

After being all mounted we generally steered for the

Mission, which was about 3 miles, sand knee deep all the
way, and I assure you quite enough for Jack and his horses,
for no sooner [was] Jack on his horse than the horse was on
the move, and he continued until the rider was thrown,
which was soon the case with some of them. Our object
was in forming a straight line and wheeling from right to
left, keeping our respective stations at a full Gallop. We
first commenced with a walk, then with a Gallop, which we
all performed by some means or other tolerable well; but
when the word was given to alter our pace to a walk again,
it was sad work for all hands. . . . Those that would not
stop put their riders in a worse perdicument than those that
did, and truly it was a laughable scene for any looker on
to see Jack grinning and holding on, some round the horse's
neck, some holding of the tail, others the saddle, Jack losing
all command of the helm. . . .

Thus we were put into confusion, arriving at the Mission
one by one, some an hour after the others, which pleased
the old Fathers much, who were always glad to see us,
and always had the table spread for us to refresh, whenever
we called.

Another of the visitors' favorite pastimes was hunting
for what the writer called "foxes," but which were probably California coyotes, then numerous on the peninsula.

After taking a snack, those that had not had enough . . .
would proceed to the Downs, beyond the Mission [for]
Fox hunting, which was my favorite sport. This place
abounded in those animals, who would stand and Stare you
in the face untill you came close to them; then they would
start. The slyest rascals I ever saw, they were exceedingly
large and being so numerous, attack the oxen and horses
which run wild. But the Spaniards are so cursedly lazy that

they would rather see them come into their houses than exert themselves to destroy them.

We generally kept this up till we all got separated, for some would take after one Fox and others after another, or till our company became small, on account of our horses being knocked up, as they were not the first breed. Indeed they were but poorly fed, nothing but the grass they grazed at night, or when they were at rest, which was not often. Though they were so very numerous all around, Jack began to find them scarce latterly. Well enough they may, for it was very rare to see Jack come in with his horse.

## iv

THREE YEARS after the visit of the *Racoon,* another foreign ship, this one flying the flag of the Russian imperial navy, entered the harbor. The *Rurik,* a two-masted brig commanded by Otto von Kotzebue, was on a three-year-long exploring cruise of the Pacific. The little 180-ton craft had left her home port of Kronstadt early in 1815, crossed the South Atlantic, rounded Cape Horn and, after spending some months in the South Seas, had headed north, reaching Bering Strait in the summer of 1816. After some time mapping the coast of Alaska, diminishing supplies forced a return to the south.

The *Rurik* spent most of October in the bay. The following excerpts from the narrative of the party's naturalist, Adelbert von Chamisso, tell some of the high lights

of the party's stay. His description of the ship's arrival
follows:

On the afternoon of the 2nd of October, 1816, at four
o'clock, we sailed into the harbor of San Francisco. A great
deal of movement in the fort at the southern entrance to the
channel was apparent. They hoisted their flag; we hoisted
ours, which did not seem to be recognized, and saluted the
Spanish by firing seven times. The salutation was returned
by the same number of shots, less two, according to the
Spanish custom. We anchored before the Presidio, but no
boat started from shore to us, since the Spaniards possess
not a single boat in this glorious water-basin. I was immediately commanded to accompany Lieutenant Schischmareff to
the Presidio. Lieutenant Don Luis de Arguello, Commandant *ad interim,* since the death of the Captain, received us
in an exceptionally friendly manner, and cared for the most
pressing needs of the *Rurik,* by sending fruit and vegetables
on board. On the same evening, he dispatched a courier to
Monterey to apprise the Governor of New California of our
arrival.

The next day, the 3rd, I met the artillery-officer, Don
Miguel de la Gomez, and a padre of the Mission here, who
came on board the ship just as I was going to the Presidio
on a commission for the Captain. I accompanied them on
board; they brought with them the most friendly offers of
aid from the Commandant, and from the wealthier Mission.
The reverend father invited us for the next day, which was
a feast day, to the Mission of San Francisco, and promised
horses in readiness to carry us thither. According to the
express wish of the Captain, we were promptly furnished
with the greatest abundance of beef and vegetables. In the
afternoon, the tent, observatory, and Russian bath were

erected on the shore. In the evening we paid a visit to the Commandant, and eight cannon shot were fired from the Presidio, by way of reception to the Captain.

As a further means of entertaining their guests, the hospitable Californians set about preparations for what had long been one of their favorite spectacles. Of this Chamisso wrote:

A combat between a bear and a bull had been promised to us. On the 21st, ten or twelve soldiers went over to the northern shore, in the shallop of the Mission, in order to capture bears with the lasso. Late in the evening, we could distinctly hear loud cries, which came from the bear hunt on the opposite shore; no bivouac fires, however, could be seen. The Indians must have had remarkably shrill voices.

On the evening of the 22nd, the hunters brought in a small bear. They had also caught a larger one, but so far in the interior, they were unable to bring him to the shore. As for the bear which was to fight on the following day, he remained all night in the shallop, having his head and mouth free, contrary to custom, that he might be fresher for the combat. . . .

On the 23rd, the bear-baiting took place, on the beach. Unwilling and bound as the animals were, the spectacle had in it nothing great or praiseworthy. One pitied the poor beasts, who were so shamefully handled.

The *Rurik's* scribe was a keen observer and his report makes clear the deplorable conditions then existing at the mission and the presidio, a state of affairs brought about by the indifference and neglect of the authorities at Mexico City. Moreover, he presently became aware that considerable friction had developed between the officers at the presidio and the mission padres.

The Captain here, as in Chile, succeeded in making the Commandant and his officers familiar guests at our table [he reported]. We ate on shore, in the tent, and our friends at the Presidio were always promptly on hand. This condition of things arose spontaneously. The misery in which they languished, forgotten and deserted for six or seven years by Mexico, their mother-land, did not permit them to be hosts; and the need felt to pour out their hearts to some one, drove them to us, with whom they live easily and comfortably. They spoke with bitterness of the missionaries, who, with all the lack of provisions, yet lived, having abundance of the produce of the earth. Now that their money was spent, the missionaries would deliver to them nothing without a requisition, and even then only that which was absolutely indispensable to their sustenance; this not including bread or meal; so that for years, without seeing bread, they lived on maize. Even the garrisons, which were in all the missions, for their protection, were provided with necessities only upon requisition. "*Los Señores* are too good," exclaimed Don Miguel (meaning the commandants); "they should insist on supplies." A soldier went further, and complained to us that the commandant would not permit them to press natives from the opposite shore, in order to force them to work for the soldiers, as they did in the missions.

Discontents arose, also, because the new governor of Monterey, Don Pablo Vicente de Sola, had, since his entry upon the duties of his office, set himself in opposition to smuggling, which alone had provided them with the indispensable necessaries.

The *Rurik*'s visit provided the Spanish authorities

with an opportunity to reopen a question that had long
been a matter of contention; namely, the presence of the
Russian settlements at Fort Ross and Bodega, some fifty
miles farther up the coast.

On the 25th of October [wrote Chamisso], Herr Kuskoff,
with several shallops, arrived from Bodega—a clever, and,
with regard to his business, an experienced man. On the
26th, during the morning, the diplomatic conference took
place at the Presidio. Don Pablo Vicente de Sola, Governor
of California, set forth, duly emphasized, the indisputable
right of Spain to the territory of the Russian settlement
occupied by Herr Kuskoff, and demanded that Kuskoff
should evacuate the settlement, as he possessed it only in
opposition to international law. Herr Kuskoff, agent of the
Russian-American Company, and superintendent of the
settlement at Port Bodega, without entering upon the legal
question, which did not concern him, showed the greatest
willingness to evacuate Port Bodega as soon as he was
authorized to do so by his superior, Herr Baranoff, who had
ordered him thither. Thereupon, the Governor demanded
of Herr von Kotzebue to use his authority in the name of the
Emperor and to effect the evacuation of Bodega. The Lieutenant of the Russian Imperial Navy, Captain of the *Rurik*,
Otto von Kotzebue, explained that he was incompetent to
act in the matter, though, otherwise, the right appeared so
clear to him, that its bare announcement only was necessary
to be at once conceded. And so we were just as far advanced
as before.

Thereupon, it was resolved to draft a protocol of the day's
transactions, and the condition of things; the same, in dupli-
cate, to be signed and sealed by all the participants in the

said transactions, that it might reach the hands of both their sovereign majesties—the Emperor of Russia, through the Captain of the *Rurik;* the King of Spain, through the Governor of New California.

The drafting of this document, which was written in Spanish, I, as interpreter, had to supervise. I rejected the first plan, in which something was missing. Then I said to Don Pablo Vicente: "By bringing this matter before the thrones of the high sovereigns, and by expecting the Emperor of Russia himself to remedy this injustice, and to punish his responsible servants, you resign your otherwise incontestable right of self-defense against the intruders, since you find yourself obliged not to forestall the high decisions of the monarchs."

Don Pablo Vicente de Sola had no objections to raise; he praised my judgment, and caused the protocol to be rewritten and, when it was signed on the evening of the 28th at the Presidio, he gave his solemn word of honor to undertake no violent measures against Kuskoff and his settlement at Bodega, and to allow the matter, until the decision of the two courts, to remain *statu quo.* . . .

I do not mean to boast about this development of the affair, for even if the valiant Don Pablo Vicente had not given his solemn promise, he would scarcely have begun hostilities, and undertaken an expedition against the Russian fort at Bodega.

I have heard that the foregoing protocol has not missed its proper destination at St. Petersburg and, without being referred to the Emperor, has been filed with the proper ministerial department. But it is said that to Don Pablo Vicente de Sola, *Gobernador de la Nueva California,* a Russian decoration has been transmitted. I received from Herr

Kuskoff, as a gift of respect, a beautiful sea-otter skin, which may be seen in the Zoological Museum at Berlin, to which I presented it.

It needs only to be added that the Russians retained their settlements at Fort Ross and Bodega for nearly a quarter century longer. It was not until 1842 that they having sold their property to Captain John A. Sutter, withdrew permanently from the province.

The time for our sojourn in California had ended [Chamisso's narrative concludes]. On the 26th day of October, on Sunday, after a ride to the Mission, a feast and a parting dinner were given under our tent. The artillery of the *Rurik* accompanied the toasts to the union of the monarchs and the nations, and the health of the Governor. A good missionary dipped his mantle too deep in the juice of the grape, and reeled visibly under the burden. On the 28th, the camp was broken up, and we again embarked. While we sealed the protocol at the Presidio, Herr Kuskoff, with the knowledge of Herr von Kotzebue, sent two shallops into the rear of the bay, for catching otters.

## V

THE *Rurik* was but one of a number of foreign ships that put into the harbor during the early decades of the nineteenth century. In general the purpose of such visits was not only to replenish supplies but to learn something of the nature and resources of the province and to determine how strongly it was held. It was a period when a number of European nations—England, France, Holland and Russia—were ambitious to extend their holdings in the New World, and all these, as well as the United States, were casting speculative eyes on Alta California and the territory that lay to the north.

Another such visitor was His Britannic Majesty's ship *Blossom*, a 16-gun sloop commanded by Captain Frederick William Beechey and carrying a crew of one hundred. The *Blossom* left Portsmouth on May 19, 1825, bound on an exploring expedition to the North Pacific. After spending the summer of the following year in the vicinity of Bering Strait, the ship dropped down the coast and, on November 6, entered San Francisco Bay.

Beechey's account of the expedition, *A Narrative of a Voyage to the Pacific and Beering's Strait in the Years 1825–28*, was published in London, in two thick volumes, in 1831. The part relating to the California visit occupies the first eighty-seven pages of Volume II, and it is from that chapter that the following is quoted:

When the day broke, we found ourselves about four miles from land. . . . The tops of the mountains, the only part of the land visible, formed two ranges, between which our port was situated, though its entrance, as well as the valleys and the low lands, were still covered with the morning mist condensed around the bases of the mountains. We bore up for the opening between the ranges, anxious for the rising sun to withdraw the veil, that we might obtain a view of the harbor, and form our judgment of the country in which we were to pass the next few weeks. As we advanced, the beams of the rising sun gradually descended the hills, until the

mist, dispelled from the land, rolled on before the freshing
sea wind, discovering cape after cape, and exhibiting a
luxuriant country apparently abounding in wood and rivers.
At length two low promontories, the southern one distinguished by a fort and a Mexican flag, marked the narrow
entrance of the port.

We spread our sails with all the anxiety of persons who
had long been secluded from civilized society, and deprived
of wholesome aliment; but after the first effort of the breeze,
it died away and left us becalmed in a heavy N.W. swell.
. . .

At length a breeze sprung up, and we entered the port,
and dropped our anchor in the spot where Vancouver
[George Vancouver, the English explorer, who several times
visited the bay in the early 1790's] had moored his ship
thirty-three years before. As we passed the entrance, a
heavy sea rolling violently upon a reef of rocks on our left
bespoke the danger of approaching that side too close in
light or baffling winds; while some scattered rocks with
deep water around them skirting the shore on our right,
marked that side also as dangerous; so that the entrance may
justly be considered difficult. Beyond the rocks, however,
near the fort, there is a bay in which, if necessary, ships
may drop their anchor.

The fort, which we passed on our right, mounts nine
guns, and is built upon a promontory on the south side of
the entrance, apparently so near to the precipice, that one
side will, before long, be precipitated over it by the gradual
breaking away of the rock. Its situation, nevertheless, is good,
as regards the defense of the entrance; but it is commanded
by a rising ground behind it. As we passed, a soldier pro-
truded a speaking-trumpet through one of the embrasures,
and hailed us with a stentorian voice, but we could not

distinguish what was said. This custom of hailing vessels has arisen from there being no boat belonging to the garrison, and the inconvenience felt by the governor, in having to wait for a report of arrivals, until the masters of the vessels could send their boats on shore.

The port of San Francisco does not show itself to advantage until after the fort is passed, and then it breaks upon the view, and forcibly impresses the spectator with the magnificence of the harbour. He then beholds a broad sheet of water, sufficiently extensive to contain all the British navy, with convenient coves, anchorages in every part, and, around, a country diversified with hill and dale, partly wooded and partly disposed in pasture lands of the richest kind, abounding in herds of cattle. In short, the only objects wanting to complete the interest of the scene are some useful establishments and comfortable residences on the grassy borders of the harbour, the absence of which creates an involuntary regret that so fine a country, abounding in all that is essential to man, should be allowed to remain in such a state of neglect. So poorly did the place appear to be peopled that a sickly column of smoke rising from within some delapidated walls, misnamed the presidio, or protection, was the only indication we had of the country being inhabited.

Having further described the great extent of the harbor and its adjacent inlets and rivers, the writer continued:

As we opened out the several islands and stopping places in the harbour, we noticed seven whalers at anchor at Sausalito, not one of which showed their colours; we passed them and anchored off a small bay named Yerba Buena, from the luxuriance of its vegetation, about a league distant from

both the presidio and the mission of San Francisco. I immediately went on shore to pay my respects to Don Ignacio
Martínez, lieutenant in the Mexican army, acting governor
in the absence of Don Luis, and to the priest, whose name
was Tomaso, both of whom gave me a very hospitable and
friendly reception, and offered their services in any way
they might be required. Our first inquiries naturally related
to supplies, which we were disappointed to find not at all
equal to what had been reported; in short, it seemed that
with the exception of flour, fresh beef, vegetables and salt,
which might be procured through the missions, we should
have to depend upon the American vessels for whatever
else we might want, or upon what might chance to be in
store at Monterey, a port of more importance than San
Francisco. . . .

It was evident from this report that our supplies were
likely to be very inadequate to our wants, but that no opportunity of obtaining them might be lost, I dispatched Mr.
Collie the surgeon, and Mr. Marsh the purser, overland to
Monterey with Mr. Evans as interpreter, with orders to
procure for the ship what medicines, provisions and other
stores were to be had. . . . The governor politely furnished
a passport and a guard for this service; and our hospitable
friend Tomaso, the padre of the mission, provided horses
for them free of charge. In the meantime we arranged with
a relation of the governor for the daily supply of the ship's
company, an arrangement which it afterwards appeared
increased the jealousy that had long existed between the
presidio and the missions, by transferring to the pocket of
the commandant the profits that would otherwise have been
reaped by the padre.

We were happy to find the country around our anchorage
abounding in game of all kinds, so plentiful, indeed, as

soon to lessen the desire of pursuit; still there were many inducements to both officers and seamen to land and enjoy themselves; and as it was for the benefit of the service that they should recruit their health and strength as soon as possible, every facility was afforded them. Horses were fortunately very cheap, from nine shillings to seven pounds apiece, so that riding became a favorite amusement, and the Spaniards finding they could make a good market by letting out their stud, appeared with them every Sunday opposite the ship, already saddled for the occasion, as this was a day on which I allowed every man to go out of the ship. Some of the officers purchased horses and tethered them near the place, but the Spaniards finding this to interfere with their market, contrived to let them loose. . . . The only difficulty to the enjoyment of this amusement was the scarcity of saddles and bridles, some of which cost ten times as much as a decent horse. The ingenuity of the seamen generally obviated these difficulties, while some borrowed or hired saddles from the natives; for my part, I purchased a decent looking horse for about thirty-five shillings sterling, and on my departure presented it to a Spaniard, who had lent me the necessary accoutrements for it during my stay, which answered the purpose of both parties, as he was pleased with his present, and I had my ride for about a shilling a day: a useful hint to persons who may be similarly circumstanced.

Such of the seamen as would not venture on horseback made parties to visit the presidio and mission, where they found themselves welcome guests with the Spanish soldiers. These two places were the only buildings within many miles of us, and they fortunately supplied just enough spirits to allow the people to enjoy themselves with their friends, without indulging in much excess—a very great advantage in a seaport.

The sadly neglected condition of the presidio and the all but complete isolation of officers and men were thus described by the visitor:

Martínez [Ignacio Martínez, then the acting commandant] was always glad to see the officers at the presidio, and made them welcome to what he had. Indeed, nothing seemed to give him greater pleasure than our partaking of his family dinner; the greater part of which was dressed by his wife and daughters, who prided themselves on their proficiency in the art of cooking. It was not, however, entirely for the satisfaction of presenting us with a well-prepared repast that they were induced to indulge in this humble occupation: poor Martínez, besides his legitimate offspring, had eighteen others to provide for out of his salary, which was then eleven years in arrears. . . .

The governor's abode was in a corner of the presidio, and formed one end of a row, of which the other was occupied by a chapel; the opposite side was broken down, and little better than a heap of rubbish and bones, on which jackals, dogs, and vultures were constantly preying; the other two sides of the quadrangle contained storehouses, artificers' shops, and the gaol, all built in the humblest style with badly burnt bricks, and roofed with tiles. The chapel and the governor's house were distinguished by being whitewashed.

Whether viewed at a distance or near, the establishment impresses a spectator with any other sentiment than that of its being a place of authority, and but for a tottering flag-staff, upon which was occasionally displayed the tri-colored flag of Mexico, three rusty field pieces, and a half-accoutred sentinel parading the gateway in charge of a few poor wretches heavily shackled, a visitor would be ignorant of the

importance of the place. The neglect of the government to
its establishments could not be more thoroughly evinced
than in the dilapidated condition of the buildings in question; and such was the dissatisfaction of the people that
there was no inclination to improve their condition, or even
to remedy many of the evils which they appeared to us
to have the power to remove.

The plain upon which the presidio stands is well adapted
to cultivation; but it is scarcely ever touched by the plough,
and the garrison is entirely beholden to the mission for its
resources. Each soldier has nominally about three pounds a
month, out of which he is obliged to purchase his provision.
If the governor were active, and the means were supplied,
the country in the vicinity of the establishment might be
made to yield enough wheat and vegetables for the troops,
by which they would save that portion of their pay which
now goes to the purchase of these necessary articles.

The garrison of San Francisco [that is, the district of
which San Francisco was the center] consists of seventy-six
cavalry soldiers and a few artillerymen, distributed between
the presidios and the missions, and consequently not more
than half a dozen are at any time on one place. They appear
to be very dissatisfied.

Because medicines and other urgently needed supplies
were not to be had locally, the party presently set sail
for Monterey, where they remained only a short time,
then proceeded to China and Kamchatka, and during
the summer of 1827 resumed their explorations in the
vicinity of Bering Strait. The end of October found them
back at Monterey, and in mid-December they paid a
second visit to San Francisco Bay. Three weeks later, on

January 3, 1828, the *Blossom* sailed out the Golden Gate on the first leg of the long voyage back to England, via Cape Horn.

Of this, their final visit to the port, Beechey wrote:

While we remained in San Francisco refitting the ship, the boats were constantly employed sounding and surveying the harbour, in which duty we received every assistance from Martínez, the governor, who allowed us to enter the forts, and to take what angles and measurements we pleased, requiring only in return for this indulgence a copy of the plan when finished for his own government. . . .

On the 12th of December a salute was fired from the battery; High Mass was said in all the missions, and a grand entertainment, to which all the officers were invited, was given at the presidio, in honour of Santa Señora Guadalupe. There was also to be a fight between a bear and a bull, but for some reason not known to us—probably the trouble required to bring the animal so far, as bears do not come within many miles of the presidio—it did not take place; and we were all greatly disappointed, as we had heard so much of such exhibitions from everybody that our curiosity had been greatly excited. This is a favourite amusement with the Californians, but it is of rare occurrence, as there is much trouble in getting a bear alive to the scene of combat, and there is also some risk and expense attending it. We were informed that when a fight is determined upon, three or four horsemen are dispatched with lassos to the woods where the bears resort, and that when they come to an advantageous spot they kill a horse or a bullock as a bait, and hide themselves in the wood. Sometimes they have to wait a whole day or more before any of the animals appear, but when they come to partake of the food, the men seize a favorable opportunity, and rush upon them at different points with their lassos, and entangle one of them until he is thrown to the ground, when they manage to suspend him between the horsemen, while a third man dismounts and ties his feet together; he is then extended upon a hide and dragged home, during which time it is necessary, they say, to keep him constantly wet to allay his thirst and rage, which amounts almost to madness—and woe to him who should be near if he were to break away from his fastenings. . . .

The bear being caught, two or three men are dispatched for a wild bull, which they lasso in an equally dexterous manner, catching him either by the horns or by whichsoever leg they please, in order to trip him up and retain him between them. It is necessary to begin the fight as soon as the animals are brought in, as the bear cannot be tempted to eat, and is continually exhausting himself in struggling for his liberty. The two animals are then tied together by a long rope, and the battle begins, sometimes to the disadvantage of the bear, who is half dead with exhaustion, but in the end almost always proves fatal to the bull. It is remarkable that all the bears endeavour to seize the bull by the tongue, for which purpose they spring upon his head or neck and first grapple with his nose, until the pain compels the bull to roar, when his adversary instantly seizes his tongue, pierces it with his sharp talons, and is sure of victory. These battles were the everlasting topics of conversation with the Californians, who indeed have very little else to talk about, and they all agreed as to the manner of the fatal termination of the spectacle.

By Christmas day we had all remained sufficiently long in the harbour to contemplate our departure without regret; the eye had become familiar to the picturesque scenery of the bay; the pleasure of the chase had lost its fascination, and the roads to the mission and presidio were grown tedious and insipid. There was no society to enliven the hours, no incidents to vary one day from the other, and to use the expression of Donna Gonzalas, California appeared to be as much out of the world as Kamchatka.

On the 26th, being ready for sea, I was obliged to relinquish the survey of this magnificent port, which possesses almost all the requisites for a great naval establishment, and is so advantageously situated with regard to North America and China, and the Pacific in general, that it will, no doubt, at some future time, be of great importance. We completed the examination of those parts of the harbour which were likely to be frequented by vessels for some years to come, in which it is proper to mention, in order to give as much publicity to the circumstances as possible, that we discovered a rock between Alcatrasses [Alcatraz] and Yerba Buena islands, dangerous to both shipping and boats. . . . [This was "Blossom Rock," named for Beechey's ship. Under this rock, in 1870, twenty-one tons of powder were placed. The resulting explosion, which destroyed it, was witnessed by great crowds on Telegraph Hill and other points of vantage.]

On the 28th we took leave of our hospitable and affable friends, Martínez and Padre Tomaso, full of gratitude for their kindness and attention to our wants; weighed anchor, and bade adieu to the Port of San Francisco, in which we had all received material benefit from the salubrity of its climate, the refreshing product of its soil, and the healthy exercise we had enjoyed there. In the ship's company in particular there was the most apparent amendment; some of them, from being so emaciated on their arrival that the surgeon could scarcely recognize them, were now restored to their former healthy appearance, and we had the satisfaction of sailing without a single case of sickness on board. We had to regret during our stay the loss of one of our best men, Joseph Bowers, a marine. He had accompanied one of the officers on a shooting excursion, and was led by his naturally ardent and bold disposition to plunge into a lake after a wild fowl that had been shot, forgetting that he could not swim. His eagerness led him beyond his depth, and in his attempt to regain his footing, he unfortunately perished before any aid could be brought. His body was interred at the burial ground near the presidio landing place, and was followed to the grave by all the officers. As the coffin was lowering into the ground, the good understanding that existed between the ship's company and the inhabitants was testified in the most gratifying manner, by the latter approaching and performing the last office for the deceased, by dropping the earth in upon his coffin. I cannot recollect ever having met with such conduct in any other foreign port, and the act, most certainly, did not lessen our regard for the inhabitants.

## vi

ALMOST WITHOUT exception, visitors to the bay during the early 1800's were impressed by two things: the size, beauty, and potential importance of the great landlocked harbor and the sadly neglected appearance of the presidio and mission, the area's only inhabited spots.

Another newcomer who shared that view was Philip Leget Edwards, a twenty-five-year-old ex-schoolteacher turned frontiersman, who, with several companions, arrived in the spring of 1837. The party's intention was to buy a herd of the half-wild California cattle and drive them north to the pioneer settlements in the Willamette Valley of Oregon—a difficult feat that they were eventually able to accomplish. The group arrived aboard the brig *Loriot*, which crossed the Columbia River bar on February 10 and reached a point off the Golden Gate three weeks later.

Edwards kept a diary, and in it he thus described the difficult—and dangerous—entry into the harbor:

This morning found ourselves drifting between the Farallone Islands and Sir Francis Drake's Bay, having made little advance during the night. During the day but little wind. At 4 P.M. it became so feeble that we found ourselves drifting with the tide towards the shore of Drake's Bay. There was a short distance below us a reef of rocks which extended as far up as we were. The anchor was thrown out in 13 fathoms of water and after letting out 80 fathoms of chain, our bow was in 9 and our stern in 7 fathoms water. In this unenviable situation night set in with a heavy wind from S.S.E. and rain. Tremendous seas were breaking over our bows, and it was pretty evident even to the inexperienced land lubber that we would not weather it until morning. The violent motions of the vessel had induced so violent a headache that I was fain to retreat from the scene of terror to the cabin. Spreading my pallet on the cabin floor, I fell in a slumber. At 9 o'clock I was aroused by a frightful crashing on deck, and the cry that the cable had parted. All were immediately on deck to assist in throwing out the second anchor, when, to our great satisfaction, we ascertained that only the windlass had capsized. The captain now calling his officers to the quarter-deck declared the ship in danger. Should the other cable fail, there was, he said, no hope the smaller would hold. That therefore the only hope of saving the people was in running the vessel aground in a small bay to the northward, which might possibly be effected, if the reef to the N. W. did not prevent. . . . With the same wind there was, he said, no hope of retaining our hold, for the seas would continue to increase. Unless the wind shifted we must therefore be ready for the worst, and the harsh grating of the chain as a furious sea dashed over the ship's bow and washed her decks . . . augured his apprehensions too rational.

But that kind Providence who had "clothed and fed us all our lives long" did not forsake us. Before 10 o'clock the wind had changed to the N.W., and at 10 we began to draw up our anchor, which, the windlass being useless, we were forced to do with tackles. It is peculiarly trying to labor unsuccessfully when life, perhaps, depends on the issue. It was, however, our fate. The old tackles parted three or four times, and consequently we must lose chain before it could be arrested. In three hours, however, of tugging at the tackles, the anchor was got up and sails unfurled. It required the entire force on board, and my blistered hands could attest my own exertions. The decks were so slippery from the rain that they were necessarily sprinkled with sand, and even then many were our slips and a few falls. Hardly had we got under way, when the stupid Sandwich Islander at the helm, either through inattention or fright, brought the vessel about. She was, however, soon brought right again, and in a few minutes we were considered safe.

Next day the *Loriot* entered the bay and dropped anchor at what was then called Whalers' Harbor, off present-day Sausalito. On March 9 Edwards and a shipmate visited the presidio and the fort that stood at the southern entrance to the bay. His diary entry for that day contains these philosophical comments:

These buildings were erected about fifty-five years ago for the accommodation of the Spanish garrison. The Presidio is a building, the walls of adobes and the roofs of tiles, enclosing a square area, the sides of which are perhaps three hundred feet long. Since the expulsion of the Spaniards in the revolution [of 1821, when Mexico gained its independence from Spain], the place has been going to ruins. One entire side is fallen and parts of the others. All of the outer buildings, of which there were many, are now fallen except one. It is now inhabited by a half dozen families, too indolent to do anything to arrest the progress of decay. A sort of military burlesque is here still supported at times. I found the fort, which once commanded the entrance to the bay in the same ruinous condition. Some of the cannon bore inscriptions dated A.D. 1648. Ruins, however diminutive, are melancholy mementoes of human blindness and folly. These humble ruins, thought I, vie not with those more extensive and magnificent found in the old world, but are equally indicative of debased propensities. I am not gazing upon the ravages of war. These are simply the ravages of time— of a little time! A little circumspection and industry would have averted all. One American colony, supposing itself aggrieved, has dissolved its connection with its transatlantic parent, and assumed a "separate and equal station"—has risen to grandeur and happiness; another, without the same causes of complaint, and without the essential qualifications in itself, ventures upon the same experiment, and sinks down into an anarchy more abhorrent than despotism.

## vii

FOR WELL over half a century after their founding in the mid-1770's, the mission and presidio remained the sole outposts of civilization on the shores of the bay. Not until 1835 was the first house put up on the site of the future city—a spot that Richard Henry Dana, who arrived toward the end of that year aboard the *Pilgrim*, described as "the little harbor, or bight, called Yerba Buena, in which sailing vessels anchor." This lone structure, which Dana called "a shanty of rough boards," stood at approximately the spot where Grant Avenue and Sacramento Street now intersect. It was built by William A. Richardson, a British sea captain. Richardson carried a small stock of merchandise for trading both with the Indians and with Californians engaged in the transport of hides, tallow, and other products between ships in the harbor and the missions and pueblo at the lower end of the bay.

Of this, the first commercial activity of any importance to take place in the area, Dana wrote:

The Mission of Dolores, near the anchorage, has no trade at all; but those of San Jose, Santa Clara, and others situated on the large creeks or rivers, which run into the bay, and distant between fifteen and forty miles from the anchorage, do a greater business in hides than any in California. Large boats, or launches, manned by Indians, and capable of carrying from five to six hundred hides apiece, are attached to the Missions, and sent down to the vessel with hides, to bring away goods in return. Some of the crews of the vessels are obliged to go and come in the boats, to look out for the hides and goods. These are favorite expeditions with the sailors in fine weather; but now, to be gone three or four days, in open boats, in constant rain, without any shelter, and with cold food, was hard service. Two of our men went up to Santa Clara in one of these boats, and were gone three days, during all of which time they had constant rain, and did not sleep a wink, but passed three long nights walking fore and aft the boat, in the open air. When they got on board they were completely exhausted, and took a watch below of twelve hours. All the hides, too, that came down in the boats were soaked with water, and unfit to put below, so that we were obliged to trice them up today, in the intervals of sunshine or wind, upon all parts of the vessel. We got up tricing-lines from the jib-boom-end to each arm of the fore-yard, and thence to mast-heads, from the fore to the main and cross-jack yard-arms. Between the tops, too, and the mast-heads, and from the fore to the main swifters, and thence to the mizzen rigging, and in all directions athwart-ships, tricing-lines were run, and strung with hides. The head stays and guys, and the spritsail-yard, were lined, and, having still more, we got out the swinging-booms, and strung them and the forward and after guys with hides. The rail, fore and aft, the windlass, capstan, and sides of the ship, and every vacant place on deck, were covered with wet hides, on the least sign of an interval for drying. Our ship was nothing but a mass of hides, from the cat-harpins to the water's edge, and from the jib-boom-end to the taffrail. . . .

Having collected nearly all the hides that were to be procured, we began our preparations for taking on a supply of wood and water, for both of which San Francisco is the best place on the coast. A small island, about two leagues from the anchorage, called by us "Wood Island," and by the Mexicans "Isle de los Angelos," was covered with trees to the water's edge; and to this two of our crew . . . were sent every morning to cut wood, with two boys to pile it up for them. In about a week they had cut enough to last us a year, and the third mate, with myself and three others, were sent over in a large, schooner-rigged, open launch, which we hired of the Mission, to take in the wood and bring it to the ship. We left the ship about noon, but owing to a strong wind, and a tide which runs about four or five knots, did not get into the harbor, where the boats lie, until sundown. No sooner had we come-to, when a strong southeaster, which had been threatening us all day, set in, with heavy rain and a chilly air. We were in rather a bad situation: an open boat, a heavy rain, and a long night; for in winter, at this latitude, it was dark nearly fifteen hours. Taking a small skiff, which we had brought with us, we went ashore but discovered no shelter, for everything was open to the rain, and, collecting a little wood . . . and a few mussels, we put aboard again, and made the best preparations in our power for passing the night. . . .

Toward morning the rain ceased, and the air became sensibly colder, so that we found sleep impossible, and sat up, watching for daybreak. No sooner was it light than we went ashore, and began our preparations for loading our vessel. . . . We were not mistaken in the coldness of the weather, for a white frost was on the ground, and—a thing we had never seen before in California—one or two little puddles of fresh water were skimmed over with a thin coat of ice. In this state of the weather, and before sunrise, we had to wade off, nearly up to our hips in water, to load the skiff with wood by armfuls. The third mate remained on board the launch, two more men stayed in the skiff to load and manage it, and all the water-work, as usual, fell upon the two youngest of us, wading forward and back, from the beach to the boat, with armsful of wood, barefooted, and our trousers rolled up. When the skiff went off with her load, we could only keep our feet from freezing by racing up and down the beach on the hard sand, as fast as we could go. We were all day at this work, and toward sundown, having loaded the vessel as deep as she would bear, we hove up our anchor and made sail.

Dana and his companions spent Christmas of 1835 in the harbor, and two days later the *Pilgrim* weighed anchor and got under way.

We sailed down this magnificent bay [he wrote on December 27] with a light wind, the tide, which was running out, carrying us at the rate of four or five knots. It was a fine day, the first of entire sunshine we had had for more than a month. We passed directly under the high cliff on which the presidio is built, and stood into the middle of the bay, from whence we could see small bays making up into the interior, large and beautifully wooded islands, and the mouths of several small rivers. If California ever becomes a prosperous country, this bay will be the center of its prosperity. The abundance of wood and water; the extreme fertility of its shores; the excellence of its climate, which is as near being perfect as any in the world; and its facilities for navigation, affording the best anchoring-grounds in the

whole western coast of America—all fit it for a place of
great importance.

## viii

THE HOUSE Captain Richardson put up on the shore of
Yerba Buena Cove was presently followed by others.
For by the mid-1830's California's abundant resources
had become known in many parts of the world and—
despite efforts of the Mexican authorities to keep them
out—the number of foreigners who settled there increased from year to year. To the newcomers it soon
grew clear that Mexico's hold on the province could not
be much longer maintained, and it became a question
of to which of several nations the rich prize would fall.

It was the declaration of war by the United States
against Mexico on May 13, 1846, that decided the issue.
Thereafter events moved swiftly. On June 14 a group of
Yankee settlers seized the town of Sonoma and set up
the short-lived California Republic. On July 7 Commodore Sloat raised the American flag at Monterey and declared the province a part of the United States, and two
days later the flag was hoisted above the little village of
Yerba Buena.

The passing of California from the control of Mexico
to that of the United States was accomplished with a
minimum of bloodshed, the most serious engagement
being that at San Pascual, in which the casualties on

both sides numbered less than fifty. At Yerba Buena the transfer was made without incident, no opposition being offered to the landing of a detachment from the U.S. ship *Portsmouth* on the morning of July 9, and the raising of the Stars and Stripes on the flagpole of the plaza.

A number of eyewitness accounts of that event have come down to us; one of the liveliest is that of "Filings," a petty officer aboard the *Portsmouth*, who in the early 1850's contributed a number of reminiscent articles to a San Francisco weekly, the *Golden Era*, under the title "Filings from an Old Saw."

The morning of the ninth of July broke bright and beautiful [recalled "Filings"], and long before the sun rose, the crew of the *Portsmouth* were roused from their hammocks, and contrary to usual custom, the decks were left to their own fate for the nonce, for far more important affairs were on the *tapis* than the mere cleaning of decks and scouring of brass. Breakfast was served at six A.M., and the word passed for all hands to clean in white frocks, blue pants, black hats and shoes, and prepare for muster. Breakfast was soon dispatched, for everybody was too much interested in the crowding events of the day to have much appetite, and long before the sound of the drum called us to muster, the boys might be seen each in his respective station around the guns.

Precisely at eight, the drum beat to quarters, and the captain made a speech of (as one of the foretopmen called it) eleven or eight words, which conveyed to us the idea that he, in obedience to orders from the commodore [John D. Sloat], should hoist the Stars and Stripes in the public square that day, and take possession in the name of the United States of America. The first lieutenant then called over a list of carbineers, who were for the nonce to become soldiers and form a part of the city detail. The marines under the command of Lieutenant Watson were in full dress, and every officer of the ship, save two who remained on board to fire a national salute, were to accompany the party.

As soon as the retreat was beaten, the boats were ordered alongside, and the marines and carbineers filed into them. We were landed on what is now Clark's Point, and when all were on shore, formed into sections, and to the soul-inspiring tune of Yankee Doodle from our band, consisting of one drum and fife, with an occasional put-in from a stray dog or disconsolate jackass in the line of march, trudged proudly up through Montgomery Street to Clay, up Clay to the Plaza, and formed a hollow square. Here we rested on our arms, while the aides of the commander in chief disseminated themselves through the town and gathered together some thirty or forty persons of all nations, colors, and languages, and having penned them in the square formed by the soldier-sailors, the captain, putting on all his peculiar dignity, walked up to the flagstaff and gave a majestic nod to his second in command. The first lieutenant gave a similar nod to one of our quartermasters, who came forward, flag in hand, and bent it on the halyards.

This was an eventful moment. Something was about to be done that could not be easily undone, and as I gazed upon that crowd of manly faces, I fancied I could read a settled determination to do or die in defense of the act of this day, should it become necessary. Captain M. [Montgomery] had a proclamation ready prepared, and our first lieutenant now read it to the assembled crowd, and when he finished, gave the signal, and in a moment, amid a roar of cannon from the ship, the hurrahs of the ship's company, the *vivas* of Californians, the cheers of the Dutchmen, and barking of dogs, the braying of jackasses, and the general confusion of sounds from every living thing within hearing, that flag floated proudly up, which has never yet been lowered to mortal foe. When the ceremony was over and the captain had proclaimed himself governor of the northern portion of Upper California, he constituted Lieutenant Watson of the marines as commander of the town of Yerba Buena, and giving him a garrison consisting of twenty-four rank and file marines, installed him in the adobe custom house, which from thenceforth assumed the name of barracks, and made him at once, from a poor lieutenant of marines, the great and noble potentate of the village.

The flag-raising ceremonies over, the sailors returned to the *Portsmouth.* "Filings'" account continues:

As soon as the Jacks had marched away, a guard was placed at the foot of the flagstaff, and the assembled crowd of . . . Mexicans, convinced that they had by some magical proceeding suddenly been metamorphosed into citizens of the United States, unanimously voted to go where liquor could be had, and drink a health and long life to that flag. The Indians consequently rushed frantically to one pulperee, Captain Leidesdorff and the aristocracy to Bob Ridley's barroom, and the second class and the Dutch to Tinker's. The houses being on three of the four corners of the square, one standing in the door of the barracks could see the maneuvers of each of them. For the first hour, things went quiet enough, but soon the strong water began to work, and such a confusion of sounds could never have been heard . . . as came from these three corners. . . . This pandemonium lasted for some hours, in fact, until sundown, when the commandante sent a guard to warn the revelers that as the town was now under martial law, they must cease their orgies and return to their respective homes.

Next day work began on the building of a fort designed to protect the town against possible attack by the dispossessed Mexicans.

A hill a few hundred yards below the point was selected as the position, and the guns from the old fort, which had been spiked by the Frémont party, were to be brought up, drilled out, and constitute the armament. . . . We had captured a launch schooner called the *Sarmienta,* and having commissioned her under the command of Bobby Whitaker, the boatswain, she was dispatched to convey a sufficient amount of material to construct the fort. Other boats under the charge of Dave Bruce, the sail-maker, were ordered to dismount the guns at the fort and bring them to the landing where the carpenter and his gang were busy at work making carriages for them, and the armorer and his man drilling them out and putting them in order.

As soon as the spot was leveled off, the work of laying the adobes [of which the walls were to be made] commenced, and as we had some of the bricklaying craft on board, they were appointed bosses. All day long might be seen a steady stream of Jacks, each with an adobe perched on top of his head, toiling up the steep hill, while in the valley below the clang of hammer on anvil rang merrily out. . . .

The fort was at last finished. The floor was planked over, the guns amounted, a beautiful flagstaff erected, and though no garrison was stationed there, an artillery company was formed and always held in readiness on board to man the battery whenever a vessel was signalized as entering the harbor, from a station we had erected on Telegraph Hill.

Meanwhile, extensive improvements were going on in the town. The laddies, who at the first alarm of war had retired to their ranchos, now finding that we were no cannibals, began to return. By degrees we assumed the appearance of a comfortable, quiet-looking little country town.

The barque *Olga*—Captain Libby—one of the hide droghers belonging to the Boston company, was the first to enter the harbor after the hoisting of the flag. She brought a large addition to our stock of male companions in the person of W. D. M. Howard, W. H. Thompson, a merchant, Frank Mellus, a supercargo in the employ of the company, H. Teschmaker, a clerk, and last though not least, W. H. Smith, or as he was then called, Jim Crow Smith, a fellow of infinite jest and humor, who was always on hand for a frolic, a fight, or a footrace. Time, however, began to hang heavily on our hands, and many a growl was sent up at our long tarry here. Grub began to grow short and no chance for a new supply. Jack began to grow morose and sullen, when all at once on Saturday afternoon, July 17, 1846, without signal or warning, round the point came booming along a full-rigged ship, crowded with men and bearing our flag at her peak. She came to anchor, our boats boarded her, and on their return reported her to be the American ship *Brooklyn* from New York via the Sandwich Islands, with a load of Mormon immigrants.

The unexpected appearance of this visitor, carrying some two hundred and thirty men, women and children, was, in "Filings'" words, "an event which caused great surprise and no little excitement in our colony." For the Mormons were then an object of intense curiosity throughout the country, one of the tenets of their religion—namely, the practice of polygamy—having shocked and scandalized members of other sects. It had, indeed, been in the hope of escaping further persecution at the hands of their critics that this party had set off for the far coast, their intention being to found a colony in the remote Mexican province where they could practice their religion without outside interference. They were, accordingly, both disappointed and dismayed to learn on arriving that California had become a part of the United States.

How this unexpected appearance of the *Brooklyn* party was greeted by residents of the little town is thus described by "Filings":

Curiosity was raised to the highest pitch, and surmises ran rife among all the inhabitants. The stories of their adventures in Illinois and Missouri had preceded them, and a vague idea seemed to predominate that they were a wild, desperate people, and that trouble would soon raise from their arrival. Captain M., however, was a man equal to any emergency, and with him to will was to do. Consequently he at once decided upon a plan to curb them if hostile, or to foster them if they came in peace.

Our boat was again dispatched to the *Brooklyn* and soon returned, having on board their leader, Samuel Brannan, and two or three of his coadjutors who were designated as elders. Upon being ushered into the recesses of the private cabin of the *Portsmouth*, the views and plans of the newcomers were at once explained, preliminaries arranged, the harmony so necessary to good government concerted, and the parties departed for their own ship again.

The next day being Sunday, Captain Montgomery invited the newcomers to attend morning services on his ship. These were conducted by the captain himself, the *Portsmouth* having no chaplain. "Filings' " account makes clear that curiosity among members of the crew was keen, particularly as regards the "female portion of this strange sect."

At the appointed hour [he continues] the quarter deck was cleared, the awnings spread, the chairs from the ward room and cabin placed for the ladies, the capstan bars ranged as seats for the men, and the boats called away to bring the visitors. When on their return with their live cargoes they hauled alongside the gangway, the whole ship's company was collected on the larboard side of the spar deck, and every eye was fixed on the ladder, anxious to get a first peep at that portion of the human family which is generally denominated the better half of man.

Over they came, and as they followed one another, curiosity faded away, and ere the last had seated herself in the chair appropriated for her, the long-drawn sigh of disappointment escaped from that large crowd, and a . . . quarter gunner growled out in no very sweet tones: "Damnation! Why they are just like other women." And so they were. Sect, creed, nor religion had changed the human form divine, and they sat smiling as though they had no religion at all. Service over, they one and all partook of a lunch with the captain and lieutenants, inspected the ship, and took their leave, having created a most favorable impression among the hearty tars of the good ship *Portsmouth*.

On Monday morning all the boats of the ship were dispatched to aid in disembarking the Mormons and their plunder, and before night they were all snugly on shore and their white tents pitched in the lot bounded by Kearny, Montgomery, Clay, and Washington Streets, directly oppo-

site the barracks. . . . The cargo of the *Brooklyn* consisted
of the most heterogeneous mass of materials ever crowded
together. . . . Agricultural, mechanical, and manufacturing tools were in profuse abundance. Dry goods, groceries,
and hardware were dug out from the lower depths of the
hold and speedily transferred on shore, our men working
with a will. A printing press and all its appurtenances next
came along. And last though not least, three beautiful pieces
of brass cannon, with the necessary complement of powder
and shot. . . . The cannon were pressed into the service
of the United States, and all the immense supply of ammu-
nition transferred to the powder house, which was erected
on the Square, under the special guard of the sentry who
paced beneath the flagstaff.

## ix

O NE OF the most spirited accounts of life in Yerba
Buena during its first years is to be found in the
*Reminiscences* of John Henry Brown—a curious little
book first published in 1886. Brown, a sailor, reached
California aboard a British ship in 1843. Soon thereafter
he settled in the village then taking shape beside the
bay, where his genial disposition—plus a native shrewd-
ness—speedily made him one of its first citizens.

Of his arrival at the little frontier settlement, he wrote:

The first person I met . . . was a Mr. Thompson [the
owner, with a man named Finch, of an early-day bar], who
had formerly had a blacksmith shop in the Cherokee Nation.

. . . I made his house my home, but I had not been there very long before I came to the conclusion that my chances of securing employment of any kind were very poor. There was one small general merchandise store in the place, one billiard-room and one liquor saloon; the latter having just opened by my friend, in partnership with another man. They promised me if their business improved that they would pay me ten dollars per month together with my board and washing if I chose to stay over and work for them.

Brown turned down their offer, feeling that he "could do better elsewhere," and made his way to Sutter's Fort, where he became "overseer of the cook-house and butcher-shop" for Captain Sutter. However, his stay there was brief, for the Yerba Buena partners presently renewed their offer, and he returned to the bay.

I was then in the employ of Finch and Thompson [he recalled], having charge of the bar, and also keeping the accounts. Mr. Finch . . . could neither read nor write and he had a peculiar way of his own in keeping accounts. He had an excellent memory for names and was in the habit of noting any peculiarity about a person as regards his dress or general appearance. Captain Hinckley [then the town's alcalde] wore brass buttons on his coat and was represented on the books by a drawing of a button. A certain sawyer in the place was represented on the books by a drawing of the top saws of a saw pit, and many others were thus represented. . . . Many of the drawings showed considerable ingenuity and originality. I remained with Finch about three weeks, during which time I became acquainted with Robert T. Ridley, the proprietor of a liquor and billiard saloon. He made me an offer of fifty dollars per month to

take charge of his place. I accepted the offer and commenced my work there in the early part of February, 1846.
. . .

The billiard-room was at that time the headquarters of all strangers in the city, both foreigners and Californians. All persons wishing to purchase lots would apply to Ridley; as the first map of surveyed land was kept in the bar-room, the names of those who had lots were written on the map. The map got so much soiled and torn from the rough usage it received that Captain Hinckley volunteered to make a new one. He tried several times, but, being very nervous he could not succeed in making the lines straight, so he got me to do the work, according to his instructions. The original map was put away for safe keeping. The maps were left in the bar-room until after the raising of the American Flag, when they were demanded of me by Washington A. Bartlett, of the United States Ship "Portsmouth," by order of Captain Montgomery.

Brown went on to describe another "first"—that is, the first wedding to take place in Yerba Buena after it came under American rule.

The ceremony [he wrote] was performed in a large room on the ground floor [of the Portsmouth House], which was generally used by the Mexicans as a calaboose. . . . The marriage took place among the Mormons, who had arrived so short a time before. The contracting parties were: Lizzie, the second daughter of Mr. Winner, and Mr. Basil Hall. The marriage ceremony was performed by Mr. Samuel Brannan, according to the Mormon faith. I was one of the guests, and I never enjoyed myself at any gathering as I did there. There was a general invitation extended to all, a large quantity of refreshments had been prepared, and as there was plenty of music and singing, we had lots of fun. The festivities were kept up until twelve o'clock, when everyone returned to their homes, perfectly satisfied and ready to pronounce the first wedding a great success.

Shortly after the village was taken over by the Americans, it grew clear to Brown that "as there were a large number of officers [from the *Portsmouth*] coming ashore daily, besides many other persons who wanted accommodations, a good lodging house and restaurant was badly needed." This need he, with the help of several friends, proceeded to fill, thereby becoming the town's first innkeeper.

Here is his explanation of how the new hotel got its name:

The noncommissioned officers on board the "Portsmouth," Whittaker, the sail-maker, and Whinnsay, the ship carpenter, offered to make the sign-board, paint it and find everything needed, if I would call it by this name. I agreed; the sign was made on board the "Portsmouth," brought ashore, and put on the building; and it was the first sign-board ever put up in the now large city.

As host of the Portsmouth House, Brown soon found that guests were appearing in such numbers that he was hard put to accommodate them.

After the arrival of the "Brooklyn" I found I could employ help, on very reasonable terms. I engaged a lady housekeeper, a widow with one young son; her name was Meramore; also a waitress, and a good cook. . . . I was just in time, [for] on the second day of August . . . there arrived in port from eight to ten whaling ships, and, on the advice of Captain Montgomery, they staid in port four months. . . .

I must relate how I obtained furniture in those days: I got a couple of carpenters (who arrived in [the] "Brooklyn") to make benches, tables and bedsteads. Our beds were mostly made of Sandwich Island moss, excepting four feather beds, which I purchased from the Mormons. The blankets were made of heavy flannel, with a seam in the center. The quilts were made of calico. . . . I had one bedstead made of extra length, thinking it would be long enough for my tallest lodger. Dr. Semple [Robert Semple, co-owner of San Francisco's first newspaper, the *Californian*] tried it, as he was a few inches taller than any of the rest, and the next morning he asked me if I had any chickens I wanted to roost, as his legs came out at the foot of the bed sufficient to roost about a dozen. The bedstead was six feet in length; but the next day I had one made that measured seven feet six inches, which the doctor said was a perfect fit.

The first ordinance passed by the newly organized town council after the place came under American rule had to do with the apprehension of sailors who had deserted from ships in the harbor.

In early days it was a very common thing for sailors to run away from their vessels [wrote Brown]. It was pretty generally understood that the captain would give five dollars reward to anyone returning a runaway. . . . One person whom I will mention here by the name of Peckham, is now [1886] living in San Jose and he will, no doubt, remember the circumstances. When Peckham arrived here during the Mexican War on the whale ship "Cabinet," he deserted the vessel, thinking he could get away without being known.

A few days later, while the Captain was in the billiard-room, Tom Smith, (a man who made a regular business to catch runaway sailors) informed the Captain that one of the men had deserted. The Captain was surprised and inquired what kind of a looking man he was. Tom told him he was a "seven footer," and after thinking a moment the Captain made up his mind who he was. He then asked Smith what he got for bringing in runaway sailors. He said five dollars was the regular price. The Captain said he thought five dollars was too much; but he would be willing to give him two dollars and a half if he would let the runaway sailor go wherever he pleased, as he was no earthly account on board ship.

During the first months after the town was taken over by the Americans the place was lightly held, and there was some uneasiness on the part of the residents that the native Californians might attempt to recapture it. It was during that period that the following amusing incident took place:

Captain King, who arrived from the Islands [Brown recalled], brought with him a newly patented coffee-pot, the like of which I had never seen. It held about a gallon and a half. On the top was a large iron wheel, which fitted tight to the rim; over that was a cover; on the outside was a screw, which could be screwed down so tight no steam could escape. Captain King had with him a Kanaka steward who had learned how to use the coffee-pot with safety. . . . It was their habit to make coffee in this pot every day; but it so happened at this time that the steward had other work to do, and after fixing the coffee-pot, as he supposed, all right, he left it in charge of the second cook, with instructions that if too much steam escaped, to turn the screw tighter; and the cook turned it down so tight that no steam could escape. The consequence was that the coffee-pot exploded, blowing the cook twenty yards from the kitchen, also scattering the cooking utensils in different parts of the room.

At that time Captain Hull's headquarters were on the north side of the hotel. When he heard the explosion he ran immediately to the Barracks (which were in the old Custom-House), and ordered the long roll to be beat, as the Spaniards had come to take the city. George McDougal and I were in the bar-room at the time, and on looking out of the window, we saw the cook lying on the ground badly scalded; we went immediately and picked him up. . . . Captain King with two other gentlemen came to our assistance, and told me to run to the military quarters for a doctor. In the meantime Captain Hull demanded the call of the citizens, who very promptly responded, and he ordered them to fall in line, and to be ready to fire at the word of command. He also sent out some marines as scouts to find out the strength of the Californians. He made signals for the men on ship to be ready, if required on shore. When I arrived at the quarters I met Captain Hull as I was going up the steps, and he began to scold me for not being on hand, one of the very first, as he thought I had as much at stake as anyone. I then told him he could stop beating his long roll; all I wanted was a doctor, as the coffee-pot had exploded in the hotel and the cook was badly scalded. . . . He turned to his company . . . and thanked them for their ready response to his call, and in case they should be needed in the future he hoped they would show as great a readiness to respond as they had that day. They were then discharged from further duty. This, I think, was the last call to fight an imaginary battle in San Francisco.

Yet another incident that throws light on the life of the time is related by the genial innkeeper. One of the ships arriving in the harbor in the summer of 1847 was the bark *Whiting*, and among its passengers was a clergyman named Roberts who, with his wife and daughter, was en route to Oregon Territory.

While the vessel lay in the harbor [wrote Brown] Roberts often came ashore. He informed me that if it was convenient and would be agreeable to the citizens to have him do so, he would like to hold services on Sunday. I told him he could have the use of the dining-room, and that I knew he would have a good congregation. On Sunday morning in June, 1847, I posted a notice that there would be preaching that day at the hotel. The room was filled, and the Reverend Mr. Roberts preached a good sermon, and it was the first Methodist sermon ever preached in the city. . . . The congregation was not very fashionable, but deeply attentive, and well pleased with the sermon. I can say that many who were at that meeting had not been in any place of worship for ten or fifteen years previous to that occasion. One old sailor, who was greatly pleased with the sermon put a five dollar gold piece in his own hat and went around the room and collected over fifty dollars, which he gave to the minister, and with tears in his eyes tapped the minister on the shoulder in a sailor-like way and exclaimed: "That was a d - - n good sermon." He further showed his appreciation by inviting the minister and his family to take dinner with him the next day at the hotel. The dining-room was in the corner of the house; on the other side was a billiard-room and saloon; on the other were two rooms, used for card-playing. I do not suppose another instance could be cited where under the same roof there was preaching, drinking, card-

playing and billiards all going on at the same time. . . .
Those who did not wish to attend the religious services in
the room had too much respect for the minister to make
the least noise or disturbance. Let this much at least be said
to the credit of the early pioneers.

X

WHEN THE Americans took over in the summer of
1846 Yerba Buena was a small frontier community
with a population of less than two hundred and fifty.
Like other California towns, it had been governed by
an alcalde, or mayor, and an ayuntamiento, which cor-
responded to a town council. On its transfer to the
United States, Washington A. Bartlett, lieutenant in the
U.S. navy, was appointed alcalde, succeeding José Jesús
Noé. Bartlett served but a short time and is remembered
chiefly because it was he who caused the name of the
village to be changed to San Francisco. On February 22,
1847, he was replaced by Edwin Bryant, and three
months later Bryant, in turn, was succeeded by George
Hyde.

Up to that time the American alcaldes had served without town councils. Such one-man government, however,
seems to have been unsatisfactory, and in the summer
of 1847 Colonel R. B. Mason, then military governor of
California, wrote Hyde directing him to form an ayuntamiento to aid him in administering the growing settle-

ment. Mason's letter, written from Monterey on July 15, read as follows:

Sir: There is wanted in San Francisco an efficient town government, more so than is in the power of an alcalde alone to put in force. There soon may be expected a large number of whalers in your bay, and a large increase in your population by the arrival of emigrants; it is therefore highly necessary that you should, at an early day, have an efficient town police, proper town laws, town officials, & c, for the enforcement of the laws for the preservation of order, and for the proper protection of persons and property.

I therefore desire you to call a town meeting for the election of six persons, who, when elected, shall constitute the town council, and who, in conjunction with the alcalde, shall constitute the town authorities until the end of the year 1848.

All the municipal laws and regulations will be formed by the council, but executed by the alcalde in his judicial capacity, as at present. The first alcalde will preside at meetings of the council, but shall have no vote, except in cases where the votes are equally divided.

The town council (not less than four of which shall constitute a quorum for the transaction of business), to appoint all necessary town officers, such as treasurer, constables, watchmen, &c., and to determine their pay, fees, &c. The town treasurer to enter into ample and sufficient bonds, conditioned for the faithful performance of his duties, the bonds to be fully executed to the satisfaction of the council before the treasurer enters upon his duties.

The second alcalde shall, in case of the absence of the first alcalde, take his place and preside at the council, and perform all the proper functions of the first alcalde. No soldier, sailor, or marine, nor any person who is not a "bona fide" resident of the town, shall be allowed to vote for a member of the town council.

These orders were duly carried out, and for the next eight months—that is, until May, 1848, when the rush to the gold fields drew lawmakers and governed alike into the Sierra foothills—the town continued to be administered by the system inherited from the Mexicans. Meanwhile, in 1847, there was issued from the press of the town's pioneer newspaper, the *Californian,* an eight-page pamphlet bearing the title, *The Laws of the Town of San Francisco.* This—one of the rarest of all items of Californiana—throws interesting light on some of the difficulties with which the newly elected town officials had to cope. Thus the first ordinance passed by them had to do with the problems posed by runaway sailors. Entitled "To Prevent Desertion of Seamen," it read:

Be it ordained by the Town Council of the Town of San Francisco, that if any person within the limits of this Town, shall entice or advise any Sailor or other person employed on board of any vessel within this harbor or bay, to leave the vessel on which he or they may be employed, upon conviction thereof, shall be fined not exceeding five hundred dollars, nor less than twenty, and be imprisoned for not exceeding three months.

Be it further ordained, that if any person or persons shall feed, harbor or employ, any runaway Sailor within the limits of this Town without permission from the Alcalde, such person or persons shall be fined on conviction thereof, not exceeding five hundred dollars, nor less than twenty, and be imprisoned not exceeding three months.

Be it further ordained, that if any Sailor or other person employed on board any vessel now in this bay, or which may hereafter come into it, run away and be caught within the town, said Sailor or other person shall, on conviction of having run away, be ordered to hard labor on the public works not exceeding six months.

Be it further ordained, that this ordinance take effect from and after the sixteenth day of September, A.D. 1847.

The second section of the *Laws* was headed "Police Regulations," which, after fixing fines and/or prison terms for those convicted of burglary, assault, and other breaches of the peace, continued thus:

Be it ordained that any person firing a gun or pistol within one mile of Portsmouth Square, shall be fined upon conviction thereof, not less than three nor more than five dollars.

Be it further ordained, that any person killing or maiming the carrion fowls or birds within the limits of this town, shall be fined one dollar for each offense, upon conviction thereof.

Be it ordained that from and after the 12th day of November, 1847, all property holders desiring to dig wells upon their premises, or who now may have them dug, shall, under a penalty of fifty dollars, carefully close and fence, or box them up.

The matter of licensing sellers of "every description of merchandise" was next taken up, the fees being fixed at $100 per year for those dispensing spiritous liquors, a like amount for shopkeepers in general, and, in the case of the former, requiring the applicant to post a $250 bond as a guaranty that his resort would be conducted in an orderly manner.

Of particular interest is the following, which authorized the first city-financed public improvement of the waterfront; namely, the Broadway pier:

Be it ordained . . . that the sum of one thousand dollars is hereby appropriated for the erection of a pier at the foot of Broadway.

Be it ordained, that the pier shall be not less than ten feet wide, and of sufficient height to resist the action of the sea and tide, and one hundred and fifty feet in length, commencing at the rocks projecting from the bank, to be continued eastward in a parallel with Broadway.

Be it further ordained, that a committee of three be appointed to direct, superintend, and make contracts for the materials and work for the same, and report progress from time to time, when called on.

Named to oversee this project were three prominent citizens, Messrs. Clark, Howard, and Parker. The pier was completed in the fall of 1848.

# Part Two

# Gold Spawns a City
# 1848–1849

# i

O**N JANUARY** 24, 1848, James Marshall picked up a few flakes of yellow metal from the tailrace of Captain John A. Sutter's new sawmill on the American River. The Treaty of Guadalupe Hidalgo, which ended the war with Mexico, was signed on February 2 of that same year. Thus by one of the major ironies of history Mexico relinquished its ownership of California only nine days after the discovery that was to focus the world's attention on the then little-known province and set off the greatest gold rush of all time.

What effect Marshall's find had on the quiet little village beside the bay is described by the authors of *The Annals of San Francisco*, the most comprehensive of the early histories of the town, which was published in New York in 1855. Under date of May 18, 1848, they wrote:

Early in the spring of this year, occasional intelligence had been received of the finding of gold in large quantities among the foot hills of the Sierra Nevada. . . . Small parcels of the precious metal had also been forwarded to San Francisco, while visitors from the mines, and some actual diggers, arrived to tell the wonders of the region and the golden gains of those engaged in exploring and working it. In consequence of such representations, the inhabitants began gradually, in bands or singly, to desert their previous occupations, and betake themselves to the American River. . . . Labor, from the deficiency of hands, rose rapidly in value, and soon all business and work, except the most urgent, was forced to be stopped. Seamen deserted their ships in the bay and soldiers from the barracks. Neither threats, punishment nor money could keep men to their most solemn engagements. . . . The infection spread on all sides, and led to a general migration of every class of the community. The day laborer, who had worked for the good and at the command of another, for one or two dollars a day, could not be restrained from flying to the happy spot where he could earn six or ten times the amount, and might possibly gain a hundred or even a thousand times the sum in one lucky day's chance. Then the life, at worst, promised to be one of continual adventure and excitement, and the miner was his own master.

While this was the case with the common laborer, his employer, wanting his services, suddenly found his occupation at an end; while shopkeepers and the like, dependent on both, discovered themselves in the same predicament. The glowing tales of the successful miners all the while reached their ears, and threw their own steady and large gains in the shade. They therefore could do no better, in a pecuniary sense even, for themselves, than to hasten after their old servants, and share in their new labor and its extraordinary gains, or to pack up their former business stock, and travelling with it to the mines, open their new stores and shops and stalls, and dispose of their old articles to the fortunate diggers at a rise of five hundred or a thousand percent.

In the month of May it was computed that at least one hundred and fifty people had left San Francisco, and every day since has added to their number. Some were occasionally returning . . . but they had little time to stop and expatiate upon what they had seen. They had hastily come back, as they had hastily gone away at first, leaving their household and business to waste and ruin, now to fasten more properly their houses, and remove goods, family and all, at once to the gold region. Their hurried movements even more than the words they uttered, excited the curiosity and then the eager desire of others to accompany them. And so it was. Day after day the bay was covered with launches filled with the inhabitants and their goods, hastening up the Sacramento. This state of matters soon came to a head; and master and men alike hurried to the *placeres,* leaving San Francisco like a place where the plague reigns, forsaken by its old inhabitants, a melancholy solitude.

On the 29th of May, 1848, the West Coast's first newspaper, the *Californian* (which had moved from Monterey to San Francisco the previous year), temporarily suspended publication.

The whole country [wrote its editor], from San Francisco to Los Angeles, and from the sea shore to the base of the Sierra Nevada, resounds to the sordid cry of *gold!* ! , *gold!* ! , GOLD! ! , while the field is left half planted, the house half built, and everything neglected but the manufacture of shovels and pick-axes, and the means of transportation to the spot where one man obtained one hundred and twenty-eight dollars' worth of the *real stuff* in one day's washing, and the average for all concerned is *twenty dollars per diem!*

Conditions in the all-but-deserted town were thus described by the authors of the *Annals,* who themselves had joined in the exodus:

About the end of May we left San Francisco almost a

deserted place, and such it continued during the whole summer and autumn months. Many ships with valuable cargoes had meanwhile arrived in the bay, but the seamen deserted. The goods at great expense had somehow been landed, but there was nobody to take care of them, or remove them from the wharves where they lay exposed to the weather, blocking up the way. The merchants who remained were in a feverish bustle. They were selling goods at high prices, and could get no hands to assist them in removing and delivering the articles. By and by, some of the miners came back to their old homes; but most of them were emaciated, feeble and dispirited. Here, therefore, as at the mines, the prices of labor and all necessities rose exceedingly. The common laborer, who had formerly been content with his dollar a day, now proudly refused ten; the mechanic, who had recently been glad to receive two dollars, now rejected twenty for his day's services. It was certainly a great country, this—there was no mistake about it; and every subject was as lofty, independent, and seemingly rich as a king. . . .

Within the first eight weeks after the "diggings" had been fairly known, two hundred and fifty thousand dollars had reached San Francisco in gold dust, and within the next eight weeks, six hundred thousand more. These sums were all to purchase, at any price, additional supplies for the mines. Coin grew scarce, and all that was in the country was insufficient to satisfy the increased wants of commerce in one town alone. Gold dust, therefore, soon became a circulating medium, and was readily received by all classes.

## ii

WHAT this mighty influx of treasure did to the economy of the little town is made clear by its genial first innkeeper, John Henry Brown, excerpts from whose "recollections" were quoted in Part One.

When gold was first brought to Yerba Buena [he wrote] I had no idea of what its real value was, and most people had an idea that gold dust would depreciate in value, judging from the quantity which was brought to the city; consequently, I would pay out the gold dust as fast as possible, fearing I might lose by keeping it, selling it often at the rate of ten or twelve dollars per ounce. Cash seemed to be money, but gold dust was looked at more in the light of merchandise. I have often purchased it for six dollars per ounce. . . . At this time [that is, the fall of 1848] the gamblers would not play for it. Those having no coin were obliged to come to the bar and sell their dust for eight dollars per ounce; and when I was short of cash I would pay only six dollars. . . . All persons that were boarding in the hotel, also those running bar bills, on making payments we would buy their dust at the rate of eight dollars per ounce.

The first shipment [of gold] which I made was with Captain Newell of the schooner "Honolulu," which was going to the Sandwich Islands for goods. I remember giving Newell twenty pounds of gold dust in bottles, with which to purchase goods, and he was to sell the balance of the dust and bring back what cash remained. The next was Captain John Young. I gave him a gallon pickle bottle full of gold dust; just how much it weighed I could not tell. . . .

At the commencement of my taking gold dust, I thought it would be to my advantage to send it away; I did not expect it was going to bring me over twelve dollars per ounce; but, to my great surprise, I did not ship any that brought less than sixteen dollars per ounce, and often more than that amount. . . .

I had a great advantage over most persons in obtaining coin. During the latter part of the summer, a great many persons came to the city, all of whom had coin, and we accommodated as many as we possibly could at the hotel. . . . I think I may say that one-half of the cash which was brought here by the passengers was spent in the hotel. I was well acquainted with the captains with whom I had dealings . . . and felt quite sure that I ran no risk in trusting them with the gold dust; their percentage, aside from the freight, was ten per cent on the cash returns, and ten per cent on the goods purchased.

So crowded was the town that winter that by the end of November there were, Brown estimated, "over one hundred and sixty persons in the hotel." He added:

We had to put two beds or more in a room; and as we rented the rooms for twenty dollars per week, it made no difference to us how many slept in them. Those who gambled would use the beds during the day, and others would occupy them at night, so they were well taken up, night and day. . . .

It seems almost incredible now, the many stories that are told of the manner in which persons would waste the gold dust in those early times. In front of Mr. Howard's store, on Montgomery Street, from the sweepings of a floor a man got over fifty dollars in one day. Another instance occurred in the City Hotel bar-room. [The City Hotel, which Brown leased in the summer of 1848, was located on Kearny Street, near Clay.] The man who did the sweeping would save the sweepings in a barrel until full; and on washing it out he obtained over two hundred dollars in gold dust.

At the time it seemed that the mines were inexhaustible; hence, few hoarded their dust, the general feeling being that there was "plenty more where it came from." Brown cites this example of the length some went to toss their earnings away:

A person arrived from the Sandwich Islands by the name of Montgomery, who carried on the business of auctioneering. . . . He found it very profitable, as some goods that were brought here would not sell at any price, and he would often purchase them at private sale and lay them over until they were in demand. . . . One time he rode up to the barroom window (which was very large), and said he was going to ride through. I informed him that if he did so it would be a very dear ride. He asked how much it would cost him. I made the figures rather high, thinking it would keep him from coming through. The price was $500. The words were hardly out of my mouth when he threw a bag of dust through the window to me and said, "Weigh out your $500, and take enough out for a basket of wine," and before I could pick up the bag he and his horse were through the window into the bar-room.

Although he had no lack of customers who willingly paid high prices for such services as he had to offer, Brown made clear that running a hotel in a spot so far removed from sources of supplies presented many problems.

I found it very difficult to keep up the boarding department of the City Hotel [he recalled], and would have failed entirely had it not been for the fact that I was personally acquainted with the captains of vessels, and consequently had an opportunity of procuring from them a portion of what they had for the use of their ships. Although they charged me enormous prices, I still considered that they were doing me a great favor by letting me have such provisions, as I really needed them and could not well do without.

By every vessel that left for Oregon I would send for such articles as butter, onions, pickled tripe, ham, bacon, eggs, or anything I could obtain in the way of provisions. . . . Fresh meats, such as beef and mutton were very reasonable; much cheaper than they are now [1885]; pork was very dear. . . . An old gentleman by the name of Herman supplied the hotel with vegetables, such as lettuce, cabbage, turnips, radishes, carrots. These he brought daily; I had to pay him from fifteen to twenty dollars per day. . . . Another item of considerable expense to me was the hiring of two hunters and a whale boat to go off up the creeks after game; they would make two trips a week, and were usually very successful. If I had been compelled to purchase in this city everything I needed in the way of provisions for the table, I would have lost every day at least one hundred dollars. Had it not been for the large amount of wine that was generally consumed at the dinner-table, I could never have stood the losses made in the boarding department. . . .

In the Fall of 1848 the miners began coming to Yerba Buena for the purpose of spending the winter, and they continued to come until the latter part of December. In those days there were no towns or houses at the mines, and the

only place that afforded any shelter was at Sutter's Fort. . . .
That winter between eighty and ninety were boarding and
lodging at the City Hotel.

At the commencement of the winter the miners would
pass the time away by playing billiards; but they soon tired
of that, and wished me to take the billiard-table out and
turn it into a gambling saloon. They said they would pay
me two hundred dollars per day; or pay five dollars an hour
after six o'clock up to twelve at night; later than that, they
would pay ten dollars per hour. The size of the room was
thirty feet by twenty-four. I got eight tables made for this
room, and before the tables were finished they were all
taken. One man was so afraid he would not be able to
obtain one that he gave me one hundred dollars in advance.
. . . When it was in full blast, we found that there were
not enough tables to accommodate all who wished to join
in the games. I could have rented, in the same room, a dozen
tables; but the room was not large enough. I had three more
tables made and placed them in an adjoining room. All three
rooms were used for gambling purposes; such games as
Monte, Faro, Roulette, and others being played. Most of
the tables were spoken for in advance; sometimes they were
engaged by the week, and I could have rented as many more
if I had room for them. There were two other rooms used
for gambling purposes in the back of the hotel. I feel almost
ashamed to put in print some of the things that happened
in those early days, as they seem almost incredible, and still
it is the truth.

## iii

THE unprecedented richness of California's gold fields is the sort of news that travels fast, and before the year 1848 was out the initial stages of a world-wide gold rush were under way. To be sure, when rumors of the discovery first reached the East Coast they were received in many quarters with marked skepticism. However, evidence in the form of impressive quantities of "dust" (including a $3,000 tea caddy sent President Polk by Colonel R. B. Mason) soon began to arrive, whereupon all doubts vanished.

While thousands of those bound for the new El Dorado chose to follow one or another of the overland trails, many others—particularly those who lived close to the Atlantic seaboard—made ready to travel by sea. At a dozen ports from New England to the Gulf, ships of all sorts and conditions were pressed into service, hastily refitted and supplied and, crowded to capacity, dispatched on the months-long voyage to San Francisco. As time passed, however, and the first wave of gold hunters began to subside, those planning the trip proved less willing to accept any route or means of transportation that might be offered. The result was that those offering passage by sea, whether by steamer via Panama or Nicaragua, or by sailing ship round the Horn, were presently competing for a share of the lucrative trade.

One reminder of that period when the merits of the different routes were being advertised to the public was a forty-six-page pamphlet entitled *Gregory's Guide for California Travellers*. Published in New York in 1850, this curious little guidebook purports to set forth "all the requisite information needed by persons taking the route via the Isthmus of Panama."

With a view of guiding *all* travellers to California by way of the Isthmus [the text begins], the following directions have been prepared, by one who has twice travelled this journey, and who asks favor for them only for their *brevity* and *correctness*. Good health is essential to anyone who desires success in California, and the saving of expense, is no small object with most travellers. It is confidently believed that best results will be attained by a strict adherence to the following suggestions.

From New York to Chagres, the route may be considered plain sailing, and we will commence with the anchorage off Chagres, which is usually from one to two miles distant. The Steam Ship Company provides for the landing of the passengers and their baggage, using the ship's quarter-boats for the former, and the launch of the steamer *Orus* for the latter. . . . The captain of the *Orus* is paid by the Steam Ship for landing both passengers and baggage. Three or four taverns are kept at this landing by white men, one or two of whom are Americans.

After seeing your baggage safely landed from the *Orus,* your first object should be to secure a good canoe—one holding four or five persons is the most preferable.

Then make your contract to convey yourself and baggage to Cruces, which will cost you from thirty to forty dollars the trip (six to eight dollars each person), usually occupying three days, during which time your pleasure will be greatly enhanced, if you have been provident in supplying yourself with a sufficient stock of provisions.

The ranchos and huts on the river are poor "sights" for hungry travellers.

The next several pages deal with the crossing to the Pacific side, with hints as to where to stop en route, what prices to pay for accommodations and other services and, in particular, warnings not to trust one's baggage in the hands of unauthorized persons.

On arrival in Panama [the account continues] your first business is to ascertain from the Agents when the Steamer is to leave, and if you are to be delayed a week or more, it is advisable for four or five persons to engage a room, with a cot in it for each, and arrange for a supply of drinking water. All this will cost a dime a day for each person. Taking meals at Restaurants or Eating houses, a person may lodge in a good room, and thus live moderately at about three and a half dollars a week.

The day before the Steamer leaves, notice is posted up by the Agents of the hour that passengers are required to be at the Mole, in front of the Custom House.

Passengers are required to pay the expense of conveying themselves and their baggage to the Steamer.

Travellers on the Steamships between New York and Chagres, are of course much better provided, than on the Pacific Steamers.

Having the New York Markets to resort to, once in each month, makes a very essential difference. The Pacific Steamers are supplied with stores from New York, via Cape Horn,

with the exception of such as are obtainable on the Pacific
Coast. . . .

Steerage passengers will find one or two jars of preserves,
and one or two pecks of dried fruit, (peaches or apples)
very acceptable. A few jars of pickles, and a few pounds of
Milk, Soda, or Butter Crackers, some Bologna Sausages and
Cheese, a Ham and a piece of Smoked Beef, would not only
prove very palatable and comfortable, but more agreeable
in case of seasickness than Ship's fare. . . .

Take sufficient coffee, tea, loaf sugar, &c., for five days
consumption in crossing the Isthmus, and should there be
anything left on arriving at Panama, *anything* you have is
preferable to tropical fruit, *which should be avoided* by all
means.

A similar outfit of provisions is desirable for the steerage
on the Pacific, and more so, for reasons above stated; each
steerage passenger is provided with his own *plate, knife and
fork, spoon, drinking-cup, mattress and pillow.*

During the delay, (always more or less at Panama), persons who regard their health, will avoid exposure or hard
work in the sun, during the middle of the day. Perhaps more
persons have died from imprudence in this respect than
from any other cause. It is considered highly dangerous, and
by many residents on the Isthmus as almost certain death, to
drink ardent spirits after eating tropical fruit, as it produces
fermentation in the bowels, which seems to defy the influence
of all medical skill.

The use of Milk should be avoided, in any form, while on
the Isthmus. Numerous cases of distressing illness are
known from its use.

Light clothing, such as is worn in the United States, during
the Summer months, is all sufficient for travelling purposes,
from three days out of New York, to within five or six days

short of San Francisco, after which, the usual warm clothing will be necessary.

In consequence of the great and bitter disappointment incurred by many persons, in being delayed, for weeks and months in Panama, *it has become indispensably necessary,* for each person to be provided with a ticket for the Pacific Steamer, before leaving New York. . . .

For want of this precaution, many have been compelled to wait at Panama, until they could send for a ticket. . . . The expense of landing at San Francisco, is borne by each passenger; the Steamer coming to anchor as near the city as the landing is safe and practicable.

This route to California, although more expensive than that by way of Cape Horn, is by far the most desirable for those who can afford the additional outlay . . . not the least of which is the very great saving in time, and the avoiding of a tedious and monotonous life on shipboard. . . .

After a perusal of the foregoing, any practical man can, before leaving home, estimate very nearly what his expenses will amount by the time he lands in San Francisco. Some allowance for detention at Panama should be made, which you can easily estimate after learning from the Steam Ship Company in New York, on what day the Steamer will leave Panama.

As a matter of course, no prudent person will undertake so long a journey without making some provision in his calculations for unforeseen events that may require some outlay beyond the estimate of his entire expenses. Any surplus of funds he may have on hand on his arrival at San Francisco, will not be found very burdensome, and he may feel quite sure that his money will not trouble him long, if he remains, even for a little while, in a state of *masterly inactivity.*

## iv

GREGORY'S GUIDE was not the only work of the sort that found its way into print during the first year or two of the gold rush. While virtually all such works were, in the words of the California bibliographer, Robert E. Cowan, "highly colored accounts . . . compiled with little regard for accuracy," they have a particular interest to present-day readers because, far better than more temperate later writings, they make clear the picturesque extravagancies of the period.

As it happened, the first book to be published in San Francisco belongs in that category. This is F. P. Wierzbicki's *California as It Is and as It May Be: Or, A Guide to the Gold Fields,* which appeared in 1849 from the press of one of the town's pioneer printers, Washington Bartlett, whose shop was at Number 8 Clay Street. A native of Poland, Wierzbicki reached San Francisco in March, 1847, as a member of Stevenson's regiment, and on his discharge a month later began the practice of medicine, becoming one of the town's first physicians. On the discovery of gold the following spring he joined the rush to the Sierra foothills. However, after a few weeks he returned to San Francisco, where he continued to practice until his death in 1860, at the age of forty-five.

One of the chapters of his little book is called "The Towns of California," and in it he thus described San Francisco as it appeared in the spring of 1849:

The town has led the van in growth; there is nothing similar on record. . . . In fact, it looks very much like one of those cities only built for a day. Its houses, built of planks and cotton sheetings cannot last but for a day; however, whatever it may lack in quality they make up in quantity. Four months ago the town hardly counted fifty houses, and now it must have upwards of five hundred, and these are daily increasing, even a theater is spoken of as being built. From eight to ten thousand inhabitants may be afloat in the streets . . . and hundreds arrive daily; many live in shanties, many in tents, and many the best way they can. The magic power of gold marks every spot here; vessels from different parts of the world press into the harbor, and make already a floating city in front of the *terra firma;* goods of all descriptions are scattered on the shore in open streets that are too narrow for men, animals and carts that pass up and down. The freaks of fortune are equally as remarkable in this place as everything else connected with it; some men who two years ago had not a cent in their pocket, count by thousands now; property that a year ago could have been bought for five or six thousand dollars, now pays a rent of thirty thousand dollars per annum; mechanics who formerly were glad to get a job at two dollars a day, now get from six to twelve; in fact, mechanics, and particularly carpenters, are the most independent aristocracy of the place.

In this writer's opinion, the town's most grievous lack —one that he felt might well prevent the place from ever becoming a permanent city—was the scarcity of women.

In the midst of abundance of every kind [he wrote] women are very scarce; the domestic circle does not exist; domestic pleasures are wanting, and household duties are unfulfilled. We touch here upon a subject which, if we allowed ourself to speak feelingly as a bachelor, we might be even eloquent. . . . We will, however, say nothing of ourself—we will speak of the situation of others; we will try to advocate the cause of poor and forlorn bachelors, and persuade some respectable heads of families that have daughters to settle in life, to come to California and build up the society, which, without women, is like an edifice built on sand. Women, to society, are like cement to the building of stone; the society here has no such cement; its elements float to and fro on the excited, turbulent, hurried life of California immigrants. . . . Such is the society of San Francisco. But bring women here, and at once the process of crystallization, if we may be permitted the expression, will set in the society, by the natural affinities of the human heart. There are here many worthy men who have had the good luck to make a respectable competency, who would like to be married and settled in life, as honest and sensible men should do; but for want of fair ones, they think only of getting away from here as soon as possible. . . . This would not be so if some pleasant families from the States, rich in nothing else but in intelligent, home educated daughters, were to migrate to California, they could well provide for all their members here with much more ease, as yet, than in any portion of the Union.

It was not on romantic grounds alone, however, that the good doctor deplored the lack of women in the early town. He went on to point out other reasons why he found their absence distressing.

The greatest privations that a bachelor in this country is exposed to [he wrote], consist in not being able to furnish himself with clean linen when he desires, as domestic service is too difficult to be kept up here for want of working women. To induce some of the few women that are here to condescend to wash their linen for them, they have to court them besides paying six dollars a dozen.

We know an instance of an inveterate bachelor who married a spinster because she refused to wash his clothes for him, but he was determined she should do it at any price, as he was a great lover of cleanliness; in the dilemma he resolved to pay her all he was worth, rather than forego his habit of cleanliness. He is in the habit of saying, "He who goes without a clean shirt on, keeps his conscience open to suspicion"—too severe a judgment upon us, the inhabitants of this town.

The doctor summed up his impressions of the place in these words:

When this uneven slope of the hill on which the town is situated, shall be built up with fine and solid houses, what now looks dreary and desolate will then look very picturesque and smiling; so will it be with the society here; when elements that are now daily accumulating get through their fermentation and become settled, they also will present a smooth and transparent surface to the moral eye of the beholder, but as yet, one needs a little philosophy to bear him through the present that he may lean on the future.

### v

PERHAPS the most widely read of all books on the gold rush is *Eldorado, Or Adventures in the Path of Empire,* first published in London and New York in 1850

and many times reprinted. Its author, Bayard Taylor, a twenty-four-year-old correspondent for the New York *Tribune*, had an uncommonly observant eye for the more novel aspects of life in the helter-skelter city then taking shape on the bay shore, and he wrote of them in so graphic a fashion as to entertain not only his own generation but ours.

Taylor left New York on June 28, 1849, aboard the steamer *Falcon*, transferred to the *Panama* at the Isthmus, and reached San Francisco toward the end of August. Here he records his impressions on first stepping ashore:

A furious wind was blowing down through a gap in the hills, filling the streets with clouds of dust. On every side stood buildings of all kinds, begun or half-finished, and the greater part of them mere canvas shacks, open in front, and covered with all kinds of signs, in all languages. Great quantities of goods were piled up in the open air, for want of a place to store them. The streets were full of people, hurrying to and fro, and of as diverse and bizarre a character as the houses: Yankees of every possible variety, native Californians in *serapes* and sombreros, Chileans, Sonorians, Kanakas from Hawaii, Chinese with long tails, Malays armed with their everlasting creeses and others in whose embrowned and bearded visages it was impossible to recognize any especial nationality.

We came at last into a plaza, now dignified by the name Portsmouth Square. It lies on the slant side of the hill, and from a high pole in front of a long one-story adobe building used as the Custom House, the American flag was flying. On the lower side stood the Parker House—an ordinary

frame house of about sixty feet front—and towards its
entrance we directed our course.

Our luggage was deposited on one of the rear porticos,
and we discharged our porters, after paying them two dollars each—a sum so immense in comparison to the service
rendered that there was no longer any doubt of our having
actually landed in California. There were no lodgings to be
had at the Parker House—not even a place to unroll our
blankets; but one of the proprietors accompanied us across
the plaza to the City Hotel, where we obtained a room with
two beds for $25 per week, meals being in addition $20 per
week. I asked the landlord whether he could send a porter
for our trunks. "There is none belonging to the house," said
he; "every man in his own porter here." I returned to the
Parker House, shouldered a heavy trunk, took a valise in one
hand and carried them to my quarters, in the teeth of the
wind. Our room was a sort of garret over the only story of
the hotel; two cots, evidently of California manufacture,
and covered only with a pair of blankets, two chairs, a
rough table and a small looking-glass, constituted the furniture. There was not space enough between the bed and the
rafters overhead, to sit upright, and I gave myself a severe
blow on rising the next morning without the proper heed.
Through a small roof-window of dim glass, I could see the
opposite side of the bay. The wind whistled around the eaves
and rattled the tiles with a cold, gusty sound, that would
have imparted a dreary character to the place, had I been
in a mood to listen.

Like every other visitor, Taylor was filled with wonder at the strangeness of the scenes that met his eye
wherever he went, scenes unlike any he had ever witnessed before.

Every new-comer to San Francisco [he wrote] is overtaken by a sense of complete bewilderment. The mind, however it may be prepared for an astonishing condition of affairs, cannot immediately push aside its old instincts of value and ideas of business, letting all past experience go for naught and casting all its facilities for action, intercourse with its fellows or advancement in any path of ambition into shapes which it never before imagined. . . . One knows not whether he is awake or in some wonderful dream. Never have I had so much difficulty in establishing, satisfactorily to my own sense, the reality of what I saw and heard.

I was forced to believe many things, which in my communications to *The Tribune* I was almost afraid to write, with any hope of their obtaining credence.

Along with other recent arrivals, Taylor was astonished at the fantastic prices charged for goods and services of every sort. However, there was one occasion when he was able to profit by the situation:

Many of the passengers began speculation at the moment of landing [he commented]. The most ingenious and successful operation was made by a gentleman of New York, who took out fifteen hundred copies of *The Tribune* and other papers, which he disposed of in two hours, at one dollar apiece! Hearing of this, I besought me about a dozen papers which I had used to fill up crevices in packing my valise. There was a newspaper merchant at the corner of the City Hotel, and to him I proposed the sale of them, asking him to name a price. "I shall want to make a good profit on the retail price," said he, "and can't give you more than ten dollars for the lot." I was satisfied with the wholesale price, which was a gain of just four thousand percent!

Of other phases of the inflated economics of the town the bemused visitor wrote:

The Parker House rented for $110,000 yearly, at least $60,000 of which was paid by gamblers, who held nearly all the second story. Adjoining it on the right was a canvas tent fifteen by twenty-five feet, called "Eldorado," and occupied likewise by gamblers, which brought $40,000. On the opposite corner of the plaza, a building called "Miner's Bank," used by Wright & Co., brokers, about half the size of a fire-engine house in New York, was held at a rent of $75,000. A mercantile house paid $40,000 rent for a one-story building of twenty feet front; the United States Hotel, $35,000; the Post Office, $7,000, and so on to the end of the chapter. A friend of mine, who wished to find a place for a law-office, was shown a cellar in the earth, about twelve feet square and six deep, which he could have at $250 a month. One of the common soldiers at the Battle of San Pasquale was reputed to be among the millionaires of the place, with an income of $50,000 *monthly*. A citizen of San Francisco died insolvent to the amount of $41,000 the previous autumn. His administrators were delayed in settling his affairs, and his real estate advanced so rapidly in value meantime, that after his debts were paid, his heirs had a yearly income of $40,000. These facts were indubitably attested; everyone believed them, yet hearing them talked of daily, as matters of course, one at first could not help feeling as if he had been eating of "the insane root."

The prices paid for labor were in proportion to everything else. The carman of Mellus, Howard & Co. had a salary of $6,000 a year, and many others made from $15 to $20 daily. Servants were paid from $100 to $200 a month, but the wages of the rougher kind of labor had fallen to about $8. Yet,

notwithstanding the number of gold-seekers who are returning enfeebled and disheartened from the mines, it was
difficult to obtain as many workmen as the enforced growth
of the city demanded. A gentleman who arrived in April
[four months earlier] told me he then found but thirty or
forty houses; the population was then so scant that not more
than twenty-five persons would be seen in the streets at any
time. Now, there are probably five hundred houses, tents
and sheds, with a population, fixed and floating, of six thousand. People who had been absent six weeks came back and
could scarcely recognize the place. Streets were regularly
laid out, and already there were three piers at which small
vessels could discharge. It was calculated that the town
increased daily from fifteen to thirty houses; its skirts were
rapidly approaching the summits of the three hills on which
it is located.

The journalist presently set off on a tour of the gold
towns. When he returned, after a comparatively brief
absence, he wrote:

When I landed there, a little more than four months
before, I found a scattering town of tents and canvas houses,
with a show of frame buildings on one or two streets, and a
population of about six thousand. Now, on my last visit, I
saw around me an actual metropolis, displaying street after
street of well-built edifices, filled with active and enterprising people and exhibiting every mark of permanent commercial prosperity. Then, the town was limited to the curves
of the Bay fronting the anchorage and bottom of the hills.
Now, it stretched to the topmost heights, followed the shore
around point after point, and sending back a long arm through
a gap in the hills, took hold of the Golden Gate and was
building its warehouses on the open strait and almost front-

ing the blue horizon of the Pacific. Then, the gold-seeking sojourner lodged in muslin rooms and canvas garrets, and ate his simple though substantial fare from pine boards. Now, lofty hotels, gaudy with verandas and balconies, were met with in all quarters, furnished with home luxury, and aristocratic restaurants presented daily their long bills of fare, rich with the choicest technicalities of the Parisian cuisine. Then, the vessels were coming in day after day, to lie deserted and useless at their anchorage. Now scarce a day passed but some cluster of sails *outward* bound through the Golden Gate, took their way to all corners of the Pacific. Like the magic seed of the Indian juggler, which grew, blossomed and bore fruit before the eyes of his spectators, San Francisco seemed to have accomplished in a day the growth of half a century. . . .

There had been a vast improvement in the means of living since my previous visit to San Francisco. Several large hotels had been opened, which were equal in almost every respect to houses of the second class in the Atlantic cities. The Ward House, the Graham House, imported bodily from Baltimore, and the St. Francis Hotel, completely threw into the shade all former establishments. The rooms were furnished with comfort and even luxury, and the tables lacked few of the essentials of good living. . . . The sleeping compartments of the St. Francis were the best in California. The cost of board and lodging was $150 per month—which was considered unusually cheap. A room at the Ward House cost $250 monthly, without board. The principal restaurants charged $35 a week for board.

But, as the *Tribune*'s correspondent made clear, not all the town's residents lived in such opulent surroundings. The majority slept in one or another of numerous

lodging houses where, stated Taylor, "a berth or 'bunk'
—one out of fifty in the same room—might be had for
$6 a week."

The model of these establishments [he continued]—which
are far from being "model lodging-houses"—was that of a
ship. A number of staterooms, containing six berths each,
ran around the sides of a large room, or cabin, where the
lodgers resorted to read, write, smoke and drink at their
leisure. The staterooms were consequently filled with foul
and unwholesome air, and the noises in the cabin prevented
the passengers from sleeping, except between midnight and
four o'clock.

The approach of winter brought other trials and in-
conveniences, the rains transforming the unpaved streets
into bottomless quagmires.

The wind now and then blew a heavy gale [continued
the journalist], and the cold, steady fall of rain was varied
by claps of thunder and sudden blasts of hail. The mud in
the streets became little short of fathomless, and it was with
difficulty that the mules could drag the empty wagons
through. A powerful London dray-horse, a very giant in
harness, was the only animal able to pull a full load; and I
was told that he earned his master $100 daily. I saw occa-
sionally a company of Chinese workmen, carrying bricks
and mortar, slung by ropes to long bamboo poles. The plank
sidewalks, in the lower part of the city, ran along the brink
of pools and quicksands, which the street inspector and his
men endeavored to fill by hauling cart-loads of chaparral and
throwing sand on the top; in a day or two the gulf was deep
as ever.

The sidewalks, which were made at a cost of $5 per foot,

bridged over the worst spots, but I was frequently obliged to go the whole length of a block in order to get on the other side. One could not walk any distance without getting at least ankle-deep, and although the thermometer rarely sank below fifty degrees, it was impossible to stand still for even a short time without a death-like chill taking hold of the feet. As a consequence of this, colds and bronchial affections were innumerable. The universal custom of wearing the pantaloons inside the boots threatened to restore the knee-breeches of our grandfathers' times. Even women were obliged to shorten their skirts, and wear high-topped boots.

But for all their discomfort, the winter storms had one redeeming feature, as Taylor pointed out in this paragraph:

As the rains drove the deer and other animals down from the mountains, game of all kinds became abundant. Fat elks and splendid black-tailed does hung from the doors of all the butcher-shops, and wild geese, duck and brant, were brought into the city by the wagon-load. "Grizzly bear steak" became a choice dish at the eating-houses; I had the satisfaction one night of eating a slice of one that had weighed eleven hundred pounds. The flesh was a bright red color, very solid, sweet and nutritious; its flavor was preferable to that of the best pork. The large native hare, a specimen of which occasionally found its way to the restaurants, is nowise inferior to that of Europe.

At the end of his stay, the journalist summed up impressions of San Francisco—and of California in general—in these words:

The practical equality of all the members of a community, whatever might be the wealth, intelligence or profession of each, was never before so thoroughly demonstrated. Dress was no gauge of respectability, and no honest occupation, however menial in character, affected a man's standing. Lawyers, physicians and ex-professors dug cellars, drove ox-teams, sawed wood and carried luggage; while men who had been army privates, sailors, cooks or day laborers were at the head of profitable enterprises. . . . A man who would consider his fellow beneath him, on account of his appearance or occupation would have had some difficulty in living peaceably in California. . . . The security of the country is owing, in no small degree, to this plain, practical development of what the French reverence as an abstraction, under the name of *Fraternité*. To sum up all in three words, *labor is respectable:* may it never be otherwise while a grain of gold is left to glitter in California soil!

## vi

ANOTHER who knew the town well during the great boom of '49, and who wrote both accurately and entertainingly of what he saw, was Walter Colton. Colton arrived in California in 1845 as chaplain aboard the United States ship *Congress*, and following the American conquest, served for a time as alcalde at Monterey. In *Deck and Port*, the first of his two books on California, he, too, commented on the wildly inflated prices San Franciscans were obliged to pay for whatever they needed.

But you are hungry—want a breakfast—turn into a restaurant—call for ham, eggs, and coffee—then your bill—six-dollars! Your high boots, which have never seen a brush since you first put them on, have given out: you find a pair that can replace them—they are a tolerable fit, and now what is the price—fifty dollars! Your beard has not felt a razor since you went to the mines—it must come off, and your frizzled hair be clipped. You find a barber; his dull shears hang in the knots of your hair like a sheep-shearer's in a fleece matted with burrs—his razor he strops on the leg of his boot, and then hauls away—starting at every pull some new fountain of tears. You vow you will let the beard go—but then one side is partly off, and you try the agony again to get the other side something like it; and now what is the charge for this torture—four dollars! Night is approaching, and you must have a place where you can sleep: to inquire for a bed would be as idle as to hunt a pearl in the jungle of a Greenland bear. You look around for the lee of some shanty or tent, and tumble down for the night; but a thousand fleas dispute the premises with you—the contest is hopeless—you tumble out as you tumbled in, and spend the remainder of the night in finding a place not occupied by these aborigines of the soil.

But you are not perhaps a gold-digger, as I had supposed; you are a supercargo and have a valuable freight, which you wish to land. You have warped your vessel in till her keel rakes, and yet you are several hundred yards off. Some lighter must be found that can skim these shallows; your own boats will not do so: so after waiting two or three weeks, you get the use of a scow, called a lighter, for which you pay one hundred and fifty dollars a day.

Tomorrow you are going to commence unloading, and wake betimes; but find that during the night every soul of your crew has escaped, and put out for the mines. You rush about shore to find hands, and collect eight or ten loafers, who will assist you for fifteen dollars a day each. Your cargo must be landed, and you close the bargain, though your fresh hands are already half-seas over. The scow is shoved from shore, brought alongside, loaded with goods, which are tumbled in as an Irishman dumps a load of dirt, and then you up oars and poles and push for the landing; but the tide had ebbed too soon: you are only halfway, and there your scow sticks fast in the midst of a great mud bottom, from which the last ripple of water has retreated. You cannot get forward and you are now too late to get back: night is setting in and the rain-clouds are gathering fast; down comes a deluge, drenching your goods and filling your open scow. The returning tide will now be of no use, the scow won't float. . . . So out you jump, and by crawling and creeping, make your way through the mire to the landing. . . .

Your loafers must be paid off in the morning, and the scow recovered, or its loss will cost you half the profits of your voyage. But the storm last night has driven another brig into yours: and there they both are, like a bear and bull that have gored and crushed each other. But "misery loves company," and you have it. The storm which swept your scow and stove your brig last night, has been busy on shore. Piles of goods heaped up in every street are in a condition which require wreckers as well as watchmen. But no one here is going to trouble himself about your misfortunes, nor much about his own. The reverses of to-day are to be more than repaired by the successes of to-morrow. Those are only the broken pickaxes and spades by which the great mine is to be reached. What is the loss of a few thousands to one who is soon to possess millions? Only a coon back in his hole, while the buffalo remains within rifle-shot,—only a periwinkle lost, while the whale is beneath the harpoon,—only a farthing candle consumed, while the dowered bride, blushing in beauty and bliss, is kneeling at the nuptial altar. . . .

But you are not alone in your destitution and dirt. There are hundreds around you who are quite as daintily reared, and who are doing out here what they dodged at home. Do you see a youth in red flannel shirt and coarse brogans wheeling a wheelbarrow? He was once a clerk in a counting-house in New York, and came here to shovel up gold as you scoop up sand. He has been to the mines, gathered no gold, and returned, but now makes his ten dollars a day by rolling that wheelbarrow; it costs him six, however, to live, and the other four he loses at monte.

## vii

Early-day San Francisco was a truly cosmopolitan community, for the gold discoveries drew adventurers from all parts of the world, and, like the Yankees themselves, many of the outlanders recorded their impressions of the town's tempestuous beginnings. Thus it is possible today to see the spot through the eyes of men of many different backgrounds.

One of the most observant of such visitors from overseas was Vicente Pérez Rosales, a native of Santiago, Chile, who sailed from Valparaiso on the French bark *Stangueli* late in 1848 and reached San Francisco toward the middle of the following February.

Rosales' first impression of "this most extravagant and singular town" (as he called it) was far from favorable.

There were no sidewalks in the streets [he wrote], nor anything resembling them, and the center was a slough of trampled mud whose solidest parts were formed by the thousands of broken bottles thrown from the buildings as emptied. The inhabitants, of heterogenous nationality, numbering about fifteen hundred permanent residents and as many transients, might have been thought to be celebrating a vast and noisy masquerade ball, such were their exotic costumes, their language, and the very nature of their occupations. . . . At every step we were compelled to get out of the way, plunging our legs into the mire to give passage to some former dandy now arrayed in woolen shirt and rolled up pants and sweating under the weight of some load he was carrying. . . . Quiet and ease were words without meaning in San Francisco. In the midst of the tremendous din of hammering that went on all about, some men were setting up tents, others were sawing boards; one man rolled a barrel, another struggled with a post or pounded loudly to fix it in the ground. A tent was scarcely erected when business was in full swing, the goods displayed in the open: boots and flimsy clothing, Chanco cheeses, bundles of jerked beef, piles of dried pears, shovels, picks, powder and liquors, objects which, like toasted and untoasted flour, brought their weight in gold. Chilean brandy sold for seventy dollars a four-gallon jug, and the sweetened soda water they called champagne for eight to twelve dollars a bottle. The prices were due not so much to the small supplies of commodities, as to the necessity for economy of time, which no one wasted in haggling, even though things might be cheaper a bit further on.

Rosales and his companions spent little time in the confused and noisy town; like most newcomers, they hurried on to the gold fields. When, something less than a year later, having failed to make their fortunes, they returned to the city, the diarist wrote:

How different was the San Francisco of my second visit! The city of canvas and a few more or less pretentious structures had disappeared. Tents and shelters had been metamorphosed into buildings in regular rows, though of hurried and rough construction. Foundations had been laid for splendid hotels, and the streets, formerly cut off by mire at the high water level, had been extended out over the water by means of piers resting on redwood logs driven into the bottom. Lots that had diligently been given away were now measured by feet, and their value was more than sky high.
. . .

The bay was crowded with ships, all of them deserted. Passengers and crews were raising the unstable population to over 30,000. And so intense was the activity of transient and permanent residents alike, that the city was growing and being transformed as if by magic. Long wharves had already been built out over huge redwood piles, but were being lengthened; and others, only half finished as yet, ran out from every street that came down to the water's edge, disputing with the mud of low tide room for thoroughfares and new buildings. Owing to the shortage of other material right at hand for pier construction, boxes and sacks of earth were heaped up at the waterline in one place, while in another spot piers, warehouses and streets were improvised by grounding a row of ships in a line from the ends of the city streets. Shops were then built over beams and boards resting upon the ships.

## viii

AMONG the scores of accounts of early San Francisco that have come down to us, few are more revealing than that of Jessie Benton Frémont. Daughter of the Missouri senator, Thomas Hart Benton, and wife of the Pathfinder, she was a figure of consequence in the political and social life of the nation (a fact of which she herself was well aware), and throughout her stay she was treated with a deference befitting her station.

More than a quarter century later, in a little book called *A Year of American Travel,* Mrs. Frémont recalled some of the highlights of her visit. Of her arrival in the spring of 1849, she wrote:

We found a bleak and meager frontispiece to our Book of Fate. A few low houses, and many tents, such as they were, covered the base of some of the wind-swept treeless hills, over which the June fog rolled in chilling mist. Deserted ships of all sorts were swinging with the tide. A crowd of men swarmed about what is now Montgomery Street, then the mud shore of the bay. It was Aladdin's old lamp, however, homely as it seemed, and fortune was there for those who had what my father used to call "a stomach for a fight," and for those who, born lucky, succeed by virtue of the unknown force to which we concede the term.

The mere landing of the passengers was a problem. The crews who took boats ashore were pretty likely not to come back. The *Ohio,* Captain Ap Catsby Jones commanding, was there. Captain Jones very kindly invited me on board to remain until Mr. Frémont should arrive, for I had the disappointment of finding he was not yet here. Mr. Howard, a wealthy merchant, had brought out his boat, and I accepted his invitation, as after so much sea travel the land was best for me.

There were then some three or four regularly built houses in San Francisco, representing the Hudson Bay and the Russian hide business; the rest were canvas and blanket tents. Of course there was no lumber for building, and there were not even trees to be cut down; nor would any man have diverted his attention from the mines to go house building. A little later when they found the hardships of mining life too great and the returns too uncertain, the tide turned, and many men came back to make fortunes at steady work in building up the town. Sixteen dollars a day was ordinary pay for carpenters. The young officers of the army and navy there used to lament to me that their business was so far less profitable. . . .

I was taken out to one of these houses, which had been the residence of Leidesdorff, the Russian consul, who had recently died. It was a time of wonderful contrasts. This was a well-built adobe house, one story high, with a good veranda about it, and a beautiful garden kept in old world order by a Scotch gardener. Luxuries of every kind were to be had, but there were wanting some necessaries. Fine carpets and fine furniture and a fine Broadwood piano, but no housemaid. The one room with a fireplace had been prepared for my sleeping room, and had French furniture and no end of mirrors, but lacked a fire. . . . There was no fuel proper; and little fagots of brushwood, broken up goods boxes and sodden ends of old ship timber were all that could be had.

The club of wealthy merchants who had this house to-

gether had excellent Chinese servants, but to make everything comfortable for me they added the only woman that
could be procured, who accepted a temporary place as
chambermaid at two hundred and forty dollars a month
and perquisites. One of the perquisites was the housing of
her husband and children as well as herself. She had been
washerwoman to a New York regiment, and was already the
laundress of these gentlemen. She was kind enough to tell
me that she liked my clothes, and would take the pattern
of certain dresses, and seemed to think it a matter of course
that I would let her carry off gowns and wraps to be copied
by her dressmaker, a Chinaman. I declined this as civilly as
I could, but the result was that she threw up the situation.

The only really private house was one belonging to a
young New Yorker, who had shipped it from home, house
and furniture complete—a double two story frame house,
which, when in place, was said to have cost ninety thousand
dollars. At this price, with the absence of timber and the
absence of labor, it will be seen that it was difficult to have
any other shelter than a tent. The bride for whose reception
this house was intended arrived just before me, but lived
only a few weeks; the sudden and great changes of climate
from our Northern weather into the tropics, and from the
tropics again into the raw, harsh winds of that season at San
Francisco, were too much for her, even with all the comforts
of her own beautiful home. At a party given to welcome her
the whole force of San Francisco society came out, the ladies
sixteen in number.

Visits in the daytime were held as a marked attention.
I was told that "time was worth fifty dollars a minute," and
that I must hold as a great compliment the brief visits which
were made to me constantly through the day by busy men.

After a stay of several weeks, Mrs. Frémont joined her husband at Monterey, and for several years San Francisco saw no more of her.

## ix

FIRE was an ever-present hazard to the early city; no less than six major blazes swept over the business section during '49, '50, and '51. After the second such visitation—that of Christmas Day of '49, which destroyed above fifty buildings with a loss of over a million dollars —the town council passed an ordinance levying heavy fines on all who refused to join in fighting fires or removing goods from the path of the flames. The ordinance also provided for the digging of artesian wells and the building of reservoirs, and required each householder to keep six buckets filled with water constantly in readiness. Before these precautionary measures could be put into effect, however, a third and still more costly blaze broke out. This was the great fire of June 14, 1850, which before it burned itself out three days later consumed buildings and goods valued at from three to five million.

The journal of Captain George Coffin, whose ship, the *Alhambra,* was then in the harbor, gives this account of the catastrophe:

. . . It was mail day, and I had gone to the post office to deposit my letters. It was open at eight o'clock. I arrived at half past seven, and found two long lines of waiting depositors. Just before the window slides were drawn, the alarm bell of the Montgomery engine house rang out its frightful ding-dong-clang. Looking down the hill, I saw a volume of smoke bursting out of the bakery of the Sacramento House on the east side of Portsmouth Square. In an instant the square was a dense mass of human beings. The post office files were broken instanter. Enginemen and traders dashed down the hill like an avalanche.

I deposited my letters and started to assist my friends Plummer and Keith. Certainly fifteen minutes had not elapsed when through smoke and fire and confusion indescribable I reached their store in time to assist Mr. Keith in removing a chest containing thirty thousand dollars in gold dust. It was a lug, but we managed to drag it down to the lower end of Howison's pier where it could be thrown overboard as a last resort.

It was at once seen that nothing could stay the furious element. A fire engine was no more use than an old maid's teapot.

Leaving Mr. Keith mounted on his box of gold dust, I went over to the Long Wharf to look out for my sloop, which lay there among fifty other small craft in the mud, no water within a cable's length. Between the pier and the wharf, the communication was by a narrow causeway in front of the large building of the Pacific Steamship Company and another building occupied by the military quartermaster. The former was in flames, and a posse of men were engaged in futile attempts to save the merchandise there, by throwing it onto the dock, where it was burned before the flood tide came in.

By great exertion I forced myself through the confusion and, smoked and scorched, I reached my sloop just as a cartman came driving furiously down the wharf and dumped a large military chest at my feet and drove furiously back. I looked at the box and saw that it was marked gunpowder. I gave the alarm, and two or three neighboring boatmen coming to my assistance, we pitched it overboard and buried it in the mud. I then cut my sloop sails from the spars and put them under deck, and jumping onto the dock with my shovel, I covered her decks with soft mud.

The quartermaster's warehouse was said to contain five thousand stands of loaded muskets. The constant discharging of these would at any other time have sounded like a military engagement, but amid the roar of this awful conflagration they were not heard. The rapid and constant succession of flashes showed they were being discharged. Our escape was owing to the fact that these muskets were fitted in perpendicular racks so that the shells were thrown upward.

The wharf was a continuance of Clay Street. About five hundred of us were cut off from communication with the city, and we had nothing to do but gaze at the devouring monster, who at every blast of the hurricane came surging down the wharf in clouds of smoke and cinders, obliging us to lie flat on our faces.

The fire had now reached the extensive premises of Simmons, Hutchinson and Company, S. H. Williams and Company, and McCondray [Macondray] and Company. These were the most important mercantile houses in the city, and the merchandise in these warehouses was of immense value. They were east of Clay Street and fronted the Bay. In an hour they were all a heap of ashes, except the pyramids of lumber piled up in their yards; probably a million feet of boards and plank were stacked up there. The scene was sublime when these pyramids of lumber got well on fire; they continued burning for several days, and when everything else was swept away, they stood like fiery giants, with innumerable arms and tongues of flame, constantly spitting out flashes and cinders, as the knots and slivers snapped and cracked, sounding as if all the firecrackers in China were being let off at once. To my fancy they seemed the genii of the catastrophe, standing there for three days and nights, gloating over the general destruction till at last the same devouring element having eaten them off their balance, they toppled and fell in a crash of fire and smoke, the grand finale to a stupendous pyrotechnic exhibition.

x

THE aftermath of this fire of June 14 is described in some detail by an English journalist, Frank Marryat, who arrived in the harbor aboard a Panama steamer while the flames were at their height. "As we open the bay," he wrote, "we observe dense masses of smoke rolling to leeward; the town and shipping are almost undistinguishable." In his book *Mountains and Molehills* (London, 1855) Marryat thus described his impressions on going ashore the next day:

The fire was fast subsiding; and as the embers died away, and the heavy smoke rolled off . . . the site of the conflagration was plainly marked out to the spectator like a great black chart. There was nothing particularly impressive in the scene, for although four hundred houses have been destroyed, they were but of wood, or thin sheet-iron, and the "devouring element" has made a clean sweep of everything, except a few brick chimneys and iron pots. Everybody seems in good humor, and there is no reason why the stranger, who has lost nothing by the calamity, should allow himself to be plunged into melancholy reflections! Planks and lumber are already being carted in all directions, and so soon as the embers cool, the work of rebuilding will commence.

I found it amusing next day to walk over the ground and observe the effects of the intense heat on the articles which were strewed around. Gun-barrels were twisted and knotted like snakes; there were tons of nails welded together by the heat, standing in the shape of the kegs which had contained them; small lakes of molten glass all the colors of the rainbow; tools of all descriptions, from which the wood-work had disappeared, and pitch-pots filled with melted lead and glass. There was an iron house that had collapsed with the heat, and an iron fire-proof safe that had burst under the same influence; spoons, knives, forks, and crockery were melted up together in heaps; crucibles even had cracked; preserved meats had been unable to stand this second cooking, and had exploded in every direction. The loss was very great, as the houses destroyed had been for the most part filled with merchandise; but there was little time wasted in lamentation, and the energy of the people showed itself at once in action, and in forty-eight hours after the fire the whole district resounded to the busy din of workmen.

Marryat's stay in San Francisco and elsewhere in California extended over nearly two years; accordingly, he witnessed yet another destructive blaze—this one in the spring of 1851.

On the 3d of May [he wrote], at eleven in the evening, the fire-bell again startled us; but on this occasion the first glance at the lurid glare and heavy mass of smoke that rolled toward the bay evinced that the fire had already a firm grip on the city. The wind was unusually high, and the flames spread in a broad sheet over the town. All efforts to arrest them were useless; houses were blown up and torn down in attempts to cut off communication; but the engines were driven back step by step, while some of the brave firemen fell victims to their determined opposition. As the wind increased to a gale, the fire became beyond control; the brick buildings on Montgomery Street crumbled before it; and before it was arrested, over one thousand houses, many of which were filled with merchandise, were left in ashes. Many lives were lost, and the amount of property destroyed was estimated at two millions and a half sterling.

No conception can be formed of the grandeur of the scene; for at one time the burning district was covered by one vast sheet of flame that extended half a mile in length. But when the excitement of such a night as this had passed by, one scarcely can recall the scene. The memory is confused in the recollection of the shouts of the excited populace—the crash of falling timbers—the yells of the burnt and injured—the hoarse orders delivered through speaking-trumpets—maddened horses released from burning livery-stables plunging through the streets—helpless patients being carried from some hospital, and dying on the spot, as the swaying crowd, forced back by the flames, tramples all before it—explosions of houses blown up by gunpowder—showers of burning splinters that fall around on every side—the thunder of brick buildings as they fall into a heap of ruin—the blinding glare of ignited spirits. Amidst the heat that scorches, let you go where you will—smoke that strikes the eyes as if they were pricked by needles—water that, thrown off the heated walls, falls on you in a shower of scalding steam—you throw your coat away and help to work the engine-brakes, as calls are made for more men.

At daylight you plod home, half-blind, half-drowned, half-scorched, half-stunned, and quite bewildered; and from that time you never care to recall one half of the horrors you have witnessed on the night of the conflagration of the 3d of May.

The fire of May 3 burned out the heart of the city; however, only a little more than a month later came a second visitation—this one consuming much of what had been spared by the first. Marryat, who had meantime gone to the town of Vallejo, tells of having seen from there "a bright glow from the direction of San Francisco" and of hastening to the stricken city by the first available steamer.

It was with great difficulty that we landed [he recalled], for the fire had extended to the water's edge, and in many places the wharves had been disconnected; everywhere deep holes had been burnt in them, and some were drowned that night from this cause.

The ruins of the fire were quite deserted, the inhabitants had sought the suburbs, sorrowfully no doubt, for a night's rest; and the bright moon looked calmer than ever in contrast to the red angry embers which smouldered on every side.

I found myself alone after I had scrambled up a small hill that commanded a view of the fallen city, and I never remember feeling so solitary in my life. Small columns of red-tinted smoke rose lazily in every direction, the blackened shells of brick warehouses stood out here and there in bold relief against the moonlight, while every crevice and window in them was fantastically lighted by the glowing embers that still burnt within. Over the ruins of large drug stores ghostly lights of blue and green flickered in a supernatural manner. Where the fire had already been extinguished, dark pits seemed to yawn, and open wells, and deep cisterns, stood ready on all sides, their coverings being burnt, to trap the unwary adventurer who might be led to explore these regions. Not a sound broke the stillness of the night, and as the moon was overshadowed by a passing cloud, I turned and stumbled on what was either a very dead man or a very drunken one, and having seen all there was to see, I descended the hill and rejoined my companions.

Lodgings were scarce that night, as may be imagined, nor was there a sufficient number of houses standing to accommodate the burnt-out citizens.

What steps the city's volunteer firemen took to cope with these recurring blazes, and with what success, is thus described by Marryat in a passage from his journal, dated some six months later:

I found the people still very nervous about fire; and though the dreadful experiences of the past had caused extraordinary precautions to be taken for preventing the recurrence of another general conflagration, still night after night as the warning bell announced some fire in the suburbs, the whole population would turn out and follow the engines "en masse" to the scene of conflagration. Not a night passed but one or more alarms were pealed forth by that dreadful bell, of which the tone was so familiar, and so associated with misfortune, and a shanty or two would generally be consumed in the wooden portion of the city. Sometimes an hotel or hospital would blaze and furnish a furious night's work for the firemen, but these were so active and vigilant, that the flames were always confined to a small space, and it was evident that the days of general conflagrations were over. The highest praise that I can accord to the San Francisco volunteer firemen is to record the simple truth of them, and say that they are zealous and intrepid, and that their services are gratuitous.

## xi

BECAUSE the early town was made up for the most part of flimsy wooden buildings, canvas tents, and other highly inflammable materials, it was perhaps inevitable that fires should be both frequent and destructive. It presently grew clear, however, that not all such disasters were due to overturned lamps, sparks from wood stoves, unattended campfires, and like accidental causes. As time passed it became evident that many had been deliberately started by bands of hoodlums who took advantage of the resulting confusion to break into houses or shops and make off with whatever valuables they could lay hands on.

For the lure of gold had attracted not only miners, merchants, artisans, and professional men but a quota of emigrants of a quite different stamp: men—and women—who came to prey on their fellows and relieve them of their earnings by every trick and device known to the underworld. In that category were not alone gamblers, prostitutes, and assorted knaves and swindlers but many hardened criminals, most of whom had fled to California to escape punishment for their crimes at home.

It was of the latter class that J. M. Letts, another close observer of men and events in the early city, wrote in his book *California Illustrated,* which was published in New York in 1852:

San Francisco was, at this time [1849], infested by a gang of desperados disposed to repudiate all laws, and to be governed only by their own fiendish propensities. They styled themselves "hounds," and neither life nor property were secure against their depredations. They felt themselves so secure in their strength and numbers, that they did not seek the protection of night, but frequently committed the most revolting crimes at noonday, and under the eye of the public authorities. They would enter public houses, demand whatever they wished, always forgetting to pay for the same, and, perhaps, before leaving, demolish every article of furniture on the premises. This would be a mere prelude or introductory to a night of fiendish revelry. They would plunder houses, commit the most diabolical acts upon the inmates, murder in case of resistance, then commit the building to the flames to hide their infamy.

On the first Sunday after my arrival, several of the leaders of the gang returned to town after a few days' absence. They crossed over from the opposite side of the bay, having with them a fife and drum, the music of which was accompanied by yells, groans and hisses, such as one would only expect to hear from demons. After landing they marched into the main plaza . . . and commenced their foray. I was seated in a restaurant as the captain and five of his followers entered. He drew up to a table upon which were several glasses, decanters, &c., together with sundry plates of refreshments. He raised his foot, kicked over the table, smashing the crockery into atoms, then taking his cigar from his mouth, said with the utmost nonchalance, and with an oath, "Waiter, bring me a gin-cocktail." After having satisfied their thirst and hunger, they sallied forth. . . .

During the night, after having committed several robberies, they entered a Chilean tent, and, after committing the most brutal outrages upon the mother and daughter, murdered the former, and in the struggle with the latter, she, after receiving several severe wounds, caught a bowie-knife from the hand of one of them and, after dealing him a deadly blow, made her escape. She immediately gave the alarm, and although robberies had been committed with impunity, this outrage upon defenseless females, awakened an impulse that was irresistible. The excitement was most intense; citizens flocked together, armed with a determination to meet out summary punishment to the perpetrators of this inhuman outrage.

Several arrests were made, and, although many were in favor of summary vengeance, better counsel prevailed, and they were put into the hands of the authorities and locked up. . . . A few hours later, a demonstration was made by accomplices, in order to force open the jail and release their comrades. This caused the strongest feelings of indignation, and the citizens assembled en masse in the plaza, all armed to the teeth, determined to avenge this additional aggravation to the atrocious crimes already perpetrated. They immediately organized themselves into a police, and determined to act with decision upon any proposition that might be sanctioned by the meeting. Had a resolution been passed to hang the prisoners it would have been carried into immediate effect.

## xii

THE GATHERING described by the writer just quoted was the forerunner of a movement that was soon to attract attention—and stir up controversy—all over the nation; namely, the Vigilance Committee of 1851. The story of that organization, and of the circumstances that brought it about, was told some forty years later by one of its leaders, the early-day merchant, William T. Coleman. Writing in the *Century Magazine* for November, 1891, Coleman stated:

On the 3d of May, 1851, a great fire occurred that destroyed almost the entire city. . . . There were good reasons for believing that the fire was the work of incendiaries who had sacrificed these valuable lives and millions of dollars' worth of property for the sake of plunder, and a very strong and bitter feeling grew up against the newly arrived population of criminal classes. The conviction grew stronger every day that something should be done by the people themselves to rid the city of incendiaries and robbers. With a view of immediate protection, a number of mechanics, merchants and other respectable citizens agreed to form a private patrol, each member of this volunteer police to take his particular beat, and to be on duty a certain number of hours every night. In case of emergency, the entire force was to rally at a point and be prepared for duty. The effect was good, but the result was not adequate: the criminal classes continued their outrages.

A second great fire occurred on the 3d of June following,

and arrests were made of persons believed to be the incendiaries. So violent was the feeling of the people that attempts were made to hang the prisoners, but the mayor and officials promised that they should be severely dealt with. The grand jury was then in session, and found a true bill against some of the accused, but by technicalities the indictments were squashed and the persons disappeared.

The want of a strong organization among those who wished to preserve peace and enforce the laws was severely felt. Those who had the largest interests at stake felt that unless there could be united action and control there might be introduced a system of mob law, which would ultimately be more dangerous than the existing state of affairs. It was for this reason that, on the 10th of June, 1851, an organization was effected, and about two hundred names were enrolled. . . . The objects of the committee were "to watch, pursue, and bring to justice the outlaws infesting the city, through the regularly constituted courts, if possible, through more summary process, if necessary." Each member pledged his word of honor, his life, and his fortune for the protection of his fellow-members, and for purging the city of its bad characters. After arranging for a concert of action, watch-words and a signal to call the members to the rendezvous, which was three taps of a fire-bell, the committee adjourned for the evening.

Scarcely half an hour had passed before the bell was tapped. On reaching headquarters I found a number of gentlemen, and soon after there was brought in a very large, rough, vicious looking man called Jenkins, an ex-convict from Sydney, who had been caught in the theft of a safe from a store. He was well known as a desperate character who had frequently evaded justice. The committee was organized immediately into a court, and Jenkins was tried for the offense within an hour. The evidence was overwhelming; he was promptly convicted and sentenced to be hanged that night. Jenkins's bearing throughout the trial was defiant and insulting, and he intimated that his rescue by his friends might be expected at any moment. We were notified by our officers that already the roughest and worst characters throughout the city were mustering in force to resist the committee. At the same time scores of our best citizens came forward and enrolled themselves as members, while others pledged their support in anything we might do.

I strenuously resisted the proposition to execute Jenkins that night . . . and proposed that he should be held till next morning and then hanged in broad daylight as the sun rose. Only a few agreed with me; there was much nervousness; the very circumstances of his crime having been committed at the moment of our organization and in defiance of it, and the threatened attack on us by abandoned criminals, all tended to impress the committee with the necessity of prompt action. Seeing that he must be hanged, I moved that the prisoner have the benefit of clergy. This was granted, but when the minister was left with him, the hardened criminal heaped the vilest insults on his venerable head. This hastened his doom, and his career was quickly closed.

The next morning the work of the Vigilance Committee was heralded throughout the State, and hundreds of citizens came forward and tendered their approval of our acts and asked to be enrolled in our ranks. The unexpected arrest and quick execution of Jenkins spread consternation among all his class. The Governor of the State, McDougal, issued a proclamation and maintained a nominal opposition to the committee, but took no active measures against it. Many arrests were made of dangerous characters, and where clear proof of murder within the State was lacking, it was decided that banishment or corporal punishment should be the penalty. During the active operations of the committee, four men were hanged, and about thirty were banished. Nearly all were from Sydney or other British colonies, and as far as possible they were returned to the places from which they had come.

After a session of about thirty days the committee, finding that the country had been purged of a goodly number of its worst people, determined to adjourn quietly. It was decided not to disband, but to preserve the organization ready for any emergency. Happily there was no call for its services for some time; in fact, it was four years before the necessity of such a committee was again felt by the people of California.

### xiii

ANOTHER ACCOUNT of the execution of Jenkins is contained in these excerpts from the *Journals* of J. Goldsborough Bruff, miner and ex-army engineer, who was present at the time:

[June] 10th [1851]—Late last night I was awakened by the tolling of the bell of the "Monumental Engine House," and proceeded to the plaza, where a dense crowd of people were assembled, having a prisoner to *finish off*.

[June] 11th—At 2 A.M. The notorious Jenkins,—the burgler, murderer, and robber, paid the penalty of his rascalities; being hung by the populace, to the gable end of the old adobe, in the plaza, *"till dead."* . . . The body of the hanged was laid out in the Engine House, close by, and

afterwards removed to the police office. A considerable
crowd lingering about the plaza all day. I was told that
Jenkins was transported for life, to New South Wales, some
14 years since, from England; and escaped from there, and
arrived in this country about 2 years ago; since which he
has led an industrious life of villany, till it terminated, as it
should have been long ago. They say that he smoked a cigar
on the way to the plaza; and when a minister of the gospel
offered him spiritual consolation,—while the rope was around
his neck, he repulsed him in the most rude and insolent manner. On searching his pockets, preparatory to running him
up, they found 200 dolls. in gold, and enquired if he had any
friends to whom it might be given. He answered negatively,
and told them to scatter it among the mob. After death,
they found that his ankles were callous, and marked by the
long wear of shackles. While the culprit was hanging, a fellow in the crowd sang out "Sarved him right, by G-d!" and he
was instantly floored by a Sydney convict standing near;
when the last-named chap was personally seized by the mob,
decorated by the shackles which had just before graced
Jenkins, and hurried off to the Post Office. A man who had
hold of the rope—running Jenkins up the beam, had his
pocket picked of a small amount of gold while thus engaged.

As to the ethics of the committee's action in taking
over the functions of the police and courts, another observer, J. M. Letts (whose book *California Illustrated,*
was quoted earlier), commented:

Persons living in well-regulated communities, and looking
at the matter in the distance, may feel disposed to censure
the Committee and its proceedings as hasty and precipitate;
but when we take into consideration that not only property
to an immense amount, but life itself, was in jeopardy—the

want of facilities for securing and retaining criminals during the tardy process of law, the numerous rescues by accomplices, and the frequent pardons by the authorities when the accused were notoriously guilty,—I say, when we take these things into consideration, together with the fact that not an individual was executed who was not clearly proved guilty, and even confessed his guilt; we can look upon the facts of the Committee not only as just—but imperative. In the confessions of some of those who were executed they implicated men in authority, in such a manner that not a doubt was left upon the public mind. The result of these summary measures is apparent to all. Crime, since the organization of the Committee, has decreased one half, and they have now ceased to make arrests, leaving all to the jurisdiction of the proper authorities. They, however, maintain their organization, and would, no doubt, act in case of emergency.

Part Three

# The Turbulent Fifties
# 1850–1860

# i

SAN FRANCISCO's transition from raw frontier outpost to cosmopolitan city was accomplished with almost unprecedentd speed. Visitors who arrived only a year or two after the gold rush got under way invariably expressed surprise at finding, not the confused, haphazard settlement they had expected, but a community boasting most of the comforts—and many of the luxuries—of far older cities.

Among those who wrote of how rapidly the place had shunted off its crude beginnings was Frank Marryat, the British journalist quoted in Part Two. Marryat reached San Francisco in the spring of 1851, spent the summer and fall on a tour of the gold country, and in December returned to the Bay. There he proceeded to enjoy such sybaritic pleasures as the fast-growing metropolis had to offer.

Let me suppose myself to have arrived at San Francisco from the mines only this morning [he wrote]. I have no carpet bag . . . and I enter a shaving-saloon. At the counter I purchase any quantity of linen I may require for the moment, and with this I proceed to the bathroom; when I return from my ablutions, I am asked if I would like my head "shampoo-ed." With a reckless feeling in respect to shampooing, I submit to the operation.

Seating myself in an easy chair of velvet, and placing my legs on an easy stool, also of velvet, I become drowsy under the influence of the fingers and thumbs of the operator, as they are passed over my skull, as if with a view to making a phrenological chart. . . .

I am conducted to a marble washstand and a tap of cold water is turned on me. I thought I had washed my head in the bath, but it appears not, judging by the color of the water. My head is dried by hard labor, then is wetted again by a shower of eau de Cologne and water, thrown at me when least expected. "Will I be shaved, sir?" Of course I will! "Take a seat." I sink into the velvet chair, and contemplate my dirty boots, that for days have not known blacking, but have known mud, as they contrast with the crimson pile velvet on which they rest. The back of the chair is raised by means of a screw, until my head is in the proper position for operation. First I have hot water on my chin, and a finger and thumb (generally the property of a colored gentleman) feels for my beard in a dreamy way with a view to softening the stubble. Then comes the lather, and shave the first, and I am about to get up, when I am stopped by more lather, and shave the second; this is conducted in a slow methodical manner, the finger and thumb wandering about in search of any stray hairs, like gleaners after the harvest. . . .

From the barbers, I proceed to a boot-blacking saloon kept by Frenchmen. I seat myself on a comfortable fauteuil, two Gauls are at my feet, each Gaul has two brushes, and such a friction is commenced that my feet are being shampooed as much as my head was. The morning paper has been handed to me, and I have scarcely settled to the lead article when "V'la, M'sieur" announces that all is over. What a change! I pay the money with pleasure, one shilling, not before I am brushed though.

Having been shaved, shined and "shampoo-ed," the journalist set forth on his next errand.

It is [he continued] eight o'clock now, and in an instinctive search for breakfast, I enter the Jackson House. Here are a hundred small tables nearly all occupied; I secure one and peruse the bill of fare. I could have wished for fresh eggs, but these were marked at two shillings each and . . . I considered economy a duty. "Fricassée de Lapin," that sounded well, so I ordered it; I didn't tell the waiter, when he brought it, that it was not rabbit but gray squirrel, but I knew it from the experience I had had in the anatomy of that sagacious animal. . . .

But San Francisco bills of fare present at all seasons great variety, and no one has a right to complain who has but to choose from bear, elk, deer, antelope, turtle, hares, partridges, quails, wild geese, brant, numerous kinds of ducks, snipe, plover, curlew, cranes, salmon, trout, and other fish, and oysters.

According to this observer, the San Franciscans of the day demanded—and got—the best of all things, including even the draft animals that pulled the heavily loaded wagons through the streets.

An immense quantity of drays are required in the city for the transport of goods [he commented], and the stranger will be at once struck with the superiority of breed of the horses, and the high condition in which they are kept. It had not been worth while of late to send anything commonplace to San Francisco; the horses therefore that are driven across the plains are generally strong and showy animals. "Draying" is paid very well here, and many of the proprietors of these vehicles, although they drive for themselves, are well-to-do. The dray harness is often mounted in German silver; and you may see any day a respectable-looking quiet man in spectacles carting a load of hay or lumber, with a handsome four-in-hand team, well groomed, and ornamented with bear-skin trappings.

## ii

ONE of the liveliest of all accounts of the city at that stage of its development is to be found in the journal of Albert Benard de Russailh, a high-spirited and cynical young Frenchman who arrived, with a boatload of his countrymen, early in 1851. Before his untimely death in a cholera epidemic the following year, de Russailh made himself familiar with virtually every phase of the life of the town.

His journal—which dropped from sight after its owner's death and has only recently come to light again—is mainly given over to an account of the six-month voyage of his party from Le Havre to San Francisco, only the final fifty pages are devoted to the city itself. This section begins:

I went ashore the evening of my arrival. . . . By nine o'clock I was walking on the Long Wharf. I at once began to look for a hotel where I might spend the night. My friend Louis and two other cabin-passengers came ashore with me. We followed the Wharf, crossed Montgomery Street, went up Commercial and, going through Portsmouth Square, reached Dupont Street, where there is a French hotel; the *L'Hôtel de l'Alliance*. We had been assured that we could find fairly comfortable beds there. As I walked through the city, my impressions were very favorable. It could have been scarcely otherwise: after a sea voyage of six months, and so long a time spent looking at the same faces and things, the poorest Indian village would seem like a magnificent city. The brilliance of the lights on Commercial Street and the life we saw everywhere, astonished me. Like so many other emigrants, I had thought to find on my arrival here only the beginnings of a town, a cluster of tents and rude shacks, where I should scarcely obtain shelter from bad weather. But I was greatly surprised to see, instead, large and fine streets, well laid-out, and wooden and brick houses, all in regular order. Instead of on muddy clay ground, I walked on board sidewalks, roughly made, of course, but very practicable. While I was taking all this in, I reached Dupont Street with my friends; we went into *L'Hôtel de l'Alliance*. . . .

Having registered and been assigned a room containing four mattresses laid on the floor, each with a single blanket, the high-spirited group decided "to order a a supper that would make up for all the privations we had undergone during our voyage."

Lobster with mayonnaise [the newcomer continued], a roast chicken, a few slices of cold meat, and several bottles of fairly good Bordeaux, soon set us up. At one o'clock in the morning we were still at table, nearly forgetting that we had just come ashore in a foreign port, six thousand leagues from France. Poverty might await us, and riches might prove only an illusion, but we did not care. Our natural good humor revived by the end of the meal, and we became quite hilarious when we were shown to our bedroom. At daybreak we were still laughing at would-be clever remarks that the wine had put into our heads.

There is evidence that de Russailh intended to make his journal the basis of a guidebook for Frenchmen who planned to follow him to California, for much of it is given over to information likely to be of use to prospective emigrants. The following is quoted from a section dealing with living conditions as he found them:

At the time of my arrival . . . the cost of ordinary living was very high, but it is only fair to add that one could earn enough to pay one's expenses. In March, 1851, a fairly good dinner without wine cost $2.00, a bottle of wine, $1.50, which brought the price of an ordinary meal to $3.50 a person. . . . At the same period one could rent a corner of a bedroom for $1.50. You were given a blanket and had the right to wrap up in it and stretch your weary bones on the floor. Daily expenses ran up to $5.00. Everything else was in proportion: laundries charged $9.00 a dozen to do up shirts, although a new shirt cost only $2.00. The bootblacks working in front of the El Dorado, the Parker House, and the Union Hotel earned from $10.00 to $15.00 a day each. The negroes and other workmen who were always hanging around the Wharf charged $3, $4, or $5 to carry a trunk or two. A musician could earn two ounces ($32) by scraping on a squeaky fiddle for two hours every evening, or by puffing into an asthmatic flute. . . . But to make up for this, every kind of work was extremely well-paid. Almost any small business deal would eventually bring in very handsome profits. You earned money in proportion to what you spent, and you quickly got used to paying $3 or $4 for your dinner and no longer hesitated to spend five times as much as in France for a drink in the middle of the day.

The young journalist devoted a half dozen pages of his journal to the town's gambling houses. "My account of the city would be incomplete," he wrote, "if I did not describe these sordid dens, rotten with the most flagrant vice."

There are many Mexicans in California [he continued], all of them born gamblers, and all day long they fill the big rooms of El Dorado, the Verandah, the Parker House, Bella Union and California Exchange, the Empire, and other establishments. In the daytime hardly anyone is in the gambling-houses except Mexicans, seated around the monte tables and stirred to high greed by the huge banks. Occasionally a few idle Americans lean over a faro game, and perhaps a group of Chinamen are playing craps for low stakes. Italians, Germans, and Frenchmen rarely sit down; now and then they toss a few coins onto the green cloth, and the banker's rake soon gathers the money in. . . .

There are at least twenty tables in a hall, and the bank on each table is enormous. Sums as great as $12,000, $15,000, and $20,000 are piled in plain sight to lure gamblers. The proprietor of the El Dorado has made a colossal fortune with his gaming-tables. It must amount to several million dollars. They tell me that a year or two ago it was not uncommon to see a man risk $16,000 or $20,000 on a single card, but since then the stakes have come down. The most one can expect today is now and then to see a Mexican with an expressionless face calmly play 150 or 200 ounces on a card at monte ($2,400 or $3,200). The Mexicans have the reputation for being the best gamblers in the world; never a word out of them, never a complaint or an argument; they win or lose without a tremor, and during the game are as cold and impressive as stone. . . .

Across the room Americans will be bawling and cursing over faro and roulette, and scarcely a day passes without brawls that end in bloodshed. Four or five times in the El Dorado I saw Americans stab or shoot one another over some petty gambling squabble.

There was more than a touch of Gallic malice in de Russailh's comments on another phase of the San Francisco of the day. In a section of his journal entitled "Women in San Francisco," he wrote:

When I first arrived here, there were only ten or twelve French women in San Francisco, but quite a number of American women had been here for some time, and were living in attractive houses with a certain amount of comfort and even luxury. They all had come from New York, New Orleans, Washington, or Philadelphia and had the stiff carriage typical of women in those cities. Men would look hopefully at them in the streets, at least men who had just come to California, but they much preferred the French women, who had the charm of novelty. Americans were irresistibly attracted by their graceful walk, their supple but easy bearing, and charming freedom of manner, qualities, after all, only to be found in France; and they trooped after a French woman whenever she put her nose out of doors, as if they could never see enough of her. If the poor fellows had known what these women had been in Paris, how one could pick them up on the boulevards and have them for almost nothing, they might not have been so free with their offers of $500 or $600 a night. A little knowledge might have cooled them down a bit. But I'm sure the women were flattered by so much attention. Some of the first in the field made enough in a month to go home to France and live on their income; but many were not so lucky, and one still meets a few who have had a bad time and who are no better off financially than the day they stepped ashore. No doubt, they were blind to their own wrinkles and faded skins, and were too confident of their ability to deceive Americans regarding the dates on their birth-certificates.

Many ships have reached San Francisco during the past three or four months, and the number of women in town has greatly increased, but a woman is still sought after and earns a lot of money. Nearly all the saloons and gambling-houses employ French women. They lean on the bars, talking and laughing with the men, or sit at the card tables and attract players. Some of them walk about with trays of cigars hanging in front of them; others caterwaul for hours beside pianos, imagining they are singing like Madame Stoltz. Occasionally, you will find one who hides her real business, and pretends to be a dressmaker or a milliner; but most of them are quite shameless, often scrawling their names and reception-hours in big letters on their doors. There is a certain Madame Cassini who runs a collar shop and claims to be able to predict the past, present, and future and anything else you like.

To sit with you near the bar or at a card table, a girl charges one ounce ($16) an evening. She has to do nothing save honor the table with her presence. This holds true of the girls selling cigars, when they sit with you. Remember they only work in the gambling-halls in the evening. They have their days to themselves and can then receive all the clients who had no chance during the night. Of course, they often must buy new dresses, and dresses are very expensive out here.

For anything more you have to pay a fabulous amount. Nearly all these women at home were street-walkers of the cheapest sort. But out here, for only a few minutes, they ask a hundred times as much as they were used to getting in Paris. A whole night costs from $200 to $400.

You may find this incredible. Yet some women are quoted at even higher prices. I may add that the saloons and gambling-houses that keep women are always crowded and sure to succeed.

The famous beauties of San Francisco are Marguet, Hélène, Marie, Arthémise, Lucy, Emilie, Madame Mauger, Lucienne, Madame Weston, Eléonore, Madame St. Amand, Madame Meyer, Maria, Angèle, and others whose names I have forgotten.

There are also some honest women in San Francisco, but not very many.

The young Frenchman had come to California expecting to open a shop, and accordingly had brought with him a stock of merchandise. Getting his supplies ashore, however, presented a serious problem. He had arrived with but a few francs in his pocket—far less than the customs officials demanded for the release of his goods. Here he describes how he overcame that difficulty:

Among my baggage the customs officials had found some stationery goods and several cases of champagne. . . . We stood arguing on the deck, while my half-loaded boat thudded against the ship's side, and I was giving up all hope, when a sudden idea struck me. Breaking open one of the cases of champagne, I pulled out a few bottles, and gave one to the chief inspector, a burly man with a red beard. Without a word, he smashed the neck on the bulwark, gulped down the wine, tossed the empty bottle overboard, and wiped his red beard with the back of his hand. The other officers crowded around me, and in a moment half a dozen corks popped and champagne splashed onto the deck. While they were drinking, I lowered the unopened cases over the side, dropped the stationery after them, and then lifted the case from which the bottles had been taken. The wine had done its work, and by this time the inspectors were too befuddled to notice what I was doing; and in a moment I was safely away.

His stock in trade safely ashore, the embryo merchant proceeded to set up shop.

The following day [he wrote] I spent unpacking my cases in preparation for my new career. . . . Early next morning, I conquered my vanity, put on a red flannel shirt, and went down to the Long Wharf, where I chose a good place, and with a few old boards rigged up my open-air shop. My goods were soon spread out to attract customers. I had many things of no particular value: brushes, gloves, perfumes, cutlery, colored shirts, and other articles; but it was enough to begin with; and my little stock transformed me into an important San Francisco merchant. After all, my shop was not much smaller than the best in town, and my different lines were fairly complete.

My business began superbly; my sales were steady, and I made good profits. I sold a pair of suspenders for more than six times what I had paid for them, and a toothbrush for ten times its cost. Jars of cold cream, bottles of *eau de Cologne* and perfume went for high prices, $1 or $1,50 apiece. . . . But I made my biggest profit from a wholly worthless article. In Paris no restaurant charges for these articles, they are carelessly thrown away and trodden under foot, and a

man will break twenty-five a day at lunch or dinner. I am
speaking of toothpicks. I had brought with me two packages
of them (about 248 small packs) for my own use, or to give
away to friends and acquaintances. One day I decided to
lay several packs on my counter. They had scarcely left the
box when a grave gentleman paused before my shop and
began to examine my merchandise. He picked up a few
things . . . but laid them down again, and he seemed about
to walk away, when his eye happened to light on the toothpicks. He picked up a pack, held it up, and said: "How
much?"

I was quite taken back, for I had no idea what to charge.
It had never occurred to me that anyone would buy them,
and I had rather planned to give them away. But I remembered suddenly that in California nothing is given away;
everything is sold. With as serious an expression as I could
command, I replied: "Half a dollar, sir."

He gave me a long look. "It is not possible," he said finally.
"That is very little."

At first, I thought he was joking. Then I feared that he
would fly into a rage. I smiled and was about to say politely:
"That is nothing for you, sir." But he quietly gathered up
four packs, handed me $2, nodded pleasantly, and moved
away.

My happiness was even greater than my amazement, and
I congratulated myself on being such a good business man.
Next day I laid out twice as many toothpicks for sale, and
in a few minutes they were all snapped up at the same price.
"If this is a country where toothpicks are valuable," I said
to myself, "and if I have the only supply on the market, I
must certainly take advantage of the situation and do something on a grand scale." Elated by my success, I hurried
home and sat up far into the night splitting the packs of

toothpicks in two. After the process of division, packs originally containing twenty-four toothpicks had only twelve. The plan was excellent and I was not disappointed: in less than a week they had all gone for 50c a pack. I could hardly restrain my laughter whenever a man paid me half a dollar for only twelve. If I had a 1500-ton ship loaded to the gunwale with toothpicks, my fortune would have been made. . . . But, unluckily, I had only 496 packs.

### iii

IN San Francisco, as in other frontier communities, newspaper readers valued humor above all things else, and the dailies and weeklies that sprang up during the early and middle 1850's made valiant attempts to meet that demand. Of the local scribes who practiced the art, the most widely read was George Horatio Derby, a United States army engineer then stationed in the city, who wrote under the name of "John Phoenix."

Two typical examples of Derby's work are given here. The first, a burlesque description of the tri-monthly sailing of the mail steamer for the East Coast, appeared in the *Alta California* on August 21, 1853:

The *Northerner,* like the steamboat runners, was *lying* at the end of the wharf, blowing off steam, and as usual when a steamer is about to leave for Panama, a great crowd surrounded her. What made them all get up so early? Out of the three or four hundred people on the end of the wharf I don't believe fifty had friends that were about to sail. No!

they love to look upon a steamer sailing. It brings to their minds recollections of the dear ones at home to which she is speeding with fond tidings, and they love to gaze and wish to Heaven they were going in her. The usual mob of noisy fruit vendors encompassed the gangway plank; green pears they sold to greener purchasers; apples, also, whereof, everything but the shape of an apple had long since departed, and oranges the recollections of one of which doth to this day abide by me and set my teeth on edge; but high above their din, the roar of the steamer and the murmuring of the crowd, rang the shrill cry of the newsboy in his unknown tongue, Here's the *Alteruldniguntimes, Heup!* I stepped across the plank and found myself in the presence of three fine bullocks. How fat and sleek they looked; uneasy, though, as if they smelled mischief in the wind. . . .

On deck all was bustle and excitement. The sailors apparently in the last extremity of physical suffering, judging by their agonized cries, were heaving away at mysterious ropes. The mate, Mr. Dall, was engaged in busy, not tender, dalliance at the breast lines, while Burns the purser exhibited an activity and good nature only to be accounted for by the supposition that he had eaten two boxes of Russian salve (which is good for Burns—see your advertising columns) for his breakfast.

The last line fell from the dock, and our noble steamer, with a mighty throb and deep sigh at bidding adieu to San Francisco, swung slowly round, the passengers crowded to the side to exchange farewell salutations with their friends and acquaintances. "Good bye, Jones," "Good bye, Brown," "God bless you old fellow, take care of yourself!" they shouted. Not seeing any one that I knew, and fearing the passengers might think I had no friends, I shouted, "Good bye, Muggins," and had the satisfaction of having a shabby man, much inebriated, reply as he swung his rimless hat, "Good bye, my brother." Not particularly elated at this recognition, I tried again, with "Good bye, Colonel," whereat thirty-four respectable gentlemen took off their hats, and I got down from the position that I had occupied on a camp stool, with much dignity, inwardly wondering whether my friends were all aides to [Governor] Bigler, in which case their elevated rank and affection for me would both be satisfactorily accounted for.

By the mid-1850's, San Franciscans were already looking ahead impatiently to the time when a transcontinental railroad would eliminate the existing slow and tedious means of travel between the two coasts, and so end their isolation from the rest of the nation. Although well over a decade was to pass before these hopes were realized, frequent letters and editorials in the local press discussed the pros and cons of three routes that had been proposed: namely, the northern, central, and southern.

"John Phoenix" was ever on the lookout for some public question that might lend itself to satire. Accordingly, in the March, 1855, issue of the *Pioneer* he presented what he termed his "Official Report" of "a military survey and reconnaissance of the route from San Francisco to the Mission of Dolores, made with a view to ascertain the practicability of connecting these points by a railroad."

It having been definitely determined [his "Report" begins] that the great Railroad connecting the City of San Francisco with the head of navigation on Mission Creek [a distance of two and a half miles] should be constructed without unnecessary delay, a large appropriation ($120,000) was granted, for the purpose of causing thorough military examinations to be made of the proposed routes. The routes which have principally attracted the attention of the public were "the Northern," following the line of Brannan Street, "the Central," through Folsom Street, and "the extreme Southern," passing over the "Old Plank Road" to the Mission. Each of these proposed routes has many enthusiastic advocates, but "the Central" was, undoubtedly, the favorite of the public, it being more extensively used by emigrants from San Francisco to the Mission and therefore more widely and favorably known than the others. It was to the examination of this route that the Committee, feeling a confidence (eminently justified by the result of my labors) in my experience, judgment and skill as a Military Engineer, appointed me on the first instant. Having notified that honorable body of my acceptance of the important trust confided in me, in a letter wherein I took occasion to congratulate them on the good judgment they had evinced, I drew from the Treasurer the amount ($40,000) appropriated to my peculiar route, and having invested it securely in loans at three per cent a month . . . I proceeded to organize my party for the expedition.

Phoenix then named the members and duties of each of the "scientific corps" he had assembled—a list that included, besides himself as "principal engineer and chief astronomer," first and second assistant astronomers, a geologist, botanist, naturalist, ethnologist, a dentist, two draftsmen, and an interpreter. The balance of the party was made up of the following:

James Phoenix (my elder brother)     Treasurer
Joseph Phoenix (ditto)               Quarter-Master
William Phoenix (younger brother)    Commissary
Peter Phoenix (ditto)                Clerk

Paul Phoenix (my cousin)            Sutler
Reuben Phoenix (ditto)              Wagon-Master
Richard Phoenix (second cousin)     Assistant ditto

These gentlemen [he continued], with one hundred laborers employed as teamsters, chairmen, rodmen, etc., made
up the party. . . . Each employee was furnished with a
gold chronometer watch . . . [and] was suitably armed with
four of Colt's revolvers, a Minie rifle, a copy of Col. Benton's
speech on the Pacific Railroad, and a mountain howitzer.
These last-named heavy articles required each man to be
furnished with a wheelbarrow . . . which was accordingly
done; and these vehicles proved of great service to the survey in transporting not only the arms but the baggage of
the party, as well as plunder derived from the natives. A
squadron of dragoons, numbering 150 men, under Capt.
McSpadden, had been detailed as an escort. They accordingly left about a week before us, and we heard from them
occasionally on the march.

The nature of the "Official Report" rendered by the
expedition's Principal Engineer and Chief Astronomer
may be judged from these excerpts:

The climate in these latitudes is mild; snow appears to be
unknown, and we saw little ice; what there was was being
sold at twenty-five cents per pound.

The geological formation of the country is not volcanic.
I saw but one specimen of a trap during the march, which I
observed at the Valley House, with a mouse in it. . . .
From the vast accumulations of sand in these regions, I am
led to conclude . . . that the original name of this territory
was Sand Francisco, from which the final "d" in the prefix
has been lost by time, like the art of painting on glass.

Considering the innumerable villages of pigs found on the

line of march, and the consequent effect produced on the atmosphere, I would respectfully suggest . . . the propriety of changing the name of the route by a slight alteration in the orthography, giving it the appropriate and euphonious title of "*Scent*ral R. R. Route."

The survey and reconnaissance being finished on our arrival at the Mission, it may be expected that I should here give a full and impartial statement of the merits or demerits of the route, in connection with the proposed Railroad.

Some three months must elapse, however, before this can be done, as the triangulation has yet to be perfectly computed, the sub-reports examined and compiled, the observations worked out, and the maps and drawings executed. Besides, I have received a letter from certain parties interested in the Southern and Northern routes, informing me that if I suspend my opinion on the "Great Central" for the present it will be greatly to my interest—and as my interest is certainly my principal consideration, I shall undoubtedly comply with their request, unless indeed greater inducement is offered to the contrary. . . .

In conclusion I beg leave to return my thanks to the Professors, Assistants, and Artists of the Expedition for the energy, fidelity and zeal with which they have ever cooperated with me and seconded my efforts; and to assure them that I shall be happy at any time to sit for my portrait for them, or to accept the handsome service of plate which I am told they have prepared for me, but feel too much delicacy to speak to me about.

I remain, with the highest respect and esteem for myself and everybody else,

John Phoenix, A.M.,
Chief Engineer and Astronomer, S.F.
A.M.D.C.R.

iv

EARLY-DAY San Franciscans were proud of the fact that their city had so speedily outgrown its helter-skelter beginnings and taken its place among the substantial cities of the nation. As early as 1853 local newspapers were pointing out that the new metropolis by the bay was as modern and safe and orderly as Boston, and looking ahead to a period of uninterrupted growth and prosperity, the problems and contentions of the pioneer period safely behind.

However, it soon grew clear that certain of these problems not only remained but were growing steadily more serious. For among the thousands who had been attracted by the gold rush were many men impatient of all restraint, including a quota of hardened criminals. It was this lawless element, together with the fact that the city government presently fell into the hands of weak or corrupt officials, that brought on a period of violence that ended only with the drastic measures taken by the Vigilance Committees of 1851 and 1856.

A typical instance of the hazards to life and property in the early town is recorded in the reminiscences of a youth named John Steele. Steele, an eighteen-year-old New Yorker, reached California in the fall of 1850 and, after spending several years in the towns and camps of the Mother Lode, returned to the East Coast in the summer of 1853. In an eighty-page pamphlet entitled *In*

*Camp and Cabin,* published in 1901, he thus described an adventure that befell him on reaching San Francisco preparatory to sailing for home:

I had planned to sail about the last of June, on the steamer *Sierra Nevada,* and was detained but a single day in the city; but in the early part of that day an incident was added to my experience, which emphasized the adage "Eternal vigilance is the price of liberty," and other valuable things.

On leaving Uniontown [in El Dorado County] a burly, rather well-dressed man occupied a seat in the stage; we took dinner at the same hotel, and when I purchased a ticket on the river steamer for San Francisco, he also was present and obtained one. Though a total stranger, he knew that I had been for some time in the mines and that I was now on my way home. I was surprised at his knowledge, for I had told him nothing about it, but I supposed he might have overheard the conversation with my uncle the night before, and therefore it excited no suspicion. He was social and pleasant, professed to be well acquainted in San Francisco, and suggested a stopping place; but I had made up my mind to stop at the Atlantic Hotel, as I had been there before. "Yes," said he, "that's a good place, and I'll go with you."

However, there were several Mexicans on the boat, and wishing to improve my Spanish, I spent most of the time during the trip in conversation with them.

At midnight or later our boat reached the wharf, and taking our satchels we started for the hotel. When almost there he invited me up to a lighted room, "to have something to drink."

"No, I want no liquor."

"Then will you be so kind as to wait here until I return?"

I begged to be excused, could be of no special service to him, and was quite ready for sleep. I was surprised in not finding him next morning at the breakfast table; in fact he had not come to the hotel.

Looking over the morning paper, I noticed that the *Sierra Nevada*, lying at Long Wharf, was announced to sail the next day; so, preparatory to the purchase of a ticket, I started for the steamer to select a stateroom. It was early in the forenoon and on a thronged street that I again met the stranger. We recognized each other, and in passing he crowded me against a door, which was on a level with the sidewalk, and with a sudden push thrust me inside.

Instead of the usual revolver, I carried two single shooters in a place prepared inside my coat; and, while with my right hand trying to prevent his shutting the outside door, with my left hand I cocked one, drew it, but just then saw another man standing in a side door, and as I raised the pistol he disappeared and shut the door. In an instant I drew the other pistol with my right hand, when the man who had pushed me in disappeared through the door on the opposite side and it was shut.

Bewildered, I stood for a moment with a cocked pistol in either hand, and on regaining presence of mind, saw that the room was only about six feet square, but containing three doors. Coming in from the street there was a door on the right and left, through which the men had disappeared.

Approaching the front door, which my assailant in his haste to get beyond the range of my pistol had failed to close tightly, I swung it open and stepped out upon the sidewalk. Meeting a policeman, I asked him to arrest the man who had assaulted me.

"Where is he?" he asked.

"In this house," I replied.

"You can't identify him."

"Yes, he followed me all the way from Uniontown. I can't be mistaken in the man who laid hands on me."

The policeman paid no further attention to my request; so congratulating myself that I was still alive and in possession of my liberty, passage and expense money, I went to Long Wharf, boarded the steamer, selected a stateroom, and going to the steamer office secured a ticket.

As I reflected on the episode of the morning, the fact that I had been pursued by a robber became apparent, and only instant resort to the pistols saved me from being robbed or worse. The room into which I was so suddenly pushed was evidently a prepared trap, into which the victims who could not be decoyed might be forced. But even with this experience, I had no idea of the actual condition of the city. The city government at that time was entirely in the hands of the saloon element, gamblers, and thugs.

Up to this time more than twelve hundred murders had been known and registered, and there were reasons to believe twice that number had been committed; and yet not a criminal had been brought to justice. Policemen, police courts, officers of all grades were implicated in crime.

## V

THE formation of the first of the town's celebrated Vigilance Committees—that of 1851—was, as stated earlier, brought about by the depredations of gangs of hoodlums known as "The Hounds" and "The Sydney Ducks," who roamed the streets day and night and, virtually unmolested, robbed and brutally assaulted defenseless citizens. Because the police and courts were unable—or unwilling—to punish the offenders, a group of the town's leaders presently banded together, took over the duties of the elected officials, and rounded up many of the worst offenders. Several of their ringleaders were hanged, others were imprisoned, and still others banished from the city. Thereupon, a semblance of order having been restored, the committee ceased to function.

The conditions that some five years later made necessary the organization of a second committee were explained in the reminiscences of its leader, William T. Coleman. In his article in the *Century Magazine* for November, 1891, he stated:

When I returned to San Francisco in January, 1856, after an absence in New York of about two years, I found a great change and much public excitement in social, political, and financial affairs. There had been a severe financial crisis in 1855, and affairs were still very unsettled. The "Bulletin" newspaper, edited by James King of William, had undertaken local reform, and was boldly assailing all evildoers who had again become aggressive. Very recently United States Marshal Richardson had been killed by an Italian gambler named Cora. The murderer had been imprisoned and tried, but all efforts to convict him had failed. The excitement over the general lawlessness and the impotence of the courts increased as the months went by, but a crisis was reached only by the assassination of Editor King in the streets, on the evening of the 14th of May. He was shot down by an ex-convict named Casey, whose infamous New York record the editor had exposed. The community was immediately thrown into intense excitement, and the engine bell on the old Plaza was rung—the familiar signal of the old Vigilance Committee.

After a hasty dinner I went to the Plaza, which I found crowded with excited citizens. Members of the old committee sought me in numbers and urged me to organize a new committee. I declined these importunities; several meetings were held in different places, and urgent appeals made not to allow a repetition of the failure of organization as was done a few months previously when Cora killed Richardson. The result was that I finally consented to take charge and organize the committee. . . . We organized, and within twenty-four hours we had fifteen hundred members, all well-known leading men of the city. Within two days after the first meeting 2500 men were enrolled and equipped with arms, while drilling was carried on constantly day and night. . . .

While this work or organization and preparation was progressing we were informed of numerous counter movements by the opponents of the committee. Word was brought that the roughs were organizing in large numbers, arming, and threatening with determined energy to defend Casey, Cora, and their friends at all hazards, and to lay the city waste if need be to accomplish that end. The next day it was developed that a strong effort was being made by the mayor and others to organize and bring into action all the militia of the State that were available. The larger and better part of the militia in the city had, however, already joined the committee. Renewed and specific threats were made on the life and property of all who were members of the committee, and a determination was announced to crush the new movement at any cost of life, money, or property.

It thus became evident that the committee had to prepare

for more serious work than was anticipated, or by rights should have been forced upon them. James King of William was honest, brave, and terribly in earnest, but often rash. Unhappily, he had arrayed against him several classes of people. He had severely, though in the main justly, castigated that portion of the press which upheld or apologized for the excesses or irregularities in political affairs. . . . Thus, the committee was assailed as his champion . . . when in fact it was merely the champion of justice and right —the child of the necessities of the hour.

With the opposition were some of the best people of the country. Their party and friends had all the City and State offices; they had with them the law and most of the lawyers, and all the law-breakers. Their chief hope was in legal, State and Government aid. We asked nothing but to be understood and judged rightly.

The days that followed were critical ones for the committee, for its opponents brought strong pressure to bear on state and federal agencies, including the West Coast commanders of the army and navy, urging them to intervene and forcibly disarm the Vigilantes. In this, however, the "Law and Order Party," as the organization was called, was unsuccessful.

Our aims and position were soon made plain and satisfactory to the leading army and navy officers on the coast [wrote Coleman] and to the Government at Washington. They soon understood us and always left us to complete our work in our own way. On May 16 I was waited upon by some gentlemen who said Governor J. Neely Johnson had just arrived, and was very anxious to see me. . . . I replied that I would do myself the honor to call on the Governor at his hotel. I did so, and the question of the committee was broached immediately. He asked what we wanted. I answered that we wanted peace. We would like to have it without a struggle, but if it must be at the cost of war, then we must have war. He asked what we wanted to accomplish. I told him, very much what the Vigilance Committee of 1851 accomplished—to see that the laws were executed upon a few prominent criminals whom the officers of the law had allowed to go unpunished; to drive away from the State some notoriously bad characters; to purify the atmosphere morally and politically, and then to disband. I told him that the names of the people in this organization were a guarantee to him that there were no personal aims, or ambitions, nothing in view except the work of the public good; that as an officer of the law, and an observer, he must be aware of the frightful condition of affairs throughout the State, especially in San Francisco; that it had been apparent to all that this could not be much longer endured, and that the climax had now arrived in the striking down of King; that the people had resolved that they would correct the mischief if possible, and that they believed they could do it; that done, they would retire from all participation in such matters, and leave the regularly constituted authorities to do their work, if they could.

"Now, Governor," said I, "you are called upon by the mayor and a class of people here to bring out the militia and try to put down this movement. I assure you it cannot be done, and if you attempt it, it will give you, and us, a great deal of trouble. It is not the way to treat the question. Do as McDougal [who was governor in 1851] did; see, as he did, that this is a mere local reform, intended to correct local abuses. Allow us to take up the work and get through with it, as he did, without anything more than formal opposi-

tion from the State. Do your duty in issuing your proclamation and manifestos, and maintaining formally the dignity
of the law, but leave to us the work, and we shall get through
with it in a short time and quit, and quite gladly." He slapped
me on the shoulder, and said, "Go it, old boy! but get
through as quickly as you can. Don't prolong it, because
there is a terrible opposition and a terrible pressure."

Thus matters stood until May 18—four days after the
shooting of King—when the committee, thirty-five hundred strong, converged on the jail and, having forced
the sheriff to give up his two prisoners, conveyed them
to the Vigilantes' headquarters.

The trial of Casey and Cora [Coleman's account contin-
ued] was soon begun and carried on with all the attention
to legal forms that marked the trials of the first committee.
No outside counsel was permitted, but all witnesses desired
by the prisoners were summoned and gave their testimony
in full. Both were convicted of murder in the first degree and
sentenced to be hanged. The execution took place on the
morning of Mr. King's funeral. The committee's entire
military force occupied the streets near the headquarters. As
King's funeral train moved, all the bells in the city chimed
in solemn requiem. The military force was brought to present
arms, and then Cora and Casey were swung into eternity
from the scaffold in front of the building. . . . No one more
than the chief actors in this drama felt the gravity and solem-
nity of the occasion. No one would more gladly have been
acquitted of these duties than they. But there was not a
scintilla of hesitation, doubt, or fear. The work was done
under solemn dictates of duty . . . and while technically
outside the law, with due and solemn reverence for the law
as it should be executed.

The committee's next moves were directed against a group known as the "ballot-box stuffers" who gathered at the polling places on election days and, in Coleman's words, "attacked, maimed, and terrified those voters who were opposed to their friends." A number of these ruffians were rounded up and, having been tried and convicted, were placed on ships bound for foreign ports and warned not to return under penalty of death, the committee paying the cost of their passage. Thereupon, feeling that its mission had been accomplished, the group prepared to disband.

We believed we were far enough along to finish our work speedily [the leader's account went on], but we were disappointed, for on June 21 there was precipitated upon us the most unexpected and severest task of the year. Judge Terry of the Supreme Bench of California, a violent, hot-headed man, and an open denouncer of the committee and its efforts . . . came to San Francisco to join in the contest against us. In a quarrel over the possession of arms, Terry plunged his bowie-knife into the neck of an officer of the committee named Hopkins, inflicting a wound which at the time was thought to be mortal. The news came like the bursting of a bomb-shell. We saw instantly the magnitude of the new labor and the new responsibility thrust upon us. It was not only to vindicate the committee law, but to punish the presiding judge of the Supreme Court for violence to one of our people. Orders were at once given and promptly executed for his arrest, and the arrest of all others who were with him. . . .

Judge Terry was treated as a high State prisoner. His trial was delayed by the uncertainty of the recovery of Hopkins, and by the efforts of Terry's friends to make a compromise.

All these efforts failed, and on June 25 the trial began. It lasted nearly a month—a long, wearisome, unsatisfactory piece of work. Terry was convicted of resistance to and assault upon the officers of the committee, but as the wound inflicted did not prove fatal, and the officer recovered, the usual punishment in the committee's power to inflict not being applicable, it was finally decided to discharge him. And it was resolved that the interests of the State imperatively demanded that he resign his position as judge of the Supreme Court.

While Terry's trial was going on, the committee had handed over to the authorities a number of men arrested for crimes and misdemeanors, and only two prisoners were held —Philander Brace for the murder of Captain West, and Joseph Hetherington for killing Dr. Randall. Both were cold-blooded crimes committed in open daylight, within the city, and demanded the full penalty. The men were tried fairly, sentenced to death, and executed. Thus ended the capital punishment of the Vigilance Committee of 1856.

On August 8, 1856, the Executive Committee decided to close their labors, and on the 18th a great parade of all the members was held, and the active work of the General Committee ended *sine die;* the Executive Committee, however, continuing in session to close up financial and other affairs.

## vi

ANOTHER view of the work of the Vigilantes of 1856 is that of the once well-known San Francisco writer, Charles Warren Stoddard, who as a child witnessed the dramatic event that led to the committee's organization:

It was on May 14, 1856. I chanced to be standing at the corner of Washington and Montgomery Streets . . . and heard a pistol-shot, and very near me—not thirty feet away. I turned and saw a man stagger and fall to the pavement. Then the streets began to grow dark with people hurrying toward the scene of the tragedy. I fled in fright. . . .

When I reached home I was dazed. On the witness stand, under oath, I could have told nothing; but very shortly the whole town was aware that James King of William (i.e., William King was his father)—the editor of the *Evening Bulletin* had been shot in cold blood by James Casey, a supervisor, the editor of a local journal, an ex-convict, and a man whose past had been exposed and his present publicly denounced in the editorial columns of the *Bulletin*. . . .

James King of William was shot on Tuesday. . . . He died on the following Monday. That fatal shot was the turning-point in the history of the metropolis of the Pacific. A meeting of citizens was immediately called; an executive committee was appointed; the work of organization was distributed among sub-committees. With amazing rapidity three thousand citizens were armed, drilled, and established in temporary armories; ample means were subscribed to cover all expenses. . . . A building on Sacramento Street, near Battery, was secured and made headquarters of the committee. A kind of fortification built of potato sacks filled with sand was erected in front of it. It was known as Fort Gunnybags. This secured an open space before the building. The fort was patrolled by sentries night and day; military rule was strictly observed. . . .

On Sunday morning, the 19th of May . . . sitting by a window, I saw people flocking past the house and hastening toward the jail. We were then living on Broadway, below

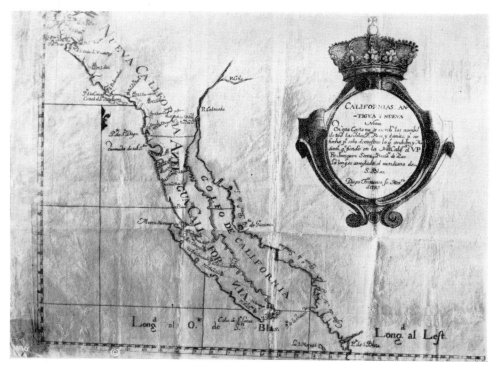

Upper and Lower California, showing early-day missions
from a map published in Mexico City in 1787


Yerba Buena (now San Francisco) in the spring of 1837

San Francisco celebrates California's admission to the Union.

Lincoln obsequies, 1865
San Francisco honors the memory of the late president.

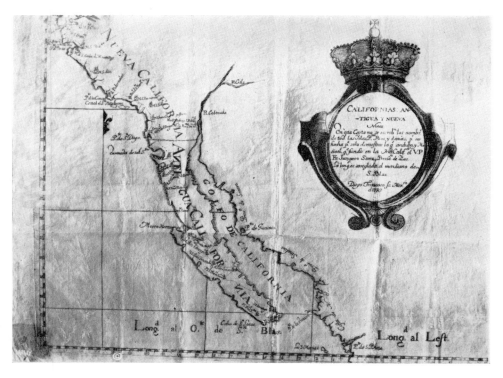

Upper and Lower California, showing early-day missions
from a map published in Mexico City in 1787

Yerba Buena (now San Francisco) in the spring of 1837

San Francisco celebrates California's admission to the Union.

Lincoln obsequies, 1865
San Francisco honors the memory of the late president.

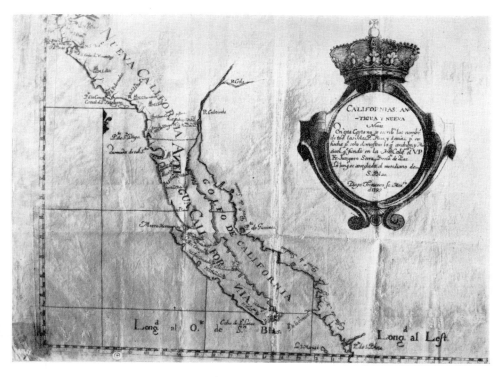

Upper and Lower California, showing early-day missions
from a map published in Mexico City in 1787

Yerba Buena (now San Francisco) in the spring of 1837

San Francisco celebrates California's admission to the Union.

Lincoln obsequies, 1865
San Francisco honors the memory of the late president.

San Franciscans watch the doomed city.

Early-day fire-fighting apparatus
showing the planked streets, long a feature of the downtown area

The Mission Dolores, founded in 1776

The Tivoli Theater
one of the most popular of the early playhouses

San Franciscans watch the doomed city.

Early-day fire-fighting apparatus
showing the planked streets, long a feature of the downtown area

The Mission Dolores, founded in 1776

The Tivoli Theater
one of the most popular of the early playhouses

Fort Gunnybags
headquarters of the Vigilance Committee of 1856

Medal worn by the Vigilantes

View of the city in 1856

Montgomery Street in 1856
At left is Wells, Fargo & Co., pioneer express and banking firm.

The Palace, the West's first luxury hotel
Lotta's fountain, another San Francisco landmark, is in the foreground.

The Montgomery Block, long the city's largest office building

One of the many types of cable-cars in use in prefire days

Henry Casebolt's "Baloon Car," a transportation novelty of the 1870's

Montgomery Street; the jail was on Broadway, a square or two farther up the street; between was a shoulder of Telegraph Hill, not yet cut away. I grabbed my hat and joined the expectant throngs. We went over the heights of the hill like a flock of goats: we were used to climbing. On the other edge of the cliff, where we seemed almost to overhang the jail, we paused and caught our breath. What a sight it was! It seems that on Saturday twenty-four companies of Vigilantes were ordered to meet at their respective armories, in various parts of the city, at nine o'clock on Sunday morning. Orders were given to each captain to take up a certain position near the jail. The jail was surrounded: no one could approach it, no one escape from it, without leave of the commanders of the committee.

The street glistened with bayonets. . . . The companies marched silently to their respective stations. Citizens . . . flocked in and covered the housetops and the heights in the vicinity. A hollow square was formed before the jail; an artillery company with a huge brass cannon halted near it; the cannon was placed directly in front of the jail and trained upon the gates. I remember how impressive the scene was; the grim files of infantry; the gleaming brass of the cannon; one closed carriage within the hollow square; the awful stillness that brooded over all.

Officials of the committee went to the jail door and demanded that the sheriff produce Casey and a second prisoner, one Charles Cora, who had murdered a United States Marshal.

The pair were hustled into the waiting carriage, and driven to the Vigilantes' headquarters on Sacramento Street. In his *History of San Francisco*, published in 1878, John S. Hittell thus described the trial that followed:

No person was present save the accused, the members of
the Vigilance Committee, and witnesses. The testimony was
given under oath, though there was no lawful authority for
its administration. Hearsay testimony was excluded; the
general rules of evidence observed in the courts were
adopted: the accused heard all the witnesses, cross-exam-
ined those against him, summoned such as he wanted in his
favor, had an attorney to assist him, and was permitted to
make an argument by himself or his attorney, in his own
defense.

The two were found guilty, and the sentence—death
by hanging—was carried out on the day Casey's victim
was buried.

On Wednesday [Stoddard recalled] James King of William was laid to rest at Lone Mountain. The whole city was
draped in mourning; all business was suspended; the citizens
lined the streets through which the funeral cortege proceeded. . . . As the procession passed up Montgomery
Street and crossed Sacramento Street, those who were walking or driving in it looked down the latter street and saw,
two squares below, the lifeless bodies of James P. Casey and
Charles Cora dangling by the neck from two second-story
windows of the headquarters of the Vigilance Committee.

Three years later, in 1859, another writer, Richard
Henry Dana, described the result of the committee's
efforts to restore law and order within the crime-ridden
city in these words:

And now the most quiet and well-governed city in the
United States is San Francisco. But it has been through its
season of Heaven-defying crime, violence, and blood, from
which it was rescued and handed back to soberness, moral-

ity, and good government, by that peculiar invention of anglo-Saxon Republican America—the solemn, awe-inspiring Vigilance Committee of the most grave and respectable citizens; the last resort of the thinking and the good, taken to only when vice, fraud, and ruffianism have intrenched themselves behind the forms of law, suffrage, and ballot.

## vii

THE passage just quoted is from a chapter called "Twenty-Four Years Later," which appears in editions subsequent to 1869 of Dana's *Two Years Before the Mast*. This, perhaps the most widely read of all books relating to California in the days when it was still a Mexican province, was first published in 1840. In 1859 Dana spent several weeks in and about San Francisco, and had this to say of the changes that had taken place since his first visit nearly a quarter century earlier:

It was in the winter of 1835–6 that the ship *Alert*, in the prosecution of her voyage for hides on the remote and almost unknown coast of California, floated into the vast solitude of the Bay of San Francisco. All around was the stillness of nature. One vessel, a Russian, lay at anchor there, but during our whole stay not a sail came or went. Our trade was with remote Missions, which sent hides to us in launches manned by their Indians. Our anchorage was between a small island, called Yerba Buena, and a gravel beach in a little bight or cove of the same name, formed by two small, projecting points. Beyond, to the westward of the landing-place, were dreary sand-hills, with little grass to be seen, and a few trees, and beyond them higher hills, steep and barren, their sides gullied by the rains. Some six miles beyond the landing-place, to the right, was a ruinous Presidio, and some three or four miles to the left was the Mission of Dolores, as ruinous as the Presidio, almost deserted, with but few Indians attached to it, and but little property in cattle. Over a region far beyond our sight there were no other human habitations, except that an enterprising Yankee, years in advance of his time, had put up, on the rising ground above the landing, a shanty of rough boards, where he carried on a very small retail trade between the hide ships and the Indians. Vast banks of fog, invading us from the North Pacific, drove in through the entrance, and covered the whole bay; and when they disappeared, we saw a few well-wooded islands, the sand-hills on the west, the grassy and wooded slopes on the east, and the vast stretch of the bay to the southward, where we were told lay the Missions of Santa Clara and San José, and still longer stretches to the northward and northeastward, where we understood smaller bays spread out, and large rivers poured in their tributes of waters. There were no settlements on these bays or rivers, and the few ranchos and Missions were remote and widely separated. Not only the neighborhood of our anchorage, but the entire region of the great bay, was a solitude. On the whole coast of California there was not a lighthouse, a beacon, or a buoy, and the charts were made up from old and disconnected surveys by British, Russian, and Mexican voyages. Birds of prey and passage swooped and dived about us, wild beasts ranged through the oak groves, and as we slowly floated out of the harbor with the tide, herds of deer came to the water's edge, on the northerly side of the entrance, to gaze at the strange spectacle.

Having thus pictured the scene as he had known it in the mid-1830's, Dana went on in these words:

On the evening of Saturday, the 13th of August, 1859, the superb steamship *Golden Gate,* gay with crowds of passengers, and lighting the sea for miles around with the glare of her signal lights of red, green, and white, and brilliant with lighted saloons and state-rooms, bound up from the Isthmus of Panama, neared the entrance to San Francisco, the great centre of a world-wide commerce. Miles out at sea, on the desolate rocks of the Farallones, gleamed the powerful rays of one of the most costly and effective light-houses in the world. As we drew in through the Golden Gate, another light-house met our eyes, and in the clear moonlight of the unbroken California summer we saw, on the right, a large fortification protecting the narrow entrance, and just before us the little island of Alcatraz confronted us,—one entire fortress. We bore round the point toward the old anchoring-ground of the hide ships, and there, covering the sand-hills and the valleys, stretching from the water's edge to the base of the great hills, and from the old Presidio to the Mission, flickering all over with the lamps of its streets and houses, lay a city of one hundred thousand inhabitants. Clocks tolled the hour of midnight from its steeples, but the city was alive from the salute of our guns, spreading the news that the fortnightly steamer had come, bringing mails and passengers from the Atlantic world. Clipper ships of the largest size lay at anchor in the stream, or were girt to the wharves; and capacious high-pressure steamers, as large and showy as those of the Hudson or Mississippi, bodies of dazzling light, awaited the delivery of our mails to take their courses up the Bay, stopping at Benicia and the United States Naval Station, and then up the great tributaries—the

Sacramento, San Joaquin, and Feather Rivers—to the far inland cities of Sacramento, Stockton, and Marysville.

The dock into which we drew, and the streets about it, were densely crowded with express wagons and hand-carts to take luggage, coaches and cabs for passengers, and with men,—some looking out for friends among our hundreds of passengers,—agents of the press, and a greater multitude eager for newspapers and verbal intelligence from the great Atlantic and European world. Through this crowd I made my way, along the well-built and well-lighted streets, as alive as by day, where boys in high-keyed voices were already crying the latest New York papers; and between one and two o'clock in the morning found myself comfortably abed in a commodious room, in the Oriental Hotel, which stood, as well as I could learn, on the filled-up cove, and not far from the spot where we used to beach our boats from the *Alert*. . . .

When I awoke in the morning, and looked from my windows over the city of San Francisco, with its storehouses, towers, and steeples; its court-houses, theatres, and hospitals; its daily journals; its well-filled learned professions; its fortresses and light-houses; its wharves and harbor, with their thousand-ton clipper ships, more in number than London or Liverpool sheltered that day, itself one of the capitals of the American Republic, and the sole emporium of a new world, the awakened Pacific; when I looked across the bay to the eastward, and beheld a beautiful town on the fertile, wooded shores of the Contra Costa, and steamers, large and small, the ferryboats to the Contra Costa, and capacious freighters and passenger-carriers to all parts of the great bay and its tributaries, with lines of their smoke in the horizon,—when I saw all these things, and reflected on what I once was and saw here, and what now surrounded me,

I could scarcely keep my hold on reality at all, or the genuineness of anything, and seemed to myself like one who had moved in "worlds not realized."

During the next several days Dana spent his time exploring the wonders of this spot that only a few years earlier he had known as a mere cluster of barren sand hills.

I have looked at the city from the water [he continued] and islands from the city, but I can see nothing that recalls the times gone by, except the venerable Mission, the ruinous Presidio, the high hills in the rear of the town, and great stretches of the bay in all directions.

To-day I took a California horse of the old style,—the run, the loping gait,—and visited the Presidio. The walls stand as they did, with some changes made to accommodate a small garrison of United States troops. It has a noble situation, and I saw from it a clipper ship of the very largest class, coming through the Gate, under her fore-and-aft sails. Thence I rode to the Fort, now nearly finished, on the southern shore of the Gate, and made an inspection of it. . . .

Another morning I ride to the Mission Dolores. It has a strangely solitary aspect, enhanced by its surroundings of the most uncongenial, rapidly growing modernism; the hoar of ages surrounded by the brightest, slightest, and rapidest of modern growths. Its old belfries still clanged with the discordant bells, and Mass was saying within, for it is used as a place of worship for the extreme south part of the city.

In one of my walks about the wharves, I found a pile of dry hides lying by the side of a vessel. Here was something to feelingly persuade me what I had been, to recall a past scarce credible to myself. I stood lost in reflection. What were these hides—what were they not?—to us, to me, a boy, twenty-four years ago? These were our constant labor, our chief object, our almost habitual thought. They brought us out here, they kept us here, and it was only by getting them that we would escape from the coast and return to home and civilized life. If it had not been that I might be seen, I should have seized one, slung it over my head, walked off with it, and thrown it by the old toss—I do not believe yet a lost art—to the ground. . . . Meeting a respectable-looking citizen on the wharf, I inquired of him how the hide-trade was carried on. "O," said he, "there is very little of it, and that is all here. The few that are brought in are placed under sheds in winter, or left out on the wharf in summer, and are loaded from the wharves into the vessels alongside. They form parts of cargoes of other materials." I really felt too much, at the instant, to express to him the cause of my interest in the subject, and only added, "Then the old business of trading up and down the coast and curing hides for cargoes is all over?" "O yes, sir," said he, "those old times of the *Pilgrim* and *Alert* and *California*, that we read about, are gone by."

After a week of contemplating the new San Francisco, Dana boarded a coastwise steamer for San Diego. At that town, and at several stops en route, he learned that changes hardly less striking had taken place since his earlier visit.

Part Four

# Transition
# 1860–1880

# i

FROM THE TIME California was taken over by the Yankees in 1846, one of the things the new lords of the province found hardest to bear was their isolation from the rest of the nation. Then, and for close to two decades thereafter, they felt that they were an unconscionably long way from their families and friends. This feeling was understandable. During the first part of that period the only means of communication with the homeland was over one or another of the overland trails, or by sea aboard infrequent round-the-Horn sailing ships; both were tedious, weeks-long ordeals that few undertook with any degree of pleasure.

The demand for speedier, more frequent, and less arduous means of travel between the two coasts was, of course, enormously stimulated by the gold rush. However, even before Marshall's discovery, the federal authorities at Washington had taken steps to remedy the situation. On March 3, 1847, Congress passed an act authorizing the Secretary of the Navy to advertise for bids for steamships to operate on both oceans, with a crossing at Panama, the ships to carry the United States mail, passengers, and freight.

On the Pacific side, the contract was awarded to the

159

Pacific Mail Company, the owners of which set about the building of three small side-wheelers. It was, nevertheless, not until early in 1849 that the ships were completed and the line began operating. The first steamer, the 1,050-ton *California*, passed through the Golden Gate on the last day of February.

Next morning, the local *Alta California* thus described the city's delight at the inauguration of this service:

The long expected and welcome pioneer of the North Pacific Steamship Line [*sic*] arrived in our harbor yesterday morning.

She left Mazatlán on the 17th of February and Monterey on Tuesday last. General Persifor F. Smith, new Military Commander of the Territory, and his suite were among her passengers.

The "California" is truly a magnificent vessel, and her fine appearance as she came in sight of the Town called forth cheer after cheer from her enraptured citizens, who were assembled in masses upon the heights commanding a view of the bay and in dense crowds at the principal wharves and landing places. She passed the vessels of war in the harbor after a salute from each, returned by hearty cheering from the crowded decks, and at eleven was safely moored at the anchorage off the Town.

The next important move to speed communication between the two coasts was made a decade later. In 1857 the Butterfield Overland Stage Company was awarded a federal contract to operate triweekly stages between the Missouri River and San Francisco, carrying both passengers and mail. The contract was to run six years, at an annual cost to the government of $600,000.

The Post Office Department's official announcement of the inauguration of this new service read:

Sept. 16. The first overland mail to San Francisco, California, by way of Jefferson City and Springfield, Mo., Fort Smith, Ark., and Preston, Texas, takes its departure this morning from St. Louis Post Office at 7 o'clock. It goes by way of the Pacific railroad to Tipton, from whence it will be conveyed on coaches and spring wagons, the whole of the distance. Mr. J. Butterfield, who has given his personal supervision to the work of getting this mail fairly underway in all its parts, goes out with it to Springfield.

A month later, on October 16, the *Evening Bulletin* thus described how San Francisco greeted the arrival of the first coach:

At a quarter after four o'clock the coach turned from Market into Montgomery Street. The driver blew his horn and cracked his whip; at which the horses, four in number, almost seemed to partake of his enthusiasm, and dashed ahead at a clattering pace, and the dust flew from the glowing wheels. At the same time a shout was raised, that ran with the rapidity of an electric flash along Montgomery Street, which throughout its length was crowded with an excited populace. As the coach dashed along through the crowds, the hats of the spectators were whirled in the air and the hurrah was repeated from a thousand throats, responsive to which, the driver, the lion of the occasion, doffed his weather-beaten old slouch, and in uncovered dignity, like the victor of an old Olympic race, guided his foaming steeds towards the Post Office.

The next step in the long process of linking the two sides of the nation more closely together was the romantic—but short-lived—Pony Express. This service, organized by William H. Russell of the western stage and freighting firm of Russell, Majors and Waddell, began functioning in the spring of 1860. By it, the time of transit from the Missouri River to California was cut to ten and a half days. The express riders, all picked men, were mounted on swift ponies, which were changed at intervals of approximately twenty-five miles. Pressing forward day and night, the messengers each carried in a leather saddlebag letters and papers, for which a charge of $5 per half ounce was made.

On March 26 this announcement of the beginning of the service appeared in a St. Louis paper, the *Missouri Republican*:

The first courier of the Pony Express will leave the Missouri River on Tuesday, April 3rd, at 5 o'clock P.M., and will run regularly weekly thereafter, carrying a letter mail only. The point of departure on the Missouri River will be in telegraphic communication with the East and will be announced in due time.

Telegraphic messages from all parts of the United States and Canada, in connection with the point of departure will be received up to 5 o'clock P.M. of the day of leaving and transmitted over the Placerville and St. Joseph telegraph wire to San Francisco and intermediate points, by the connecting express in eight days.

The letter mail will be delivered in San Francisco in ten days from the departure of the express. The express passes through Forts Kearney, Laramie, and Bridger, Great Salt Lake City, Camp Floyd, Carson City, the Washoe Silver Mines, Placerville, and Sacramento.

Letters for Oregon, Washington Territory, British Colum-
bia, the Pacific Mexican ports, Russian possessions, Sandwich
Islands, China, Japan, and India will be mailed in San
Francisco.

Special messengers, bearing letters to connect with the
express of the 3d of April, will receive communications for
the courier of that day at No. 481 Tenth Street, Washington
City, up to 2:45 P.M. on Friday, March 30, and in New York,
at the office of J. B. Simpson, Room No. 8, Commercial Bank
Building, Nassau Street, up to 6.30 A.M. of March 31st.


## ii

THE completion of the overland telegraph, which
reached San Francisco in the fall of 1861, ended the
usefulness of the Pony Express and that picturesque
service passed into history.

However, some three months earlier, on June 28, another and far more ambitious project got under way. On
that date four Sacramento shopkeepers, Collis Huntington, Charles Crocker, Mark Hopkins and Leland Stanford, organized the Central Pacific Railroad Company,
and set about building the western half of the nation's
first transcontinental railway.

For well over a decade West Coast residents had been
advocating the construction of such a road, and warmly
supporting the series of Railroad Pacific bills that were
introduced into each session of Congress. It was, however, not until after the beginning of the Civil War that

the necessary legislation was passed and the work began. Each step in its building was followed with close interest all over the West, and the joining of the rails on May 10, 1869, set off prolonged celebrations in San Francisco and elsewhere.

This editorial, which appeared in the *Evening Bulletin* for May 8, reflects the high hopes with which the people of the city looked forward to the benefits the new line would bestow on them:

We can now leave San Francisco in the morning by the steamer *New World* and be landed in an hour and a quarter at Vallejo, from which place we shall be carried by rail to New York or whatever point we may desire to reach in the Atlantic States. Possibly within the next week the road will be in such order as to take passengers from San Francisco to New York in one week, and within a month we may anticipate making the trip in about six days from ocean to ocean. If we be not disappointed in our anticipations . . . a person will be able to leave San Francisco and be in London or Paris in from fifteen to seventeen days. . . .

It would be folly to say that quick communication will not stimulate trade. Changes must take place in the affairs of this coast, and we are on the confines of a large population, being no longer isolated from the rest of the Union. The Mississippi Valley is but four or five days from us, with its teeming millions. It is in fact not much more difficult for the inhabitants of Illinois, Missouri, Iowa, Indiana, etc., to reach us than it is for them to reach New York. . . . Railroads changed the condition of the Mississippi Valley and made it comparatively an empire. Railroads are now about to change the aspect of things in California. What this will be, and how rapidly it will come around, no man can precisely determine, but of one thing we may rest assured: we are no longer an isolated community.

In San Francisco preparations had been under way for several weeks to celebrate the joining of the rails on Saturday, May 8. Then, on the evening of the 7th, word arrived from Promontory Point that the driving of the last spike had been postponed to Monday, May 10, and suggesting that San Francisco likewise postpone its observance of the event. Local officials refused; to their mind, Saturday was clearly a better day than Monday to hold such a celebration, and the city accordingly celebrated on Saturday.

The *Bulletin's* account of San Francisco's premature but enthusiastic festivities reads in part as follows:

At sunrise a national salute was fired, and at an early hour the population of the city was astir. The slanting rays of the morning sun fell on thousands of flags and streamers which fluttered from public buildings and private residences all over the city. The scene reminded the beholder of those days when the people of San Francisco awoke to celebrate other victories—the triumph of the national arms on the fields of war. But here was a triumph bloodless, deathless, but no less glorious to the Nation and the State: a victory over space. the elements, and the stupendous mountain barriers separating San Francisco from the world. Every heart was gladdened by the contemplation of the great achievement. The people felt that it was a mighty thing for the country, for California, and for San Francisco. It was the realization of a prophecy and the confirmation of a hope.

By 10 A.M. every principal street in the city was thronged with people. Men, women and children lined the walks, and here and there was to be seen military bands and companies, associations of all kinds, detachments of the fire department, etc., marching to the place of rendezvous. On every street waved forth the glorious Stars and Stripes, and Montgomery Street was fairly shaded by the flags which waved from the housetops, or were hung in festoons across it. Wherever a flag or banner could be fastened, there one waved out.

Chief Crowley headed a troop of mounted police to clear the streets on the line of march of the procession. The banks and all principal places of business, all private offices and many public ones, were closed for the day.

The parade, in eleven sections, took four hours to pass a given spot. While it was still in progress, exercises were opened in the Mechanics' Pavilion, the orator of the day being one Judge Nathaniel Bennett, who, according to the *Bulletin*'s reporter, "held his listeners spellbound" for a period of several hours.

The celebration was heralded as one of the largest and most successful in the city's history. However, the *Bulletin*'s story contains one modern note: the festivities were marred by two traffic accidents:

While an artillery company was passing Platt's Hall one of the heavy trucks struck the corner of the temporary scaffolding erected in front of that building for the use of teachers and Normal and High School scholars, and a portion of the structure, about twenty feet in length, fell with a crash. For a few minutes considerable alarm prevailed, but as the unfortunate individuals scrambled out of the debris with smiles, quiet was once more restored, although the ladies on the remaining seats appeared relieved when the procession had passed and they again stood on terra firma.

A second runaway occurred at the corner of Stockton and Jackson streets as the procession passed along the former street. Two horses attached to a wagon became frightened at the shrill whistles and started off at a terrific rate of speed, colliding with and upsetting two buggies in their course. The occupants of the buggies were thrown to the ground with great violence and sustained severe injuries. The driver of the double team was also injured. It was impossible to ascertain the names of the parties.

### iii

THE completion of the overland railroad put a final end to San Francisco's isolation and marked the beginning of a movement that has ever since played an important part in the city's economy; that is, its growing popularity as a tourist center.

The fact that the continent had been spanned by iron rails, making it possible to travel from coast to coast with unprecedented speed and comfort, focused world-wide attention on the newly-accessible city. One result was that during the next several years a considerable number of guidebooks, volumes of travel, and similar publications appeared, all designed to supply prospective visitors with a variety of information about the city and state.

One of the earliest and most discerning of such works is a small volume called *Westward by Rail*, written by an English journalist, W. F. Rae, and published in London in 1871. After describing his trip across the country over the new railroad, and telling something of San Francisco's early history, he continued:

With the knowledge of what San Francisco had been, and unacquainted by personal observation with what it had become, my first walk along its streets on the morning after my arrival was one of peculiar interest. I went along Montgomery-street, which is the Regent-street and Lombard-street, or Broadway and Wall-street, of this city. It is lined with handsome shops. The pavement is crowded with pedestrians, the majority of whom have the anxious look and the hurried gait of business men, while the minority are ordinary sightseers, or persons who walk therein in order to be seen. Bankers' offices are very numerous. Their windows are filled with the paper-money of all nations, from the plain white notes of the Bank of England to the elaborately figured "greenbacks" of the United States. These "greenbacks" are not current in California. . . . Nothing passes current here save gold and silver coin. Small sums are reckoned in "bits," which are imaginary coins having the nominal value of twelve and a half cents. Indeed the absence of single cents causes something worse than confusion. A newspaper costs ten cents. Suppose that a quarter dollar, equal to twenty-five cents, is presented in payment for the newspaper, the seller will probably return a dime, which is equal to ten cents. Thus fifteen cents have been paid instead of ten cents. His excuse will be that he has not any half dimes, these coins being extremely scarce. In California this is taken as a thing of course by the natives and the residents. The visitors, however, are apt to regard it as an imposition. The gold coin generally current is the twenty-dollar piece. It is about the size of half a crown, and is worth nearly five pounds sterling, and is a very beautiful coin. The inhabitants, who are accustomed to high prices, part with these coins far more readily than we part with sovereigns. . . .

At its northern end Montgomery-street extends to the top of a steep hill. The latter portion is so precipitous that carriages cannot ascend it. A flight of steps enables the foot passenger to mount with comparative comfort. From the top a commanding view is to be had of the bay, the opposite coast, and the business quarter of the city. I was surprised to see the greater part of the lower town enveloped in a dense cloud of smoke. A large number of tall chimneys were emitting volumes of smoke such as in London would entail heavy fines on their proprietors. The reason was that Mount Diablo coal is burned in the furnaces . . . giving forth much black smoke during combustion. The darkness and dinginess of the city surprised me less, knowing, as I did, that the coal was in fault, than did the sight of so many manufactures. I had supposed San Francisco to be a second Liverpool: I was not prepared to find it was also a second Birmingham.

After devoting several pages to describing the city's booming industrial district, Rae went on:

A walk through the markets of this city suffices to convince the visitor that in this State the necessaries of life are furnished in unexampled profusion, and on a most extensive scale. Fish and game are plentiful and cheap. All the common fruits and vegetables are to be had for a trifle, while fruits which are luxuries elsewhere are here within the reach of the multitude. Nor is this abundance the most noteworthy circumstance. The change from winter to summer is discerned with difficulty in the market-place. As far as the supply of most fruits and vegetables is concerned there is neither seed-time nor harvest. In this favored city potatoes

are always new, and strawberries always in season. The size
of many products of the garden and orchard is gigantic. The
huge turnips, cabbages, pears, and apples which at home
form the subjects of paragraphs during the dull season, are
here substantial and purchasable realities. Now and then an
unusually large natural product is sent to the newspaper
offices of San Francisco for the inspection of the proprietors.
I was in the office of the *Alta California* when some stalks
of Indian corn . . . were examined and measured. The tallest were 17½ feet; the others were 15. Fancy a field covered
with stalks like these!

The city's newspapers next engaged the visitor's attention:

I confess to have been surprised to find the press of San
Francisco not merely flourishing, but meriting a eulogy
which cannot justly be conferred on the press of New York.
. . . The articles in the *Alta California,* for example, are
animated by a praiseworthy spirit of impartiality. Having
complex problems to solve with relation to China and Japan,
and finding that these problems are treated by the journalists of the Eastern States in a flippant and foolish style, the
journalists of San Francisco are not prone to regard the
opinions of the New York papers on subjects of general
concern as worthy of implicit confidence. . . . Unfortunately, the journals of New York are supposed in Europe to
represent the American press, and the least reputable of
these is generally, though erroneously, considered to be the
leader of that press.

In addition to the *Alta California,* there is the *Bulletin,*
also a first-class paper, while the *Morning Call* is a journal
filled with chitchat and gossip. . . . Among weekly journals, the *Golden Era* and *Morning Mercury* are what Ameri-

cans would call "real live papers." A monthly magazine entitled the *Overland Monthly* has recently been established. Already, it is acknowledged to be one of the best among American periodicals. Several English periodicals of repute are infinitely inferior to it. With considerable difficulty could many magazines be named which are both better written and more worthy of being read through from the first page to the last.

Another phase of the city's life interested Rae quite as much as its newspapers and magazines; namely, its gambling dens. For these, however, he had no words of praise. Here he describes a visit to one such resort:

The visitor rings a bell, and before the door is opened he is generally reconnoitered through a small aperture or grating. As soon as the guardian is satisfied, either from appearances, or from personal knowledge, or from the inspection of a card in the proprietor's handwriting, that no objection exists, the door is opened, the visitor takes a few steps forward, and is brought face to face with the "Tiger." He sees what he is told is a Faro table. This table is small, and will not accommodate more than six or eight persons. The dealer occupies one side, and sits with his back to the wall. . . .

I was told that the difficulty of cheating is greater at Faro than at other games of chance, and this consideration has tended to make it popular. The Californians may be great gamesters, but they naturally prefer a game played with some regard to fairness, or one which they style a "square" game. . . .

In all the hells the costume of the keepers and dealers, or rather the absence of it, was the same, shirt sleeves being their full dress. Those who superintended the games also sat without their coats. The shirts were all spotless. The superintendents, dealers and gamesters all smoked cigars. Nor were their manners more formal than their attire. All the company seemed to be on terms of intimacy; each one not only addressed the other by his Christian name, but as Tom, Dick, or Harry. . . . The losers, who appeared to be in a large majority, took their mishaps most philosophically, while the rare winners did not exult in their good fortune. Indeed, "Fighting the Tiger" in San Francisco seems to be a pastime which, if neither harmless nor praiseworthy, cannot fairly be denounced as fraught with immediate evil consequences. . . .

In some of the hells a supper is provided, but this is merely what their frequenters can get gratis at nearly every bar-room. A drink may be had for the asking; but this, again, is not a special incentive, but a part of the ordinary social arrangements. Californians do not seem happy unless they are either taking drinks or treating their friends and acquaintances with them. That they should find themselves provided with them in the gaming halls is merely what they consider themselves entitled to expect.

Having fully explored the subject of gambling, the Englishman next turned his attention to another curious phase of the curious and, to him, fascinating, city; that is, Chinatown.

My first visit to the Chinese quarter was made by daylight. I entered it without design, having no exact knowledge of its locality. The effect was as startling as the transformation scene in a pantomime. . . . The Chinamen were clothed in plainly-cut blue tunics, had straw or cloth covering their heads, and shoes on their feet resembling slippers down at the heels. The shops were adorned with pendant flags bearing inscriptions in Chinese. The entire street was filled with these strangely decorated and strangely arranged shops. In some of them merchants of the highest respectability do business, and accumulate wealth. The articles they sell are the best of their kind, and as these merchants are satisfied with small profits, the low prices attract purchasers. Other industries than those of dealers in teas, silks, lacquered ware, and porcelain are carried on in a humbler style. . . . In cellars which are certainly dark, and probably unhealthy, silent Chinamen may be seen washing and ironing clothes, manufacturing cigars, or shaving the heads of their countrymen. . . .

At night when I strolled through the quarter again, the spectacle was even more curious. The pavement was crowded with Chinamen talking incessantly and in loud tones. Entire alleys were filled with small houses, at the open windows of which painted female faces were clustered, and whence invitations, couched in broken yet broad English, were sent to every male passer-by. . . . Nearly every house is tenanted by women who, scantily clad in gaudy apparel, stand on the door steps or at the open windows, proclaiming their profession by look and gesture. Underground dancing saloons are numerous, and in them are to be seen what are here significantly styled "pretty waiter girls." These saloons are but traps for the unwary.

One other picturesque feature of the city then and later was the Chinese herb doctors, most of whom served not alone their countrymen but the whites as well.

These doctors [commented Rae] are not afflicted with modesty as to the nature of their powers. At the entrance to an alley I saw a sign-board projecting from the side of the house, and intimating that "Dr. Hung Ly cures all diseases upstairs." In the newspapers these doctors advertise regularly. Thus may be seen among other announcements one to the effect that Dr. Jay Hon Chung, graduate of the highest medical college in China, has opened an office in Washington-street:—"The most obstinate and painful chronic diseases treated with entire success, and cures guaranteed. . . ." A gentleman of majestic stature, whose head was adorned with long flowing locks, who styled himself "The King of Pain," was harvesting dollars when I arrived in San Francisco. He professed not only to cure all diseases, but also to inform the patient of his malady without asking any questions. . . . Driving through the city in a handsome carriage, he halts now and then, and makes a short speech. While he is retailing some of the miraculous cures which he has effected, a passer-by having the appearance of a sailor, or a mechanic, stops and exclaims, "What's that you say about Boston?" The quack replies, "Sir, I have just told these gentlemen how Mr. John A. Jones, a prominent citizen of Boston, was cured by a single bottle of this specific after all the other doctors had given him up." "Well, sir, that's so. I come from Boston, and I know Mr. Jones was cured by a bottle of your medicine." This independent testimony induces several among the audience to give the "King of Pain's specific a trial. He then drives off . . . and the farce is played over again in another quarter of the city, the confederate, of course, changing his attire and his story. . . .

What impressed me most in the Chinese quarter [this perceptive visitor concluded] was not any particular phase of life, but the general aspect of the place. . . . The force of contrast operates with irresistible effect. At one moment I am in Kearny-street or Montgomery-street, surrounded by tokens of Western civilization, and in a few minutes afterwards I stand in what is a small section of an actual Chinese city. It is impossible for the most cursory observer to witness these things and to fail being struck with the fact that their continued existence involves the solution of a great problem. Of this the citizens of San Francisco are perfectly conscious.

iv

ANOTHER journalist who made the trip over the new railroad was a young woman named Helen Hunt, who signed her impressions of San Francisco with her initials, "H.H." Later Miss Hunt married a Colorado banker, W. S. Jackson, added his name to her own and, as Helen Hunt Jackson, wrote such widely read books as *Ramona* and *A Century of Dishonor*—the last-named an exposé of the federal government's treatment of its Indian charges.

H.H.'s comments on what she saw in San Francisco have a pungent quality rare among writers of her day. She thought the physical setting magnificent and wrote admiringly of the beauty of the bay and its surrounding hills and the brilliance of the sunshine. Of the town itself, however, she found little to her liking.

When I first stepped out of the door of the Occidental Hotel, on Montgomery Street [she wrote], I looked up and down in disappointment.

"Is this all?" I exclaimed. "It is New York,—a little lower of story, narrower of street, and stiller, perhaps. Have I crossed the continent only to land in Lower Broadway on a dull day?"

I looked into the shop-windows. The identical hats, collars, neckties for men, the identical tortoise-shell and gold ear-rings for women, which I had left behind on the corners of Canal and Broome Streets, stared me in the face. Eager hack-drivers, whip-handles in air, accosted me,—all brothers of the man who drove me to the Erie Railroad station, on the edge of the Atlantic Ocean. . . .

"What do you ask an hour?" said I.

"Three dollars," said they all.

"Three dollars!" echoed I, in astonishment. But I jumped in, glad of any sensation of novelty, even so high-priced a one, and said:—

"Show me all you can of your city in an hour."

Presto. In one minute we had turned a sharp corner, left the dull shops behind, and plunged into scenes unfamiliar enough. I no longer wondered at the dearness of the driving. The street was as steep as the street of an Alpine village. Men and women walking up its sidewalks were bowed over, as if nobody were less than ninety.

On the crest of one of the hills the cabby stopped to rest his horses, and the visitor examined the domestic architecture of the neighborhood.

Some of the houses were almost incredibly small, square, one story high [she commented], with a door in the middle, between two small windows. Others were two stories high, or even two and a half, with little dormer or balconied windows jutting out in the second story; but there was none large, none in the least elegant, all of wood, painted in light shades of buff, yellow or brown, the yellow predominating.

. . . These were evidently the homes of the comfortable middle class of San Francisco.

Many of the houses on the highest seaward streets are handsome, and have pleasant grounds about them. But going only a few steps further seaward, you come to or look down on crowded lanes of dingy, tumbling, forlorn buildings, which seem as if they must be forever slipping into the water. As you look up at the city from the harbor, this is the most noticeable thing. The hills rise so sharply and the houses are set on them at such incredible angles that it wouldn't surprise you, any day when you are watching it, to see the city slide down whole streets at a time. If San Francisco had known it was to be a city, and if (poor, luckless place that it is, in spite of all its luck) it had not burned down almost faster than it could build up, it might have set on its myriad hills a city which the world could hardly equal. But, as it is, it is hopelessly crowded and mixed, and can never look from the water like anything but a toppling town.

Like countless other sightseers from that day to the present, H.H. visited the ocean beach, and from the windows of the Cliff House watched the sea lions (which she mistook for seals) gamboling on the rocks offshore. But this sight, too, fell short of her expectations.

It is [she wrote] so much the fashion to be tender, not to say sentimental, over the seals of the Cliff House rocks that I was disappointed not to find myself falling into that line as I looked at them. But the longer I looked the less I felt like it.

It is, of course, a sight which ought to profoundly touch the human heart, to see a colony of anything that lives left unmolested, unharmed by men; and it, perhaps, adds to the picturesqueness and interest of the Cliff House situation to have these licensed warblers disporting themselves, safe and shiny, on the rocks. But when it comes to the seals themselves, I make bold to declare that, if there be in the whole animal kingdom any creature of size and sound less adapted than a seal as a public pet, to adorn public grounds,—I mean waters,—I do not know such creature's name. Shapeless, boneless, limbless, and featureless, neither fish nor flesh; of the color and consistency of India-rubber diluted with mucilage; slipping, clinging, sticking, like gigantic leeches; flapping, wallowing with unapproachable clumsiness; lying still, lazy, inert, asleep, apparently, till they are baked browner and hotter than they like, then plunging off the rocks, turning once over in the water to wet themselves enough to bear more baking; and all the while making a noise too hideous to be described,—a mixture of bray and squeal and snuff and snort,—old ones, young ones, big ones, little ones, masculine, feminine, and, for aught I know, neuter, by dozens, by scores,—was there ever anything droller in the way of philanthropy, if it be philanthropy, or in the way of public amusement, if it be amusement, than this? Let them be sold, and their skins given to the poor; and let peace and quiet reign along that delicious beach and on those grand old rocks.

These two excerpts are typical of H.H.'s impressions of the San Francisco of her day, and go far to explain why hers is seldom included among lists of books about the city recommended by the local Chamber of Commerce and similar organizations.

## V

Y ET another visitor who found in San Francisco little to praise and much to criticize was the British novelist, Anthony Trollope. Trollope, who was on a world tour, writing "Travel Letters" for a Liverpool paper, the *Weekly Mercury*, arrived from Australia in the summer of 1875, spent a few days exploring the city, then, having paid a brief visit to the Yosemite Valley, hurried on to New York and London. The letter quoted from here—the final one of the *Weekly Mercury* series—appeared in the issue for November 13.

The general tenor of his impressions may be gained from the following passages:

My way home from the Sandwich Islands to London took me to San Francisco, across the American continent, and New York,—whence I am writing you my last letter. . . . I had made the journey before, but had on that occasion reached California too late to visit the new world-famous valley of the Yo-Semite, and the big pine trees which we call Wellingtonias. On this occasion I made the excursion, and will presently tell the story of the trip,—but I must first say a few words as to the town of San Francisco.

I do not know that in all my travels I ever visited a city less interesting to the normal tourist, who, as a rule, does not care to investigate the ways of trade or to enjoy himself in ascertaining how the people around him earn their bread. There is almost nothing to see in San Francisco that is worth seeing. There is a new park in which you may drive for six or seven miles on a well-made road, and which, as a park for the use of a city, will, when completed, have many excellencies. There is also the biggest hotel in the world,—so the people of San Francisco say, which has cost a million sterling,—5 millions of dollars—and is intended to swallow up all the other hotels. It was just finished but not opened when I was there. There is an inferior menagerie of wild beasts, and a place called the Cliff House to which strangers are taken to hear seals bark. Everything,—except hotel prices,—is dearer here than at any other large town I know; and the ordinary traveller has no peace left him either in public or private by touters who wish to persuade him to take this or the other railroad route into the Eastern States. There is always a perfectly cloudless sky overhead unless when rain is falling in torrents, and perhaps nowhere in the world is there a more sudden change from heat to cold in the same day.

I think I may say that strangers will generally desire to get out of San Francisco as quickly as they can,—unless indeed circumstances enable them to enjoy the hospitality of the place. There is little or nothing to see, and life at the hotels is not comfortable. But the trade of the place and the way in which money is won or lost are alike marvellous. I found 10/- a day to be about the lowest rate of wages paid to a man for any kind of work in the city, and the average wages of a housemaid, who is, of course, found in everything but her clothes, to be over £70 per annum. All payments in California are made in coin, whereas in the other states of the Union except California, Oregon, and Nevada, moneys are paid in depreciated notes,—so that two dollars and a half per day which the labourer earns in San Francisco are as good as three and a quarter in New York. No doubt this high rate of pay is met by an equivalent in

the high cost of many articles, such as clothing and rent; but
it does not affect the food which to the labouring man is the
one important item of expenditure. Consequently the labouring man in California has a position which I have not known
him to achieve elsewhere.

In trade there is a speculative rashness that ought to en-
sure ruin according to our old world ideas, but which seems
to be rewarded by very general success. The stranger may
of course remember if he pleases that the millionaire who
builds a mighty palace is seen and heard of and encountered
at all corners, while the bankrupt will probably sink unseen
into obscurity. But in San Francisco there is not much of
bankruptcy; and when it does occur no one seems to be so
little impressed as the bankrupt. There is a good nature, a
forbearance, and an easy giving of trust which to an old
fashioned Englishman like myself seem to be most dangerous, but which I am assured there form the readiest mode
of building up a great commercial community. The great
commercial community is there, and I am not prepared to
deny that it has been built after that fashion. If a young
man there can make friends, and can establish a character
for honesty to his friends and for smartness to the outside
world, he can borrow almost any amount of money without
security, for the purpose of establishing himself in business.
The lender, if he feel sure that he will not be robbed by his
protégé, is willing to run the risk of successful speculation. . . .

I was taken to visit the Stock-brokers' Board in San Francisco,—that is the room in which mining shares are bought
and sold. The trader should understand that in California,
and, still more, in the neighboring State of Nevada, gold and
silver mining are now very lively. The stock-jobbing created
by these mines is carried on in San Francisco and is a busi-

ness as universally popular as was the buying and selling of
railway shares during our railway mania. The housemaid of
whom I have spoken as earning £70 per annum, buys Consolidated Virginia or Ophir with that money,—or perhaps
she prefers Chollar Potosi, or Best and Belcher, or Yellow
Jacket, or Buckeye. She probably consults some gentleman
of her acquaintance and no doubt in nineteen cases out of
twenty loses her money. But it is the thing to do, and she
enjoys that charm which is the delectation of all gamblers.
Of course in such a condition of things there are men who
know how the wind is going to blow . . . who can raise the
price of shares by fictitious purchases, and then sell, or de-
press them by fictitious sales and then buy. The housemaids
and others go to the wall, while the knowing men build
palaces and seem to be troubled by no seared consciences.
In the meantime the brokers drive a roaring trade,—whether
they purchase legitimately for others or speculate on their
own account.

The Stock Exchange in London is, I believe, closed to
strangers. The Bourse in Paris is open to the world and at a
certain hour affords a scene to those who wish to go and look
at it of wild noise, unintelligible action, and sometimes apparently demoniac fury. The uninitiated are unable to com-
prehend that the roaring herd in the pen beneath them are
doing business. The Stock Exchange Board in San Francisco
is not open to strangers, as it is in Paris, but may be visited
with an order, and by the kindness of a friend I was admitted.
Paris. I thought that the gentlemen employed were going to
the fury at San Francisco is even more demoniac than at
Paris. I thought that the gentleman employed were going to
hit each other between the eyes, and that the apparent
quarrels which I saw already demanded the interference of
the police. But the uproarious throng were always obedient,

after slight delays, to the ringing hammer of the Chairman and as each five minutes' period of internecine combat was brought to an end, I found that a vast number of mining shares had been bought and sold. Perhaps a visit to this Chamber, when the Stock-brokers are at work between the hours of eleven and twelve, is of all sights in San Francisco, the one best worth seeing.

## vi

THE city's extraordinarily rapid growth, which in hardly more than a quarter century had converted the little frontier village into a metropolis of more than 250,000, was a source of wonder not only to the San Franciscans themselves but to many others. Curiosity about this new giant that had sprung up on the far coast was keen in all parts of the nation, and articles designed to explain the phenomenon regularly appeared in the magazines and newspapers of the day. One of the most interesting of these was published in *Scribner's Monthly* for July, 1875; its author was Samuel Williams, long a resident of the city, who had witnessed at first hand much of the transformation he described.

The old landmarks—pride of the pioneer—have nearly all disappeared [he wrote]. The wooden shanty, the dingy adobe hut, the crazy rookery on piles, have given place to palatial structures; and San Francisco is rapidly taking rank architecturally with the great cities of the world. Front and Battery and Sansome are already fine business streets; Kearny, Montgomery, California, and the lower part of Market suggest a town a hundred years old. Some of the public and private buildings are among the most elegant and costly in the country. . . .

The stranger, riding along Bush, Pine, Sutter, Post streets, and Van Ness Avenue, will find it difficult to realize that he is in a city only a quarter of a century old. But he will also be struck with the absence of architectural unity. Hardly any two mansions are exactly alike. The "orders" are fearfully and wonderfully mixed. He will find Corinthian, Gothic, Doric, Byzantine, huddled together in a chaotic jumble of wood and stone and brick and iron; yet there is a sort of family likeness running through all—an architectural kinship that is essentially Californian. There is the ubiquitous bay window (the San Franciscan has learned that sunlight makes the doctor's visits rare), and the ambitious Mansard roof, and the elaborate cornices—terror of timid pedestrians in earthquake times—and the somewhat "loud" front entrance. Entering a rich man's house, he will find luxury carried to the utmost limit of the possible; princely halls, and dazzling drawing rooms; the floors covered with the richest carpets; the walls adorned with costly paintings—the splendors of the East and West combined.

In discussing the source of the wealth thus ostentatiously displayed, the writer commented:

San Francisco is largely, more largely than many of our people are willing to confess, the child of the mines. They gave it its first start; they have generously, though not exclusively, nourished it ever since. They have called into

existence a very large manufacturing interest, giving employment to tens of thousands of men. They have stimulated
every branch of trade and internal commerce, quickened
every pulse of industrial life. Nearly all our finest buildings
have been erected out of the profits of mining enterprises.
Every pound of ore that is taken out of the earth, from
Alaska to Arizona, pays tribute here. A man may make his
fortune in the desert of Nevada or Idaho, but he is pretty
sure to spend it in San Francisco.

No account of the city in the mid-1870's would be
complete without reference to what was then an all-but-
universal pastime: that of speculating in mining shares.
Like many others—including Anthony Trollope—Williams described that phase of the community life in some
detail:

California Street is the speculator's paradise, or perdition.
Here the bulls bellow, and the bears growl their loudest.
Here the crowd of stock-jobbers congregate, and the opera-
tors put up their "little games." Fortunes are made or lost in
a day. A happy turn in stocks makes a millionaire of a man
who yesterday could not be trusted for a pair of boots. Nowhere is the temptation to gamble so strong, or the chances
of gain or loss so great as in mines. A single blow of a pick
may reveal millions, where before was seen nothing but
barren earth; a "horse," a streak of porphyry, a fire, a flood,
a cave, may make the richest mine on the Comstock unpro-
ductive for months. Four years ago the Crown Point and
Belcher mines were regarded as worthless. The stock of the
former went begging in the market at three dollars a share;
the stock of the latter was without buyers at any price. But
the great "bonanza" stretching across both mines was dis-

covered, and in a few months Belcher and Crown Point rushed up to $1,800 a share. Since then these mines have produced nearly $45,000,000 in bullion and two United States Senators. . . . Two years ago the Consolidated Virginia mine was denounced on the street as a "wild cat"; now its value is modestly estimated at $150,000,000; and the California mine, which a few months ago was hardly known, is likely to have an even greater future. With such marvelous revelations of the hidden riches of the earth, it is not surprising that these mercurial people occasionally lose their heads, abandon temporarily the more conservative channels of business, and seek their fortune on the street.

But a bonanza with "millions in it" is not struck every week. Stocks may "boom" today, but droop tomorrow, and with the crash come remorse and repentance, heartbreak and disgust. Then California Street curses its fate, puts on sackcloth and ashes and resolves to sin no more. The good resolution lasts till the next stock-rise, when the old appetite returns, and the speculative debauch is renewed.

Another facet of San Francisco life that has been characteristic of the spot since its beginning is the uncommonly large number of residents who live, not in private homes but in hotels or rooming houses, and who take their meals in restaurants. In consequence of this singularity the natives have long boasted of the number, variety and quality of its eating places. Of the situation as it existed in 1875, Williams wrote:

San Francisco is famed for its restaurants. In no city in America are these establishments so numerous in proportion to the population. They number between two and three hundred, and it is safe to say that at least thirty thousand people

take their meals at them. They are of all grades and prices—
from the "Poodle Dog," Martin's and the Maison Dorée,
where a meal costs from $1.50 to $20—down to the Miners'
Restaurant, where it costs only forty cents. Between these
extremes are a large number of French, German and Italian
restaurants where one may get a royal breakfast for half a
dollar, a lunch for twenty-five cents, and a dinner, including
claret, for seventy-five cents, à la carte. A tenderloin steak
(and there is no better beef in the world than here), potatoes, bread and butter, and coffee will cost fifty cents; a
lamb chop, potatoes, bread and butter, and coffee, twenty-
five cents; an omelet or eggs boiled, scrambled or fried, with
coffee, and bread and butter, thirty-five cents. A grade
lower down, but in places cleanly and entirely respectable,
one gets three dishes for twenty-five cents, and may find quite
a decent meal for twenty to thirty cents.

The writer next took up another long-established—
and justly celebrated—local institution: the free lunch:

San Francisco is the Elysium of "bummers." Nowhere else
can a worthless fellow, too lazy to work, too cowardly to
steal, get on so well. The climate befriends him, for he can
sleep out of doors four-fifths of the year, and the free lunch
opens to him boundless vistas of carnal delights. He can
gorge himself daily for a nominal sum; get a dinner that a
king might envy for fifty cents. There are two classes of
saloons where these midday repasts are furnished—"two bit"
places and "one bit" places. In the first he gets a drink and a
meal; in the second he gets a drink and a meal of inferior
quality. He pays for the drink (twenty-five or fifteen cents,
according to the grade of the place), and gets his meal for
nothing. This consists, in the better class of establishments,

of soup, boiled salmon, roast beef of the best quality, bread and butter, potatoes, tomatoes, crackers and cheese. Many of the places are fitted up in a style of almost Oriental grandeur. A stranger entering one of them casually, might labor under the delusion that he had found his way, by mistake, to the *salon* of a San Francisco millionaire. He would find immense mirrors reaching from floor to ceiling; carpets of the finest texture and the most exquisite patterns; luxurious lounges, sofas, and arm-chairs; massive tables covered with papers and periodicals; the walls embellished with expensive paintings. . . . Some of the keepers are men of education and culture. One is an art critic of high local repute, who has written a book, and a very readable one, of San Francisco reminiscences.

The saloonkeeper-author referred to above was T. A. Barry, who, in collaboration with B. A. Patten, wrote *Men and Memories of San Francisco in the "Spring of '50,"* which appeared in 1873.

San Francisco has rather more than its share of eccentric characters [Williams' account continues]. Foremost among these is "Emperor Norton," a harmless creature, who firmly believes that he is the legitimate sovereign of the United States and Mexico; issues frequent pronunciamentos; exacts tribute from such citizens as humor his delusion; spends his days walking about the streets, his evenings at the theater, and his nights at a cheap lodging-house. He has the run of the hotel reading-rooms, appears on public occasions in tattered regalia, visits the different churches to see that heresies dangerous to the peace of the Empire are not promulgated, calls at the newspaper offices to warn the conductors against the consequences of treasonable utterances—in short, is up

early and late regulating the affairs of the world in general, and the city and state in particular.

Of other of the city's idiosyncrasies, this observer wrote:

The popular speech of San Francisco is strongly flavored with localisms. You hear on every side the jargon of the mining camp, the *patois* of the frontier. If a man fails in business he is "gone up a flume"; if he makes a lucky speculation he has "struck it rich"; if he dies he has "passed in his checks." Of a man of sound sense it is said "his head is level"; a good business is said to "pan out well." The genuine Californian never says he had made a fortunate investment, but he has "struck a lead"; never says he had gotten rich, but has "made his pile." A good dinner he calls a "square meal"; a cheat is always a "bilk"; getting at the real character of a man is "coming down to bed rock." "Cleanout" and "freeze out," are synonyms for rascally operations in business. When stocks are active they are said to be "booming"; a panic in the market is expressed by the term "more mud"; a man who is hurt in a mining transaction is "cinched"; a weak man is said to have "no sand in him"; a lying excuse is denounced as "too thin." In the slang vernacular, any eating place is a "hash-house," and a pretty waiter girl is a "beer-slinger.". . .

For a young city, San Francisco is very much wedded to petty tradition. It clings to the "bit" with a death-like tenacity; clings to it against all reason and against its own interests. The "bit" is a mythical quantity. It is neither twelve and a half cents, nor half of twenty-five; it is neither fifteen cents nor ten cents. If you buy a "bit's" worth and throw down twenty-five cents, you get ten cents back; if you offer the same ten cents in lieu of a "bit," you are looked on as a mild sort of swindler. And yet the "bit" is the standard of minimum monetary value. Of no fixed value itself, it is the measure of the value of a large share of what the people buy and sell. Until within the past few years five-cent pieces were nearly unknown, and are even yet looked upon with disdain by the more conservative residents. Some time ago the leading bank tried the dangerous experiment of introducing pennies, and imported several hundred dollars' worth. They were scornfully rejected as unworthy of the notice of broad-brained Californians, and speedily disappeared. . . .

San Franciscans are remorseless critics. They pride themselves on their ability to form independent judgments, and on their contempt for the opinions of the rest of mankind. This is shown in their treatment of the distinguished dramatic and musical artists. They condemned Edwin Forrest after a single hearing, gave Madame Celeste the cold shoulder, and declined to go into raptures over Edwin Booth. But they gave Charles Kean a glorious welcome, took Boucicault to their bosoms, and went wild over "Dundreary." They opened their purses and their hearts to Parepa-Rosa, gave an ovation to Ole Bull, but permitted Wieniawsky to discourse his divine harmonies to empty benches. Gough drew, but Josh Billings cracked his awful jokes on unsympathetic ears. The Rev. Dr. Lord's historical lectures were crowded, but Charles Kingsley was generally voted a bore. They flocked to hear Depworth Dixon the first night, declared that he would not do, and left him so severely alone that he declined to make his appearance after the second attempt, and left in disgust.

Quite early in the city's history—indeed, during the first decade of its history—there sprang up a group of San Franciscans whom later generations have termed "professional pioneers." These grew in number with each passing year. Samuel Williams, writing in 1875, had this to say of the species:

He lives wholly in the past. He dates the Creation of the world from the discovery of gold at Sutter's Mill, the Deluge from the great flood at Sacramento. He went to sleep immediately after the collapse of the Vigilance Committee, and has been asleep ever since. The world has moved on; the city has increased in population sixfold; a new race of men has come upon the stage, but he knows it not. He sighs for the halcyon days when a man could get a dollar an hour for work; when the dulcet voice of the derringer was heard in the land at all hours; when one could settle his little disputes with his neighbor at Judge Lynch's Court of Last Resort. I asked a friend one day where one of these incorrigibles could be found, as I wished to deliver a message to him.

"You will find him in the ———Saloon, in the midst of a lot of bummers, drinking out of the same old bottle he drank from eighteen years ago."

"But how does he live?"

"Sponges on his friends and 'strikes' newcomers."

An amusing illustration of the conservatism of these case-hardened Argonauts occurred the other day. The recently elected officers of the Pioneer Society—men of progressive ideas, who have fully kept abreast of the times—ventured on a dangerous innovation. They removed the bar. This was an outrage on "vested rights" not to be endured. The bibulous fossils rose in their wrath, held an indignation meeting, and threatened to depose the offending officials.

"But," said the acting President, "the Pioneer Hall ought to be something more than a whiskey shop. The Society ought to do something for the future."

"You don't understand the thing at all," replied the thirsty veteran, "the Society was organized over a bar and a bar it must and shall have."

Incidentally, the die-hard group lost the argument, and many years have passed since members have been allowed to slake their thirst within the confines of Pioneer Hall.

Society has greatly changed for the better within the past few years [continued this observer of the city's mores], but is still somewhat "mixed." The lines of class and caste are often vague and shadowy. Your coachman of yesterday may be your landlord today. The man who supplied you with vegetables a few years ago may now rank with you socially. The woman who did your washing in the early days may look down with pitying eyes upon you tomorrow. Bridget, who was your maid-of-all-work when you first came to the country, lives in a grand house, rejoices in a coachman in livery, and goes to all the great parties. Don't feel hurt if she cuts you, for she is "in society," and cannot afford to be too promiscuous in her acquaintances. It is natural that in a community so largely made up of fortune-hunters, wealth should be a controlling social power; but it would be unjust to say that wealth is the sole standard of social position. Occupation, how one lives, and where one lives, have something to do with it. There is a story of a rich man—I do not vouch for its truth—who some years ago gave a famous party. He had a large circle of acquaintances, but he could not invite everybody. "We must draw the line somewhere, you know," he said, and he drew it bravely between wholesale and retail. The man who sold soap and candles by the box was decreed to be within the "sacred pale" of society's elect. The man who sold soap and candles by the pound was voted a social Philistine.

Living at a first-class hotel is a strong presumption of social availability, but living in a boarding-house, excepting two or three which society has indorsed as fashionable, is to incur grave suspicions that you are a mere nobody. But even in a boarding-house the lines may be drawn between those who have a single room and those who have a suite. Said a lady to a little woman recently arrived:

"I see, my dear, you have but one room. This will not do; you will never get into society until you have a suite."

"But, my husband can't afford it."

"He must afford it!"

But all rich people are not shoddies, and all poor people are not socially outcast. There are many—and the number is rapidly multiplying—whom wealth has not spoiled—has not made proud and insolent; to whose houses good men and women with clean antecedents, and small bank accounts, are welcome and honored guests; to whose houses successful rascals and purse-proud boobies are never admitted, and in conferring pleasures upon their less prosperous fellows, confer happiness upon themselves. I see many signs of healthful social growth.

Rich men are beginning to learn that there are nobler investments than stocks and bonds; that life has something grander and sweeter than the pursuit of sordid gain; that he who would leave an honored name behind him must do something for the future as well as for the past; for the public as well as for self. . . .

What manner of person the "Coming Man" of San Francisco is to be is not clear; but some things may safely be predicted of him.

He will be a fine man physically, clear-brained, if not

broad-minded; bold, speculative, dashing—a man of great projects, if not great fulfillments. He will be iconoclastic, unconventional, a hater of shams.

He will have little reverence for the past, little respect for traditions, little patience with precedents, little regard for the opinions of his elder brothers. He will strike out into new paths of progress, dash forward with striding step, rudely jostle more slow-going travelers, as if he were monarch of the road, and born for conquest. He will have boundless faith in himself, will be fertile in resources, quick to see his advantage, prompt to act, possibly careless in the use of means by which to attain ends. In a word, he will typify in his character of the dry, clear, intensely electric air of this land of the Setting Sun.

## vii

To present-day readers it is in many cases the writers from foreign lands who wrote most interestingly and informatively of the early city. The reason that is so is fairly obvious. For to writers from elsewhere in this country much of the physical aspect of the place, and of the behavior of the inhabitants, seemed so little different from those in other American cities that they failed to comment on them. On the other hand, to visitors from abroad such matters seemed both new and curious, and they proceeded to describe them in detail.

One foreigner whose impressions today's readers will find particularly vivid was the Mexican author, Guillermo Prieto, who reached the city early in 1877 as a member of a party of political refugees. Prieto and his group arrived aboard the Pacific Mail steamer *Granada,* and his account of his stay there and elsewhere in the United States was first published in Mexico City the following year. A translation of the section pertaining to his local stay appeared in 1938 under the title, "San Francisco in the Seventies: The City as Viewed by a Mexican Political Exile." It is from the latter that the following excerpts are quoted.

The *Granada*'s approach to the harbor he described in these words:

Daybreak of January twenty-fifth hailed us announcing the impending arrival in San Francisco. This boat was immaculately scrubbed and polished. Since three in the morning the Chinese had been working the pumps, and cascades of water had left the vessel mirror-bright. There was packing in all the cabins; children in their Sunday best tore through the passageways and over the stairs; canaries, macaws, and lapdogs came to light; ladies and escorts, spruced as if for a ball, stood waiting, with bags and parasols beside them. Only the Mexicans were sad at heart. Here for the rest was journey's end, for them the beginning of what might prove to be exile forever.

Ships began to appear from all directions, some proudly cutting out across the water, some in busy comings and goings along the shore. The bustle increased. Our crew in holiday attire covered the decks, and railings were fringed with bright hats and parasols. Steamers whistled like horses neighing as they pass. Rocks, trees, and heights unfolded in a circle to reveal in the center a forest of masts. Among them

chimneys smoked, pouring out clouds of white and black
that rose diffusely, gilded by the sun. Above, riggings and
flags formed tangled nets in the air, and all around us little
boats bobbed up and down on the waves.

Tenders of harbor-master, health officials, and postal service tossed at our side. A host of tradesmen, reporters, friends,
and mere curiosity-seekers advanced. Numerous small craft
shouted their accommodations. Swarms of agents circulated
among the passengers, brandishing cards and offering the
hospitality of hotels, restaurants, and boardinghouses. The
*Granada* proceeded through the maze in state. A babel of
shrill accents dazed our wretched ears, and soon we brushed
against a succession of wooden passages giving access to long
galleries. These were the docks.

Prieto and his companions made their way through
the throng at the dockside and eventually reached the
hotel that was to be their headquarters. This modest hostelry stood on the steep Pine Street hill, a few doors
above Kearny.

The Gailhard Hotel [wrote Prieto], like most American
buildings, is constructed on the pattern of a ship. It is a large
wooden box whose single roof covers entire floors of rooms
heaped one above the other, all joined by mahogany staircases with metal-edged steps. The rooms have windows to
the street or to various light-wells. What we call a *patio* is
unknown in this country, and its absence drives people into
the streets as if fearful of asphyxiation. For the rest, although
our hotel hesitates precariously between second class and
third, there is no lack of carpets and gas-lights in the halls,
and in the rooms, double beds, marble-topped bureaus, dress-
ing-stands, coat-racks, and tiny tables.

The dining room is on the first floor. It is crowded with small tables like our cafés at home. Tightly wedged in behind the counter stands the monumental mistress of the scene, assisted by one hunch-backed waiter with squinting blue eyes, sarcastic and long-suffering. The walls are decked with coat-hangers; here and there theater placards; a shame-faced mirror; portraits of heroes and dancers. Directly across is the office and bar, where lager beer and cocktails hold sway. Here also there are tables for the sedentary and a billiard table where bibbers may while away their boredom.

Next morning the visitor set out on a tour of the downtown area.

Kearny, Montgomery, Market, California and Sacramento streets are characteristic in their magnificence and wealth. The first of these is about two miles long. The lowest level of its buildings is made up of broad panes of glass held between slender iron columns, giving the effect of open space; so that the mass of the structures above seems to rest on air. With unvarying uniformity the walls are broken by rows of windows, all of the same size, all with green blinds. Only here and there the monotony is interrupted by elegant porticos, urns, fountains, and statues, which except for their unsubstantial materials would be miracles of architectural achievement.

Among these surprising edifices there are humble structures, always with pointed roofs and always coming singly. These are poor-appearing carriage shops, stables, laundries, or warehouses heaped with tallow and stinking hides. From them issue ragged and ill-kempt monsters whose dripping shirts are an offense to eye and nose. And behind the palaces run filthy alleys, or rather nasty dungheaps without sidewalks or illumination, whose loiterers smell of the gallows.

Eclipsing all this, however, the street floors of the great avenues form one continuous exposition of all that art and science can produce. A pauper could enter these clothing stores and in a moment step out a prince, to the eye at least. Drygoods shops like the White House, which alone contains more than our Platero Street, are stocked with a profusion of dresses, shawls, and hats; and a jewelry store like the mirrored Diamond Palace can fill its black velvet showcases with opals, emeralds, pearls and gold to the value of fourteen million dollars.

We arrived in the dead of winter, and the cold was intense. The men—I say men in general, for I never could tell one class or position from another—wore black and all had overcoats. The women, too, with a universality that became monotonous and common-place, wore coats of cloth or furs, some of them worth from three to five hundred dollars; and with them small hats with colored veils and, unfailingly, umbrellas. I saw very few beggars. Such as there were carried barrel-organs, fiddles, bunches of flowers, or boxes of matches. Through the richest sections of the city they would pass—liquory, tattered men and large, down-at-the-heel women in aprons and shawls—like evil smells in a perfumed garden.

The swarms of women on Kearny, Montgomery and Market streets is constant and unchanging at all hours of the day. The typical American woman lives in the streets. She goes everywhere, and everywhere she is received with preferential civility. Moreover, although the women of New York have a great reputation for beauty, I could never have imagined women in whom beauty and charm were more general than in these. Their figures reflect ease and self-possession, their bearing is so gracefully natural, that the writer, nostalgic with nearly sixty summers on his back, is not only moved himself but imagines that the flower of youth would cast passionate glances after them. At the edge of the sidewalk in front of the large stores there are posts where the ladies descend from their vehicles, or clerks reach comfortably up to the carriage door; women have special entrances in hotels; special sections in restaurants; and special dressing rooms, exquisitely fitted, in Pullman coaches. Everywhere they enjoy full possession of their social superiority. Whatever treatment a woman may deserve in private, in public merely because she is a woman she has every protection of man and law.

Activity in the city takes on new life at night. The darkness is crisscrossed by rivers of flame. Many of the stores remain open and crowded, their brillance heightened by the strong gas illumination of windows and showcases, the whole effect one of continuous festivity. . . .

Traffic determines the illumination of the streets. Little-used thoroughfares are dark and gloomy, their buildings looming somberly through the blackness of vacant lots marked by fallen picket fences. In the busier sections, fruit-stands, theaters, jugglers and charlatans attract the crowds by the glare of torches; and from the heights that dominate the city the lights outline every rise and fall of earth as on a relief map. . . .

The number of carts and carriages of every form and size is absolutely fantastic. First come the small handcarts. This is natural, for there is no one like the Yankee for carrying loads. His consciousness of his dignity permits him to do this with no impairment of self-respect, proving itself a sentiment of great benefit to the nation. Then no individual rises above the very humblest station without aspiring to keep a buggy.

The buggy is a small two-seated carriage drawn by one horse. It places everything within an accessible distance, and in addition offers the satisfaction of permitting its owners to rub shoulders with the most well-to-do. Thus even the baker, the vegetable-woman, the meanest farmhand, all strive to possess a vehicle as a conveyance for their goods and also for their families; who in this way enter by the doorway of labor into the enjoyment of social comforts. But here is also an abundance of finer coaches, landaus, or calèches, drawn by superb Friesian horses, flawlessly groomed and blanketed. Even here the coachman is frequently the owner as well, and elegantly attired, his legs wrapped in rich furs, he may often be seen leaving the driver's seat to step into a bank or a theater in the company of what looks to be the cream of society. . . .

Horsecars traverse the principal streets, carrying passengers a distance of four to six miles for the uniform price of five cents. Several street railway companies compete in comfort and promptness of service, but cooperate in permitting tickets, which may moreover be bought in quantities at a reduction of price, to be used on many lines. Their cars can seat up to twenty persons in comfort, though all who can find room are admitted, if they have to hang on straps in thick clusters like grapes, or squeeze like raisins into a solid mass. As usual, ladies are given the choicest places in spite of the fact that their cool assumption of title to such distinctions has made the gentlemen a bit lukewarm and themselves a good deal more polite.

Two kinds of cars attracted my special attention. Some, completely spherical in shape, veritable lottery globes on wheels, are drawn by a single horse. A wood disc set in the ground is made to turn both horse and car around to the opposite direction, the passengers mounting and descending.

Another even more original type of car runs up and down the hills of Clay and California streets for nearly two miles as if by itself, with neither draught animal, engine, driver, nor other visible means of locomotion. The mechanism consists of a slot parallel to the rails in which run iron chains whose perforations are caught in powerful claws. At the end of the chain is a steam engine, and the car stops, increases and slackens its speed according to the impulse of the operator, who has but little to do. [Prieto here is describing—not altogether accurately—the functioning of the first of the city's cable cars.]

The streets, with the exception of a few not too catholic diagonals, are very regular; they never suddenly change their names, but lead a person faithfully from one end of town to the other; the system of numbering buildings, odd numbers on one side of the street and even on the other, leaves no room for doubts, in addition to this, at intervals the street lamps bear the name of the street; coachmen, vendors and passers-by are always most willing to assist the stranger in finding his way; and finally, it is the strict duty of the police to lead to his destination anyone who requests it. The streetcars always indicate their direction, and even at night their different colors prevent the dullest person in the world from losing his way.

Now is this flawless system perfectly clear to the reader? And have I mentioned also that many citizens speak Spanish or French or Italian, so that I could never fail to understand them? Well, my sojourn in San Francisco was one long repetition of the state of being lost. I would set off toward the south, and loyally as the needle of a compass, end up due north. I would set off for the theater, and find myself horrified at the gateway to the cemetery. Thereupon I would take a streetcar, making every effort to select one I thought I knew. On it would go, and suddenly there would no longer be any streets about me. In a towering rage at my own stupidity I would pull my hat down over my eyes to exaggerate my silly look, take a *peseta* out of my pocket and hand it to the first newsboy who passed, saying only "Gailhard Hotel" and letting myself be led like a blind man to my very door.

Few phases of the life of the city escaped the eyes of this energetic visitor. Thus in due course he set down his impressions of yet another outstanding feature of the San Francisco of the day; that is, its countless bars.

The typical bar-room [he wrote] has a grille or grating to the street, a counter, a gas flame where topers may light their cigars, a box of matches, and a box of toothpicks. Against the wall behind the bar runs a bracket of glasses and bottles. Above this stands a mirror and a clock, a pad showing the day of the month, a calendar, and a travel-directory. Under the counter is a huge barrel of beer on draught. But when these prerequisites have been provided, there is still room for variations. Thus some saloons have organs that invite patrons to dally, organs often worth thousands of dollars, that play overtures, marches and tasteful variations. Other bars have bands, still others pianos. And some, in addition to a band, keep a female staff capable of waking thirst in a stone.

All bar-rooms have tables. In most of them endless bottles are opened, and drinkers smoke and carouse. But where there are women it is different. There the lady prettily takes a seat beside the stranger, and calls her friends so that there will be no odd gentlemen. And the consumption of liquor soars. For the occasional patrons who have in mind to drink in private, there are always rooms upstairs where they may do so, and where conversation is less restricted.

At one of the more select bars, the Fountain, at the corner of Sutter and Kearny streets—"a popular meeting place for bankers"—Prieto witnessed an example of Yankee ingenuity that filled him with admiration.

From one of the walls [he wrote] a slender strip of paper serpentines down like a trickle of water into a basket on the floor. I was much puzzled at the number of people who went up to consult this tiny ribbon of paper, and no less astonished when its function was revealed. This tape, it appears, contains news of the whole world, fresh at every moment, and serves as a basis for great mercantile transactions. In short, it records choice gleanings from the submarine cable. I cannot describe how affected I was by this enslavement of lightning, the object it served, its deep consequences, and the simple manner in which ideas could be transferred across intervening oceans; above all, by the conception of entrusting the mightiest concerns of the universe to a strip of paper scarcely wider than a cigar band. . . .

San Francisco has also many musical bars and dance halls. These are generally situated in little-frequented streets and underground. First, in order to understand the underground, it is necessary to recall that all buildings have a basement below the ground level, communicating with the street by a stairway. These subterranean spaces are illuminated by skylights covered with heavy little circles of glass set into iron gratings. Spread across the sidewalks, and with artificial light below, these bits of glass give the effect of tiny wells of flame. People walk upon them, and they give the sidewalks of the city a certain individuality.

The dance halls below are merely a pretext by which women are employed to stimulate the sale of liquor. The music is outrageous, the dances crowded, and the police have not infrequently to descend to restore order. Thus these justly-famed infernos are a link between lower-class restaurants and the minstrel shows.

In contrast to such wicked enterprises are the candy and pastry shops, which also dispense Vichy and soda water, and the establishments where oysters, a San Francisco specialty, are vended.

The visitor summed up his survey of that phase of the city's life with this observation: "Whatever other ingredients may enter into merry-making in this capital of the Pacific, it is obvious that love and gluttony come first."

Part Five

# The Elegant Decades
# 1880–1900

i

ALTHOUGH during the first quarter century of the city's existence many San Franciscans amassed comfortable fortunes—in mining, banking, trade, land speculation, and related fields—it was not until the seventies and eighties that a new type of financial giant—the West Coast's first multimillionaires—appeared. These were hard-driving entrepreneurs whose rise to affluence was the result of their shrewd exploitation of two sources of virtually unlimited wealth: Nevada's Comstock Lode and the Central Pacific Railroad. While a score of lesser fortunes were made from these enterprises, the chief rewards went to eight men: the "Big Four" of the Central Pacific—Huntington, Stanford, Crocker, and Hopkins—and the quartet of "Bonanza Kings"—Mackay, Fair, Flood, and O'Brien.

All eight men were San Franciscans, and it was mainly in San Francisco that they spent their wealth, pouring vast numbers of their superfluous dollars into the city's financial, commercial and industrial life, and building on the crest of Nob Hill—which had formerly been a district of modest wooden cottages—a group of ornate Victorian mansions. Until they were destroyed in the fire of 1906 these huge hilltop palaces dominated the city's skyline and were a source of unending wonder and curiosity to residents and visitors alike.

When I look back across the pageant of the years [wrote Amelia Ransome Neville in her delightful book of reminiscences, *The Fantastic City*], there is a special brightness and a touch of the bizarre about the sequence of the seventies and eighties. It was the reign of the bonanza kings who built their palaces on Nob Hill, where Jim Flood's thirty-thousand-dollar brass fence glittered in the sun. The beautifully wrought metal flashed for the entire length of two blocks on the square where the brownstone mansion stood, and it was the sole task of one retainer to keep it bright. Passing any hour of the day one discovered him polishing away at some section of it. The huge cubic house is now [1932] the home of the Pacific Union Club, and the fence is still there, but with its pristine polish gone. When I saw it last, it was black as bronze. In brighter days it might have been a symbol of all the fantastic flamboyance of the time.

An incrdible period it was, with its lavish expenditures and sudden luxury veneered over many crude ways of living. Strange homes, these Nob Hill palaces, the amazement of visitors from the Old World which had nothing like them. For that matter, they were unique in America. Very well I recall, on a visit to Chicago in later years, how insignificantly small mansions on the Gold Coast looked to one inured to Nob Hill.

Diagonally across California Street from the Flood house stood the Hopkins castle, whose gray towers could be seen from the bay and far south of the city. Terraced gardens fell away on the steep hillside at the back, and surrounding them was a mighty stone wall, forty feet high against the terrace of the lower level along Pine Street. There, massive oak doors swung on iron hinges to permit the entrance, not of armored knights on horseback, but of basket phaetons, the family barouche, rockaways, and broughams. A long looped "S" of a driveway led upward to the house, and when lamps along its way shone at night, with the castle windows alight, the effect from the city below was enchanting.

Within, the house was a mass of anachronisms. One entered portals of a feudal castle into a court of a doge's palace, all carved Italian walnut with a gallery around the second story where murals of Venetian scenes were set between the arches. They were the work of Jules Tavernier, French artist, who stopped in California after a trip to the South Seas, where he painted long before Gauguin.

A beautiful place in itself was this central court, as were many individual rooms in these anachronistic mansions filled with rare inlaid woods, marble mosaics, and rich furnishings. It is said that the architects measured shelves in the libraries of some of them and ordered yards of books from dealers to fill the spaces, as they would order fixtures. Of the truth of this I am not certain, but astonishing effects in servants' liveries I well remember. The Negro coachman of one new millionaire wore a suit of white cloth with black velvet buttons as large as butter-dishes, and orange-topped boots—his own taste, I fancy.

In spite of its absurdities, the Hopkins house achieved a general effect of stately magnificence, a sort of Mrs. Malaprop dignity. And it looked enduring. But alas, this feudal castle was built of wood painted the color of stone, and it burned like any shanty in 1906—as did all the Nob Hill palaces. . . .

Across Taylor Street [from the comparatively modest home of David D. Colton, chief counsel for the Central Pacific] the prodigious Crocker mansion billowed over its lawns; and across California Street was the homelike Tobin house, distinguished by reason of having what might be termed a hand-picked library. . . .

Just below the Hopkins castle stood the great roomy barn which was Senator Stanford's home. The death of young Leland Stanford, Jr., left a pervading sadness there, and afterwards one inevitably thought of it looking at the frowning façade of the house, painted dark brown. Built in earlier days, the vast rooms had seen elaborate entertainments. Mrs. Stanford was a plain, gentle little body who liked beautiful things. Her collection of rubies was said to be the finest in the world and her laces were as exquisite as Marie Antoinette's.

Senator Fair planned a palace to outshine them all for the hillside block facing the Hopkins and Stanford homes, but only a granite wall enclosing the grounds ever materialized. Part of it now surrounds the terrace of the Hotel Fairmont built there by his daughters. The Fair family lived in a comparatively modest mansion on the Pine Street level of Nob Hill, and there Tessie Fair married Herman Oelrichs of New York.

Flood and O'Brien had owned a restaurant on Montgomery Street, the Auction Lunch, where an especially fine fish stew drew patrons from the Stock Exchange nearby. Daily the proprietors heard talk of stocks and mining shares and together decided to invest. Results were overwhelming. Flood and O'Brien found themselves among the plutocrats and retired without delay from the restaurant business. About the same time a jolly little barkeeper at the Auction Lunch retired also into the plutocracy. He had been popular with the patrons who sometimes passed friendly tips across the bar by which Tim profited until, suddenly, he too found himself rich. Tim had been courting an Irish girl, cook at the

Toland house on Nob Hill. They were married now, and built a mansion with the surpassing splendor of a dais in the parlor where, enthroned like royalty, Hannah received visitors. It was really no more than an ingenious expression of a will to rise in the world. But when the daughter of the household returned from an Eastern finishing school expensively finished, the dais disappeared from the parlor to become a family skeleton. Since this pretty daughter married into the aristocracy abroad, the story of Tim and Hannah proves to my mind something like efficiency in the "Melting Pot." Mrs. Toland, I fear, never appreciated this. In a theater lobby, at a charity ball, whenever her way crossed that of Mrs. Tim, she always greeted her regal ex-cook with a cordial, "Good evening, Hannah."

Amelia Neville's narrative presents glimpses of San Francisco and San Franciscans during a period that extended from Civil War times until after the turn of the century. Her description of the Lick House, which remained the most elegant of the city's hotels until the mid-seventies, when it was supplanted by the Palace, follows:

Very palatial indeed, we thought it, and took great pride in the long building extending from Post to Sutter Street on Montgomery, rising to the dizzy height of three and a half stories. The opening banquet in '62 was an event of many guests, speeches, toasts, flowers, and music. It soon became the fashion to dine at the Lick on Sunday evenings. The dining-room and lobby were beautiful rooms, with their flagged marble floors and fine woodwork. James Lick had been a cabinet-maker in his youth, and for his hotel, built with California gold, he imported rare woods from South

America and the Orient, doing much of the finishing and polishing with his own hands, reveling in the work. He was a sad-looking man, more or less of a recluse, who had literally dug his gold, or much of it, from the hills himself. He worked with his pick-axe until he was rich, when, instead of a palace on Nob Hill, he built baths and planned other public benefactions. The Mercantile Library . . . owed much to him, and Lick Observatory is his memorial.

With all the new prosperity and wealth . . . San Francisco changed greatly in appearance. Downtown was suddenly more cosmopolitan. Horse-car lines and a crowd of horse-drawn vehicles filled the streets. Two new hotels were neighbors of the Lick House on Montgomery Street, the Russ House, and the Occidental, all of five stories high. . . . Under them were smart shops. Colonel Andrew's Diamond Palace was one of the sights of the town; a jewelry store of white marble with a sort of lobby where mirrors reflected the showcases and their display in flashing confusion—the final word in metropolitan splendor for a large clientele.

Kearny Street, from Market north to Clay, was the popular shopping district, and one took a Kearny Street horse-car which turned at Broadway into Stockton, to ride over toward North Beach, where Newman & Levinson's little shop kept rare imported laces. . . .

There was never anything like civic beauty in those days. In residence districts one found a varied assortment of architectural freaks, and downtown still had a haphazard aspect, with low frame structures, surviving from the fifties, scattered among well-built business blocks. The Ferry Building at the city's entrance was a long brown shed facing a plank-paved plaza, not at all an entrance to impress arriving visitors. Moreover, as they stepped off the ferry-boat which brought them from the Overland Railroad terminus across the bay, they were assailed by a battalion of hotel "runners" shouting the names of hostelries in a vociferous din. For years the Russ House runner was the star of the lot. His heavy bass boomed over and over, "Russ-ouse, Russ-ouse," with vigorous emphasis on Russ, beneath all the clamor of indistinguishable names. It was a long step toward civic beauty when the new Ferry Building finally rose in place of the shed, its tall, slender tower, copied from the Giralda of the Cathedral in Seville, dominating this foyer of the city.

We had, of course, the Mint, austerely classic and beautiful with its stone columns and the broad sweep of stone steps leading to the entrance; and there was the Post Office on Washington Street, another classic effect in gray stone. But beyond these, public buildings were unimpressive. The new City Hall, far out on Larkin Street, was simply a mess. It was never completed, but still wandering vaguely over several blocks, with its unfinished wings and peeling stucco making it look like an old ruin; it happily burned in 1906. . . .

Through residence neighborhoods of the old city passed the colorful figure of the Chinese vegetable vender in blue cotton blouse and trousers, padded slippers, and a broad hat like an inverted tray of woven bamboo. Over his shoulder he carried a flexible pole and, slung on either end of it, a huge basket overflowing with fresh greens and glowing fruit that bobbed rhythmically to his swinging gait. On Fridays the Chinese fishman followed him on his rounds and stopped at the curb to weigh silver fish in his scales. Chinese peddlers of silks and brocades, carved ivory and jade, carried their wares from house to house packed in cases that were tied in great squares of yellow cotton. It was an adventure to have one brought in with his pack. He would step softly into a room with many little bows and kneel on the floor to untie the knotted cloth; and presently the carpet would be covered with a fascinating confusion of bright silks, ivory fans, lacquer boxes, pale green tea-cups of "Canton Medallion," and carved sandalwood that scented everything.

I missed their visits when Chinatown grew progressive and a Chinese merchants' association did away with them. "Eight dolla hop," one would say holding a piece of brocade at arm's length while he knelt among his wares. "You like him? All light. Fi dolla."

Chinatown was endlessly fascinating. As early as the seventies it was said that thirty thousand Chinese were crowded into the quarter which extended northward on Dupont Street [now Grant Avenue] from California to Broadway, a distance six blocks long and a little more than a block wide. It was an enchanting little city where gentlemen in lavender brocade coats and puffed silk trousers were thick among coolies in their blue cotton. Their long queues were braided with strands of cherry silk. Little-foot women, with sleek heads and jade bracelets falling over their hands, leaned on their attendant maids in slow progress, their tiny feet shod in gold-embroidered silk; and adorable children, in green and cherry-red embroideries, laughed in the crowd of the lantern-hung street. It was, in short, a scene transported from Peking. Windows of the bazaars were a blaze of color. Sweetmeat venders were stationed along the curb, and over the gilded balconies of restaurants drifted the shrill music of the slave girls. Everywhere the scent of sandalwood mingled with that of the fish markets.

Often we went shopping in Dupont Street, for silks, carved teakwood tables, and lacquer trays, and the Canton china that found its way into San Francisco dining-rooms. And often we brought home gifts of lichee nuts, jars of ginger, or white lilies growing in jade-green bowls—good-will offerings from the merchants.

These friendly aliens, with their love of bright hues, their strange theatrical customs, the tong wars and "hatchet men," and all the mystery of life lived in subterranean levels, like geological strata, brought a flare of rich color to the pageant of the old city.

Another major attraction—then as now—was Golden Gate Park, though at the time Mrs. Neville wrote, most of it was still barren sand hills well beyond the edge of the city's built-up area. One of its major points of interest was a large glass conservatory, a gift from railroad magnate Charles Crocker. On display there were a variety of rare tropical plants, the prize being an immense pond-lily, "the largest in the world," called the Victoria Regina.

The Victoria Regina was an object of great popular interest [Mrs. Neville recalled]. As I look back now, its blooming is one of the high lights of the eighteen-eighties. Everyone talked of it. "Have you seen the Victoria Regina?" served to open conversations at dinner-parties. . . . Everyone went to the Park to look at it. In single file the citizenry passed around the pond to marvel at the great flare of petals. It was really a remarkable flower. The green leaf of its foliage measured several feet across and lay like the top of a pool table on the water.

Golden Gate Park, with its long panhandle entrance, had been laid out in lawns and driveways over several acres to become the city's favorite resort, filled with carriages on Saturday afternoons and Sundays. . . .

The Japanese Tea Garden came to the Park with the Mid-winter Fair of '93, and remained, a charming souvenir, with its cherry bloom and waterfalls, tall stone lanterns, iris pools, and little tea-houses built out over waterways with stepping-stones. It is still the loveliest of places. This Midwinter Fair . . . was a bright little exposition following the World's Fair in Chicago with some of the same exhibits and features. It was set in a valley in Golden Gate Park with charming little buildings and a Midway; and its season was a long fiesta for San Francisco. One wandered through sucalyptus avenues filled with Javanese, Arabs, Hindus, Samoans, and other picturesque aliens while Sousa's Band played, or Fritz Scheel's Orchestra. Once they both played at a concert of combined forces and this confluence of music . . . was a Niagara of sound.

In the eighteen-eighties high, cart-wheel bicycles rolled through the driveways, where horses shied at them, and no wonder. With riders perched high on the wheels, they had a curiously entomological aspect, like gigantic Daddy-Long-Legs.

## ii

ANOTHER long-time resident whose recollections of local events and personalities hold much of interest to today's readers was J. B. Levison. A native of Virginia City, Nevada, Levison reached San Francisco in the spring of 1875, when a boy of thirteen. His industry and civic-mindedness presently made him a leader in the business and cultural life of his adopted city, a position he was to maintain for close to seven decades.

The excerpts quoted here are from his privately printed memoirs, which were written in the early 1930's.

In the eighties San Francisco was a "city of neighborhoods." Most youngsters went to the nearest school. Friendships were founded on propinquity. We had not the means of swift and easy transportation that are now taken for granted. . . . We were on terms of close friendship with the letter carrier, the grocer, the butcher, the baker, the man who ran the vegetable store, and the blacksmith (there were horse-shoers in those days), to say nothing of the pleasant old ladies who kept the candy store and the "notions" store where a bell in the living rooms in the rear jangled when the front door was opened.

The district around Geary and Steiner streets was a compact neighborhood all by itself. When we lived there it was one of the most thickly settled sections of that part of San Francisco. Two full blocks—Steiner, Scott, Geary and O'Farrell—were fully built up on all sides, and this was most unusual at a time when almost every other block had a vacant "sand lot." At the corner of Geary and Steiner was Hamilton Hall (taking the name from Hamilton Square), which was used for entertainments of all sorts and as the meeting place of various orders, to some of which my father belonged.

Of his school days—which lasted only a year and a half before his father's business failure caused him to take a job to help support the family—Levison wrote:

The Boys' High School at that time [1876] was on the east side of Powell Street, between Sacramento and Clay.

. . . I used to walk back and forth between Seventh and Bryant [where the family was then living] and Powell and Clay every school day, a distance of two miles. Then, in November, the new Boys' High School on the north side of Sutter Street between Gough and Octavia was completed, and that meant even a longer walk than before.

The services closing the old building were rather interfered with by a practical joke played by a member of our class, Jack Savage. The building had previously been occupied as a church by colored people of the district and had a bell in the belfry which had not been used in years. Savage must have come to school early that morning, climbed up on the roof and attached a string to the clapper, bringing it down over the roof and through a window to his desk (he sat right next to the window). In the midst of the services the old bell, which hadn't been heard for years, started to toll, to the amazement, I might almost say consternation, of everyone. . . .

The dedication of our new school was quite an event. All the teachers and students marched in a body from the old school to the new, to take part in the ceremonies conducted by the Board of Education.

My appointment as a drummer (there were only two) was an event in my short high school life which was quite gratifying to me. I had no drum of my own, I could not afford it, but used one belonging to the school, which I was allowed to take home occasionally to practice. . . .

In those days it was not easy to find a position for a boy, but in my case one was found through an advertisement in a morning paper, with a dentist named J. L. Wilbirt who had offices at the corner of Third and Market streets, over Widber's Drug Store, where the present Claus Spreckels Building now stands. I presented my letter of recommendation [from his high school principal] to Dr. Wilbirt, and went to work for two dollars a week.

It was hard and trying work for a boy of fourteen. There was no Saturday half-holiday in those days, and I had to work Sunday mornings as well. Every morning I walked from Geary and Steiner to Third and Market, carrying my lunch with me, and every night I walked home again. Carfare was out of the question. Sometimes, after the fashion of boys in those days, I rode with a good-natured expressman who let me "nip on behind."

Working for Dr. Wilbirt were his two stepsons, boys much older than I. They were unfriendly from the start, and I was not long in learning the reason. They had been buying all the dental supplies and had been systematically robbing their stepfather by overcharging him for every item. Naturally, when I started going to the dental shop, their game was spoiled. Whether Dr. Wilbirt ever discovered this I never knew, as nothing was ever said to me, but it was not long before he entrusted all the purchasing to me, which did not tend to make me more popular with his stepsons.

A year or two later the youth got a position as clerk— at $20 a month—with an insurance company, thereby entering a field he was to follow for the balance of his life.

The New Zealand Insurance Company [he wrote] was a small office. We were five employees in all, and this gave me a chance to get a smattering of both the fire and marine business. Another good feature of this apprenticeship was the fact that Craig [the manager] was a strict disciplinarian admirably seconded by Ross, the Scotch bookkeeper. Thus I got a sound training not only in office work but in office behavior, an influence that was lasting.

The first telephone I ever spoke through was when I was sent to deliver a New Zealand policy to the Gladding, McBean yard at McAllister and Leavenworth streets. They had a direct wire to their office, which was down at the lower end of Market Street, and a good-natured bookkeeper permitted me to tak to someone at the other end of the wire, an experience which gave me a real thrill.

I may add here that the first electric light I ever saw was in the courtyard of the old Palace Hotel where, late in the seventies, were suspended several arc lights. We would go down occasionally in the evenings to look in wonderment at these lights.

In the mid-eighties young Levison became a clerk in the office of the Anglo-Nevada Assurance Corporation, a company organized by some of the city's business leaders. At first the new firm was so badly managed that some of its officers had to be replaced. As a result, the young clerk—who was still in his early twenties—found himself in charge of the Marine Department—an unexpected piece of good fortune.

The Anglo-Nevada [he recalled] had a rather motley group of employees . . . one being none other than the late James J. Corbett who subsequently became heavyweight champion of the world.

Corbett had been a clerk in the Nevada Bank and disappeared without permission to engage in a prize-fight at Salt Lake under an assumed name. He was then only a youngster. Upon his return, he obviously could not be taken back into the bank, but in view of the friendship existing between his father and J. C. Flood [one of the bank's owners] he was placed in the insurance company where he remained until he took up boxing as a profession.

He was a big, good-natured fellow with a most attractive personality and was a great favorite.

Subsequently John L. Sullivan came to San Francisco on one of his tours and had a four-round exhibition with Paddy Ryan, another well-known heavyweight. I invited Corbett to come with me to this affair which took place in the old Mechanics Pavilion. It was the first time he had ever seen Sullivan and he got quite excited during the evening, saying a number of times to me that he felt satisfied that Sullivan could never hit him. This was most amusing to me, considering that John L. was the champion of the world and Jim merely a local favorite. However, so imbued was Corbett with this idea that he went down to see William Greer Harrison, at that time president of the Olympic Club, suggesting an exhibition bout in the Club gymnasium. Harrison in turn got in touch with Sullivan's manager, who was not at all receptive, and I well remember the reason he gave, which was that if Sullivan outpointed Corbett it would not add to his reputation, whereas he was taking a chance of being outpointed by a clever young amateur, which might seriously affect his standing.

So Corbett and Sullivan never met until the historic fight in New Orleans. . . .

The Civil War heroes were real heroes to me and fired my boyish imagination tremendously. The first of these to come to San Francisco was General Sheridan, "Little Phil" as he was familiarly called. He arrived on October 12, 1875, and I can well recall my thrill when he passed in an open barouche in the procession given in his honor.

President Hayes, the first President I ever saw, with Mrs. Hayes, an unusually sweet and motherly-looking woman, came to San Francisco in September, 1880. Accompanying him was General Sherman, a grizzled veteran who interested me even more than the President. A reception was given to them at the old Mechanics Pavilion, and how I ever got in without an invitation is a mystery to me to this day.

The greatest event of all, however, was the arrival of General Grant, returning from his trip around the world, on September 20, 1879. The community had been keyed up to a high pitch of anticipation and when, just before dusk, the observer at Point Lobos reported sighting the *City of Tokio* upon which Grant was coming from Japan, the town literally went mad.

My mother, with her children and a number of neighbors, rushed up Steiner Street to Pacific and took a position on the sand dunes. . . . After waiting what seemed an interminable time the flotilla escorting the *City of Tokio* through the Golden Gate appeared, to the accompaniment of booming cannons, whistles screeching, flags waving and people cheering.

After the fleet had passed . . . I rushed down town to see the parade; dinner, of course, being out of the question. It seemed as if the entire state had poured its population into the town for the occasion, and when Grant passed, standing in an open barouche, I felt as if I had seen the Creator himself.

I am afraid I neglected my work in the office badly while the festivities lasted. A reception was given to Grant by the Chamber of Commerce in the old Merchants Exchange, and I remember standing on the edge of the crowd so that when the General passed he almost touched my shoulder. I found that I was just exactly as tall as he, and was much elated.

### iii

I N 1947 appeared a book called *920 O'Farrell Street*, in
which its author, Harriet Lane Levy, looked back on
her childhood and youth and drew a nostalgic picture
of family life in one of the city's middle-class residential
districts during the final decades of the nineteenth century. 920 O'Farrell Street, where Harriet Levy lived as
a child, was one of a row of narrow, two-story dwellings
that occupied the block between Polk Street and Van
Ness Avenue. In the next block to the east, between Polk
and Larkin, stood a residence that far outshone its neighbors in both size and elegance. These are the author's
childhood impressions of that neighborhood show place:

The south side of the 800 block held a story. I walked
along it with delight, my interest concentrated upon the
large double residence in the middle of the block which
gave balanced grandeur to the whole neighborhood. It was
the home of John Mackay, king of the Consolidated Virginia,
the mine that, at the turn of a shovel, had converted a poor
miner into a multimillionaire. Daily I passed Jewish homes
before which my spirit automatically drew back; the Frieden-
thals sat upon my heart heavily; the proud obscured the sun.
Not so the home of John Mackay. The Mackay house swept
away all small barriers; it trailed clouds of glory from the
mining centers of Nevada; it broke life into claims and stakes
and tips and noble gamblers and inexhaustible outpourings
of gold. It brought to our doors the Comstock Lode and
Virginia City.

The broad staircase, leading to the entrance, was high and the time required to climb and descend it provided moments for satisfying observation. What matter that the street door closed upon the curious; the outside offered enough. The steps democratically descended to the sidewalk, and young girls ran up and down them, swinging in to the street with easy stride. Could a prophetic eye have seen in them a future Italian princess and a Vanderbilt of New York, it would have remained glued to the entrance door. The occupants of the house and their friends filled their roles like characters in a novel, carriages stood constantly before the door; barouche, coupé, and high stanhope. Wooden coachmen sat in aristocratic immobility, footmen sprang like acrobats from their seats to hand out the ladies of the house. The solid silver-mounted harnesses clinked with the very tinkle I had read about in novels of the title. The horses *were* bays, their flanks *did* shine. On the night of a ball the elite of the city stepped, if they were women, or sprang, if they were men, from their carriages to a crimson velvet carpet, which glowed from the street to the entrance door. However, better than all this confirmation of imagined pageantry, more enlarging to experience, was the daily arrival of the milkman and the delivery into the house of huge cans of milk for the Mackays' bath. Beside such witness of fabled treasure, diamonds were pebbles, golden dinner service, plate.

I told myself that it was not the flourish of wealth but the romance of the triumphal passage from mining cabin to a city mansion that commanded my obeisance, and I made an effort to resist the argument of importance offered by the display of private parade. Before a victoria with a single driver it was easy to retain my assurance; but coachman and footman, clad in colored livery, rigid above a closed coupé, scattered my identity. At the approach of a plum-colored livery, the forehead of my spirit brushed the side-walk.

Between the Jews on the north side of the street and the Gentiles on the south a pleasant dissociation existed which no one wanted to change. The great wealth of the Mackays, and of their successors, automatically created its own barrier, but the privileged intimacy of observations provided all the enjoyment that anyone could hold. A new carriage and pair, a daring imported novelty from Paris, a bizarre visitor from abroad, and along some grapevine route the news was com-municated to the street, providing deeper flavor to already happy lives. The seclusion of the Gentiles across the street was not distorted into intentional distinction or racial prej-udice. No one desired to break through the natural barriers established by differences of race or background. The north side was satisfied that their enjoyment should be heightened by high-toned neighbors who so fortuitously embellished their view, gave distinction to their neighborhood, and pro-vided exciting entertainment by the glamorous variations of their lives.

From its earliest beginnings San Francisco had been "a good theater town," its amusement-starved populace crowding the pioneer playhouses where for an hour or two they could forget the austerities of frontier life in the glamorous world of make-believe. The result was that throughout the fifties and sixties virtually every eminent actor and actress made the long and arduous trip to the far coast, lured by the prospect of long runs in packed houses. Even as late as the period of which

Harriet Levy wrote, the city had an uncommonly high proportion of playgoers. One of the most faithful of these was her inarticulate, foreign-born father.

It was in the theater alone [she wrote] that Father found the richness of the living denied him at home. The stage had been his first English school. Had instinct been his guide, he would have walked from the gangplank of the ship, which brought him to America, straight into the nearest theater. Long before the blur of strange sounds broke into meaning for him, he was climbing the gallery nightly, absorbing the new tongue. . . . The stage became book, club, and society to him. Over a lifetime if a famous actor came to the city, Father disappeared each night after dinner as to a rendezvous. Without a word of explanation, forestalling Mother's mocking inquiry, he stole sideways across the end of the dining room and vanished into the hallway. . . .

If no actor of renown was playing in San Francisco, there was always the Tivoli Opera House. The Tivoli was the most beloved theater in the United States. At first a public garden, it developed into a concert hall for light opera and musical comedy. The price of the two thousand seats, which sold for fifty and twenty-five cents, included refreshments served by the ushers between acts—beer for the gentlemen, Queen Charlottes (ice-cold raspberry soda pop) for the ladies and children.

The Tivoli was democratic; members of the stock company and the audience were as one family. Patrons clamored their desires and their desires were rewarded. Ferris Hartman, beloved comedian, remained on the Tivoli stage for years, improvising as he sang, loving himself, permitting himself fresh extravagancies, secure in our affection.

Collamarini was made for a Tivoli audience, for families

who came night after night, whose boast was that they had not missed one opera of the long season, not one, from *Cavalleria Rusticana*, when Mascagni himself had conducted, to *The Chimes of Normandy* and *La Fille de Madame Angot*. . . .

Father's interest never palled. He laughed at the same retort every night over a long engagement, and wept as often with the same anguish, protesting the slightest departure from an initial inflection. He sat close to the stage, arriving with the opening of the door, that he might nod to the members of the orchestra, to whom he was a familiar figure, and fully enjoy the orchestral prelude. . . . The prompter's box upon the stage would have been more to his liking, but he contented himself with the first row of the orchestra. He would have felt the loss had he missed the crooking of a finger. . . .

Together Father and I went to see Clara Morris, the great emotional actress, play the New Magdalene. Word of her increasing illness and the terrible remedies she employed (hot irons on her spine) heralded her coming every season. In spite of her suffering, she held her audience under her power and moved them to anguish. Years later the muscles of my stomach contracted at the mention of her name and I could still hear Father gulp, and feel him slip his extra handkerchief into my hand beside the wet pellet which had been my own.

From behind the discreetly drawn lace curtains of the parlor bay window, the daughter of the house looked out on this scene:

At nine o'clock every morning the men of O'Farrell Street left their houses for their places of business downtown;

dressed in brushed broadcloth and polished high hats, they departed soberly as to a funeral. The door of each house opened and let out the owner who took the steps firmly, and, arriving on the sidewalk, turned slowly eastward toward the town. A man had not walked many yards before he was overtaken by a friend coming from the avenue. Together they walked with matched steps down the street.

All the men were united by the place and circumstances of their birth. They had come to America from villages in Germany, and they had worked themselves up from small stores in the interior of California to businesses in San Francisco.

From the window we watched them, foreseeing the interruptions to their march. The initial heat of a political argument halted their first advance. Another six yards and they stopped again to face each other and twist a protesting hand. A full stop came at the corner of Polk Street, where gestures were fully unsheathed and fingers touched the chest and swung into the air. If Father was walking with Mr. Levison, our neighbor, we could measure by the dislocation of his stovepipe the degree of his failure to convince the stubborn Republican that Grover Cleveland was the greatest President in American history.

## iv

IN the spring of 1889 a twenty-four-year-old journalist, en route from his native India to England, paused briefly in San Francisco and, in several letters to the *Civil and Military Gazette* in Lahore, recorded his impressions of the city. The following passages make clear that this cocksure young Briton—whose name was Rudyard Kipling—was not unduly impressed by what he saw.

> "Serene, indifferent of fate,
>   Thou sittest at the western gate,
>   Thou seest the white seas fold their tent
>   Oh warder of two Continents.
>   Thou drawest all things small and great
>   To thee beside the Western Gate."

This is what Bret Harte has written of the great city of San Francisco, and for the past fortnight I have been wondering what made him do it. There is neither serenity nor indifference to be found in these parts; and evil would it be for the Continent whose wardship were intrusted to so reckless a guardian. Behold me pitched neck-and-crop from twenty days of the High Seas, into the whirl of California, deprived of any guidance, and left to draw my own conclusions. Protect me from the wrath of an outraged community if these letters be ever read by American eyes. San Francisco is a mad city—inhabited for the most part by perfectly insane people whose women are of a remarkable beauty. When the "City of Peking" steamed through the Golden Gate I saw with great joy that the blockhouse which guarded the mouth of the "finest harbour in the world, Sir," could be silenced by two gunboats from Hong Kong with safety, comfort and dispatch.

Then a reporter leaped aboard, and ere I could gasp held me in his toils. He pumped me exhaustively while I was getting ashore, demanding, of all things in the world, news about Indian journalism. It is an awful thing to enter a new land with a new lie on your lips. I spoke the truth to the evil-minded custom-house man who turned my most sacred raiment on a floor composed of stable-refuse and pine-splinters; but the reporter overwhelmed me not to so much by his poignant audacity as his beautiful ignorance. I am sorry now that I did not tell him more lies as I passed into a city of three hundred thousand white men! Think of it! Three hundred thousand white men, walking upon real pavements in front of real plate-glass windowed shops, and talking something that was not very different from English.

The newcomer put up at the Palace Hotel—which he called "a seven-storied warren of humanity with a thousand rooms in it"—and proceeded to describe the scene presented by its famed Palm Court:

In a vast marble-paved hall under the glare of an electric light sat forty to fifty men; and for their use and amusement were provided spittoons of infinite capacity and generous gape. Most of the men wore frock-coats and top-hats,—the things that we in India put on at a wedding breakfast if we possess them,—but they all spat. They spat on principle. The spittoons were on the staircases, in each bedroom—yea, and in chambers even more sacred than these. They chased one into retirement, but they blossomed in chiefest splendour round the bar, and they were all used. . . .

Later I began a vast but unsystematic exploration of the streets. I asked for no names. It was enough that the pavements were full of white men and women, the streets clanging with traffic, and that the restful roar of a great city rang in my ears. The cable-cars glided to all points of the compass. I took them one by one until I could go no farther. San Francisco has been pitched down on the sand-bunkers of the Bikaner desert. About one-fourth of it is ground reclaimed from the sea—any old-timer will tell you all about

that. The remainder is ragged, unthrifty sand-hills, pegged
down by houses.

From an English point of view there has not been the
least attempt at grading those hills, and indeed you might
as well try to grade the hillocks of Sind. The cable-cars have
for all practical purposes made San Francisco a dead level.
They take no count of rise or fall, but slide equably on their
appointed courses from one end to the other of a six-mile
street. They turn corners almost at right angles; cross other
lines, and, for all I know, may run up the sides of houses.
There is no visible agency of their flight; but once in a while
you shall pass a five-storied building, humming with ma-
chinery that winds up an everlasting wire cable, and the
initiated will tell you that here is the mechanism. I gave up
asking questions. If it pleases Providence to make a car run
up and down a slit in the ground for many miles, and if for
two pence-half penny I can ride in that car, why shall I
seek the reasons of the miracle?

The drinking habits of Americans in general—and of
San Franciscans in particular—were another thing that
engaged the attention of this by-no-means-gentle critic.

As you know . . . [he wrote] the American does not
drink at meals as a sensible man should. Indeed he has no
meals. He stuffs for ten minutes thrice a day. Also he has no
decent notions about the sun being over the yard-arm or
below the horizon. He pours his vanity into himself at un-
holy hours, and indeed he can hardly help it. You have no
notion what "treating" means on the Western slope. It is
more than an institution; it is a religion, though men tell
me that it is nothing to what it was. Take a very common
instance. At 10:30 A.M. a man is smitten with a desire for

stimulants. He is in the company of two friends. All three
adjourn to the nearest bar,—seldom more than twenty yards
away,—and take three straight whiskeys. They talk for two
minutes. The second and third man then treat in order;
thus each walks into the street, two of them the poorer by
three goes of whiskey under their belt and one with two
more liquors than he wanted. It is not etiquette yet to refuse
a treat. The result is peculiar. I have never yet, I confess,
seen a drunken man in the streets, but I have heard more
about drunkenness among white men, and seen more decent
men above or below themselves with drink, than I care to
think about. And the vice runs up into all sorts of circles
and societies. . . .

This unhappy state of affairs has, however, produced one
good result which I will confide to you. In the heart of the
business quarter, where banks and bankers are thickest, and
telegraph wires most numerous, stands a semi-subterranean
bar tended by a German with long blond locks and a crystal-
line eye. Go thither softly, treading on the tips of your toes,
and ask him for a Button Punch. 'Twill take ten minutes to
brew, but the result is the highest and noblest product of
the age. No man but one knows what is in it. I have a theory
it is compounded of the shavings of cherubs' wings, the glory
of a tropical dawn, the red clouds of sunset, and fragments
of lost epics by dead masters. But try it for yourselves, and
pause a while to bless me, who am always mindful of the
truest interests of my brethren.

Kipling had little difficulty holding in check his admiration for most phases of the life of the city, but on one
subject—the women of San Francisco—he had nothing
but praise.

They are clever; they can talk [he commented]. Yea, it is said that they think. Certainly they have the appearance of so doing. They are original, and look you between the brows as a sister might look at her brother. They are instructed in the folly and vanity of the male mind, for they have associated with "the boys" from babyhood, and can discerningly minister to both vices, or pleasantly snub the possessor. They possess, moreover, a life among themselves, independent of masculine associations. They have societies and clubs and unlimited tea-fights where all the guests are girls. They are self-possessed without parting with any tenderness that is their sex-right; they understand; they can take care of themselves; they are superbly independent. When you ask them what makes them so charming, they say: "It is because we are better educated than your girls and we are more sensible in regard to men. We have good times all round, but we are not taught to regard every man as a possible husband. Nor is he expected to marry the first girl he calls on regularly." Yes, they have good times, their freedom is large, and they do not abuse it. They can go driving with young men, and receive visits from young men to an extent that would make an English mother wink with horror; and neither driver nor drivee have a thought beyond the enjoyment of a good time. As certain also of their own poets have said:—

> "Man is fire and woman is tow,
> And the Devil he comes and begins to blow."

In America the tow is soaked in a solution that makes it fire-proof, in absolute liberty and large knowledge; consequently accidents do not exceed the regular percentage arranged by the Devil for each class and climate under the skies.

The tempo of San Francisco life he described as a "captivating rush and whirl," and of that phase of the city he found little to criticize.

Recklessness is in the air [he wrote]. I can't explain where it comes from, but there it is. The roaring winds off the Pacific make you drunk to begin with. The excessive luxury on all sides helps out the intoxication, and you spin forever "down the ringing groves of change" . . . as long as money lasts. They make greatly and they spend lavishly, not only the rich but the artisans, who pay nearly five pounds for a suit of clothes and for other luxuries in proportion. The young men rejoice in the days of their youth. They gamble, yacht race, enjoy prize-fights and cock-fights—the one openly, the other in secret—they establish luxurious clubs; they break themselves over horse-flesh and—other things; and they are instant in quarrel. At twenty they are experienced in business, and embark on vast enterprises, take partners as experienced as themselves, and go to pieces with as much splendour as their neighbors. Remember that the men who stocked California in the Fifties were physically, and as far as regards certain tough virtues, the pick of the earth. The inept and the weakly died on route or went under in the days of construction. To this nucleus were added all the races of the Continent—French, Italian, German, and of course, the Jew. The result you shall see in the large-boned, deep-chested, delicate-handed women, and long, elastic, well-built boys. It needs no little golden badge to mark the Native Son of the Golden West—the country-bred of California. Him I love because he is devoid of fear, carries himself like a man, and has a heart as big as his boots.

v

ONE curious phase of the commercial life of the city
in the early eighties was the gathering and sale of
the eggs of the murre, a sea bird of the auk species,
which during the mating season congregated in vast
numbers on the Farallon Islands, some twenty miles off
the Golden Gate. Of this long-forgotten traffic Charles
Warren Stoddard, a well-known author of the period,
wrote:

Those who have visited the markets of San Francisco during the egg season may have noticed the abundance of large
and singularly marked eggs that are offered for sale by the
bushel. The shells of these eggs are pear-shaped, parti-col-
ored, and very thick. They range in color from light green
to grey or brown, and all of them are profusely spotted. . . .
All are a trifle stale, and the meat of coarse texture and gamy
flavor. But the Italians and Coolies are fond of them, and
doubtless many a gross finds its way into the kitchen of the
popular cheap restaurants, where, disguised in omelets and
puddings, the quantity compensates for the lack of quality. . . .
The profit on sea-eggs has increased from year to year,
and of late speculators have grown so venturesome that
competition among egg-gatherers has resulted in an annual
naval engagement known to the press and the public as the
egg-war. If two companies of egg-pickers met, as was not
unlikely, the contending factions fell upon one another with

their ill-gotten spoils—the islands are under the rule of the United States, and no one has a legal right to take from them so much as one egg without license—and the defeated party was sure to retire from the field under a heavy shower of shells, the contents of which, though not fatal, were at least effective.

Stoddard then quoted from what he called "the notes of a retired egg-picker"—an account of his experience as a member of one such party:

> On Board the Schooner *Sierra*
> May 4, 1881
>
> 5 P.M.—There are ten of us all told; most of us strangers to one another. . . . So we conclude to hang together, and make the most of an adventure perfectly new to each. At our feet lie our traps: blankets, woolen shirts, heavy boots, with huge nails in the soles of them, tobacco in bulk, a few novels, a pack of cards, and a pocket flask for the stomach's sake. . . . Drifting into the west we began to grow thoughtful; what had at first seemed a lark, may possibly prove to be a very serious matter. We have to feed on short rations, work in a rough locality, among rough people, and our profits, or our share of the profits, will depend entirely upon the fruitfulness of the egg-orchard, and the number of hundred gross that we are able to get safely into the market. No news from the town, save by the schooner that comes at intervals to take away our harvest.

Landing the party on the inhospitable islands proved a difficult and dangerous task; however, the feat was eventually accomplished. Stoddard's account continues:

We find two cabins at our disposal; the larger one containing dining-room and kitchen, and chambers above; seven of our boys store their blankets in the rude bunks that are drawn by lot. . . .

### May 9

We did the first work of the season today. . . . In front of us we each carry a large sack in which to deposit the eggs; our boots are clumsy, and the heavy nails that fill their soles make them heavy and difficult to walk in. We also carry a strong staff to aid us in climbing the rugged slopes. About us is nothing but grey, weather-stained rocks; there are few paths, and these we cannot follow, for the sea-birds, though so unused to the presence of man, are wary and shy of his tracks; the day's work has not proved profitable. . . .

### May 14

This morning all our egg-pickers went to work; gathered about forty dozen eggs and got them safely back to camp; in some nests there were three eggs, and these we did not gather, fearing they were stale. In the P.M. tried to collect dry grass enough to make a thin mattress for my bunk; barely succeeded; am more than ever convinced that desert islands are a delusion.

By the time they had spent a fortnight on the islands, the latter-day Crusoes were heartily sick of their bargain.

Affairs begin to look mutinous [wrote Stoddard on May 22]. We have searched in vain for the schooner, now considerably overdue, and are dreading the thought of having to fulfill a contract which calls for six weeks' labor on these islands. Some of the other islands are to be visited, and are accessible only in small boats over a sea that is never even tolerably smooth. This expedition we all dread a little—at least, I judge so from my own case—but we say nothing of it. While thus gloomily brooding over our plight, smoke was sighted on the horizon; we ascended the hill to watch it. . . . It was a steamer, a small Government steamer, making directly for our island. We became greatly excited, for nothing of any moment had occurred since our arrival. She drew in near shore and cast anchor. We gathered at the landing cove to give her welcome. A boat was beached in safety. An officer of the law said cheerfully . . . "I must beg you, gentlemen, to step on board the revenue cutter, and return to San Francisco." He added, this very civil sheriff, "If you do not care to accompany me, I shall be obliged to order the marines on shore. You will pardon me, but these islands are Government property, and you are requested to withdraw from them immediately." We withdrew. We steamed away from the windy rocks, the howling caverns, the seething waves, the gloomy cabins. Joyfully we bounded over the glassy waves that grew beautiful as the Farallones faded in the misty distance, and, having been courteously escorted to the city dock, we were bidden farewell. Thus ended the last siege of the Farallones by the egg-pickers of San Francisco. (Profits nil.)

And thus I fear, inasmuch as the Government proposes to guard the sea-birds until a suitable license is secured by legitimate egg-pluckers, the price of gulls' eggs will go up in proportion, and hereafter we shall have to look upon them as luxuries, and content ourselves with the more modest and milder-flavored products of the less romantic barn-yard fowl.

## vi

O N and off for more than thirty years Ambrose Bierce
conducted a column in various San Francisco journals, beginning with the *News-Letter* in 1868 and end-
ing with the *Examiner* shortly before the turn of the century. Possessed of a pretty talent for vituperation, Bierce
delighted in heaping ridicule on what he considered the
follies of his fellow townsmen in virtually every field of
endeavor. One of his prime targets was the sort of "elegant" writing then considered de rigueur in the local
society columns. The examples quoted here are typical
of countless others.

I am sorry to learn, from the *Alta*, that a man who has just
returned from the Yosemite was guilty, while there, of "holding communion with Nature in her grandest manifestation,"
and that, too, "in the presence of the speaking sublimity of
that great and unrivaled wonder." I don't clearly know what
it was he was doing with Nature, but it sounds immoral,
and I would suppose he would be afraid the "speaking sublimity" would tell. I blush to think that both the enactor and
the historiographer of this mysterious indiscretion are journalists.

When the senseless title "Esquire" shall have flickered a
little longer in the dawn of good taste it, too, will expire in
its own grease, and the *Argonaut* will have to adopt another
and perhaps clumsier device for marking its distinction between a rich man and a poor.

It is remarkable what dissimilar effects are due to slight differences in locality. The *Argonaut* office is but a short distance from the *Bulletin* office; yet when at the former it simply "grows dark," at the latter "night throws its charitable folds of darkness over the land."

Prentice Mulford is contributing to a literary weekly of this city a series of papers upon "The Invisible in Our Midst," and accounts for the delays by stating that his manuscript has to be submitted for revision to the spirits, who, he says, "have sciences for which we have no names." Judging from these revised articles, it is tolerably clear that we have at least one science more than the Invisibles—the science of English grammar.

It is rumored in society circles that Mrs. William C. Ralston is about to contract a new matrimonial alliance.—*Post*

Respected author of this paragraph, we crave a word with you. Sir, we venture to remind you that to "contract a new matrimonial alliance" is simply to "marry again." Will you kindly state the existing objections to the latter expression, and point out the merits of the former? The word "marry" is not, we hope, an immodest term. We find it in all the dictionaries but in few of the newspapers—never in the one which your talent deigns to adorn. The ingenuity that you and the gentlemen who have the honor to labor in the same literary field display in the invention of circumlocutory equivalents for that word, is above and beyond all praise, but pardon us, we do not quite perceive the necessity. To "lead to the altar," to "join in the holy bonds of wedlock," to "contract a matrimonial alliance," these are all sweet and pleasing phrases, and the fact of your employing them makes them correct and elegant. We accept them without persuasion and admire them without comprehending. But as at present ad-

vised, and pending the better instruction that it will doubtless be your pleasure to impart, we like the meaner term,
too. But if you deem that objectionable, why don't you say
"nuptiate," you royal Bengal jackass?

In a published list of "costly and elegant" wedding presents "denoted" at the "nuptials" of a "belle" whom one of the
"leaders of society" recently "led to the altar," I observe
(with pain) "two solid silver napkin-rings lined with gold"
—real gold! It is such luxury that is ruining the country—
the country George Washington soldiered to set free, eating
roasted bacon with his fingers and wiping them in his hair.

Such overblown writing was only one of the things
Bierce delighted to ridicule. Other favorite targets were
politicians, reformers, officeholders, country editors and
—in particular—amateur poets. In his *Examiner* column,
"Prattle," on February 26, 1888, he saluted one unhappy
rhymer with this verse:

> "I sing not with the minstrels
>     Who have learned the art of song;
> I sing that my heart's happy
>     As a bird the bright day long."
>         —M.W.S. in *The Pacific.*

> If less your heart were happy
>     The better were your song,
> I'm going to the minstrels—
>     By-by. Ta-ta, So long.

Below is a gathering of typical Biercian shafts in a
variety of subjects:

Last Monday a story was industriously circulated that a party of Christian young boys from the city had beaten an inoffensive Chinaman to death at San Quentin. This was afterwards discovered to be a vile Radical slander; the Chinaman *may* live.

A morning paper says three unclaimed gold watches are in the hands of the police, and that it is not definitely known who stole them. It is definitely known who will steal them.

Mr. Samuel Smith, who lives in Gyserville, exults in a calf which has no fore-legs, but which "goes backward and forward with equal facility" on his hind ones. Attach a cork right-hand to this creature, operated by strings connected with its tail, and it would write excellent "society personals" for the daily newspapers.

An eminent meteorologist who bewails the disappearance of our forests has a work in press entitled "The Climate of the Future." They are discussing it a good deal in the pulpit, too.

Two male skeletons of the "mound-builders" have been dug up in Kentucky, one lying across the other, and the fingers of each clutching the throat of the other. The skeleton of the woman has not yet been discovered, but is probably somewhere thereabout, reposing with tender trust on the breast of a third male.

"The most deplorable fact of our political life," says a contemporary, "is the national habit of making charges of corruption." Almost as deplorable is the national habit of being guilty of them.

The gentleman whose duty it was, and whose pleasure it should have been, to write for this paper the regular annual justification of the Independence Day pageant committed the indiscretion of attending it.

Of sixty-eight American cities whose death rates have been compiled by Government authority, Vallejo is the healthiest. It is so healthy up there that the editor of the Vallejo *Chronicle* has never been killed and is now seldom thrashed.

The personal property of the late Anthony Chabot, of Oakland, has been ordered sold. This is a noble opportunity to obtain Senator Vrooman.

I observe that another American *prima donna* has made a "triumphant success" in Europe. But what becomes of them all? Are they blown into interstellar space by the recoil of their vocal discharge? Do they sing under the same hard conditions as the legendary swan, whose "triumphant success" is instantly fatal? Alas for the poor daughters of song! We must remember them among the blessings which, as they brighten, take their flight. They are consumed in the flames of their own genius and their ashes thrown into the wife market.

## vii

THE final decade of the century saw a newly awakened interest in art and literature on the part of the local public, and the simultaneous rise of a group of talented young novelists, poets, painters, sculptors, actors, and musicians. It was, in fact, a veritable renaissance, one that has ever since loomed large in the artistic annals of the city.

In the field of literature one potent factor in bringing this about was a weekly paper called *The Wave*.
Founded in the late 1880's as a "society sheet," *The
Wave,* under a new editor, John O'Hara Cosgrave, attracted a group of gifted young contributors who proceeded to make it the most brightly written paper on the
coast. One of Cosgrave's small staff was Gelett Burgess,
former surveyor and draftsman, and an ex-instructor of
topographical drawing at the University of California.
Of the period when he was Cosgrave's assistant, Burgess wrote:

I must confess that, were it not for the salary (they are
not rich, those who own *The Wave*), I would rather write for
*The Wave* than any paper alive. To be sure, there are not
many weekly papers that *are* alive nowayears, not, at least,
so alive as *The Wave,* where one can have a hand at anything
from an "ad" to an editorial. For I did these, too—editorials.
I satirized the pseudo-architecture of the town,—I did good-
natured "guys" on local hypocrisies, and I rewrote mining
anecdotes, which were always in order on *The Wave.*
The best of the sport was on Tuesday nights, when we
"made up." The editor used to swear at having to stay up
to "three g.m.," as he was fond of describing the hour, waiting for the proofs from the "narrow measure" linotypes, but
he always stayed, in spite of the fact that I did not mind
climbing to the grassy top of Russian Hill at dawn, for the
pleasure of standing over the foreman of the composing room,
showing him where to put the "cuts," writing spicy headlines,
and "captions" for the pictures, and pasting the columns of
proof into the "dummy." There was one memorable occasion,
when the Chief left me to my own devices, and I had my

way with the paper. There was always an article to be cut down, or filled up to fit the page. There were little standing paragraphs to be "run in," which the Chief called "flim-flam."

But best of all were the Wednesdays, just before the copy was all in for the "second form." There was the excitement of being ordered to do a thousand words in an hour, a stern mandate that must not be denied. I could write anything required, if the Chief only did not give me too much time to do it in, for my best work was done under pressure. One becomes *blasé* after a while, and one begins to compare one's work with one's salary, but I have as yet had insufficient experience, not to kindle into a glow of delight at the words, "We *must* have a thousand words of 'copy' by four o'clock!" . . .

San Francisco is a small town, and often nothing remarkable in a journalistic way happens for a whole week at a time. One can, it is true, always fall back on a description of a prune orchard, or the "write-up" of some interesting industry, but these are as deadly to compose as they are to read. San Francisco is a pleasure-seeking community, however, and there is always sure to be some entertaining person in town, if one can discover him—or, more frequently, her! And so it fell my lot to haunt the Orpheum in search for "copy" in the wings of that unique Music Hall, which is, by the same token, one of the best that I have ever seen. It is a dull, smoky, colorless hall, with a single gallery, and it is frequented by the most varied audience in the world. Here, assemble men-about-town, gamblers, debutantes, mothers-of-families, mondaines and demi-dittos, black-legs, touts, Chinamen, Italian fishermen, bankers, princes, and tourists of all descriptions. I might, in fact, have got as interesting interviews in front of the footlights, as behind. . . .

I had the opportunity to talk to many players, but it was the third-rate vaudeville artistes of the Orpheum that were by far the most profitable to me . . . and to *The Wave*. They could be induced to buy extra copies of the paper, and very frequently purchased the half-tone portraits which we very generously printed. They were often simple, naive and as full of the elements of Romance as an American Indian, without ever being aware of the fact. Here were little families of father, mother, sister and brother, who did all sorts of riotous horse-play on the stage, and walked home, after the show, as staid and homely as the family of a country parson. They travelled all over the earth, they saw life from behind the scenes, and in half-dress, and kept themselves unspotted from the world. The sister was often not even allowed by her brother to visit Chinatown!

Burgess was a member of a little group of nonconformists who termed themselves "les Jeunes"—a group that included Bruce Porter, sculptor, Willis Polk, architect, and Porter Garnett, aesthete and man-about-town. In the late nineties "les Jeunes" launched a little magazine called *The Lark*, which despite its diminutive size and self-proclaimed lack of serious purpose, introduced so many refreshing novelties both in content and in format as to win it a permanent place in the memories, and affections, of its readers.

With the hundred dollars which was our entire capital [wrote Burgess], we started the venture. The make-up should be original from paper to typography, and we ransacked Chinatown, San Francisco's artistic treasure-house, for materials. Here we found a cheap but interesting paper of bamboo fiber which was imported in bales, each sheet double folded and stencilled upon the edges with red and green characters. All this had to be unfolded, dampened and pressed, with the result that the sheets were mildewed with strange yellow spots, and around the edges were smears of red and green dye. We set the pages without "justifying" the lines of type, letting them run out where they would, like typewritten matter, and, as the paper was thin, we printed upon only one side, in the Japanese manner. These peculiarities combined to make *The Lark* unique in aspect; it was for us then to warrant these vagaries with contents that should rescue them from the taint of "faddishness,". . .

The office of *The Lark* was, for a year, in the draughting room where I was engaged in designing [furniture]. Our town was small, but little as it was, *les Jeunes* began to be known in the Eastern cities long before San Francisco discovered us, if, indeed, it has yet. The independence of our paper which was obviously not established upon a mercenary basis, since we allowed no disfiguring advertisements, disarmed criticism. The press treated us at first with contempt, then with indulgence, and before long with frank favor. As it happened, that "one in ten" to whom we aimed our amusement, was a person of culture and influence, and . . . he took pride in his discovery, and the word was passed around that here was, at last, something "different.". . .  In a word, long before we knew it, we had made a *succès d'estime*. . . .

But we worked (or played) on, till the end, in ignorance of all this. And had we known, we would have cared no whit, for we were content with our own circle, all *les Jeunes* in a larger and more blessed medium, who watched the bird each month, with a greater interest. . . .

On the artistic side, the first reinforcement was in the drawings of Ernest Peixotto, who had lately returned from Paris with a *mention honorable,* and who provided us with happy cover illustrations for a year. When he was called to New York, the work was taken up by Miss Florence Lundborg,

who made a name for *The Lark* by her posters. . . . Mr.
Porter Garnett contributed some remarkable vagaries of style,
but these were the only regular assistants. When they could
not be induced to provide, the editor had to write the whole
number, essay, story, nonsense, poem, and "freak page" himself.

The second year began with a edition of only three thousand copies, which number we never increased. Our office
was moved, as the editor was paid a salary by the publisher
[the local book dealer, William Doxey], *The Lark* headquarters became the center of a few other activities. . . . The
Latin Quarter was for us a literary inspiration, as Chinatown,
with its wonderful feasts of color was an artistic delight,
though it was an unwritten law with us that the material
should not be used in any realistic way, for we were pledged
to Romance. . . .

But our mood was too spontaneous, or rather too enthusiastic to last, for we had dwelt over-long with gaiety; there
was the world's sober work to do. And, jealous of *The Lark*'s
prestige, which had suffered from no carelessness in our devo-
tion, after two years of the frolic, we brought the essay to a
close before it could be said that the fire of our initial enthusiasm had grown cold. So we scattered, to New York, to London, and to Paris, and California knows *les Jeunes* no more.

More than sixty years have passed since *The Lark*
made its last flight, yet the little paper has by no means
been forgotten. One reason why its memory persists is
that it was on its pages that what San Franciscans have
ever since regarded as one of their favorite and most frequently quoted bits of nonsense verse—Burgess' "The
Purple Cow"—first appeared.

## viii

IT was, of course, the gold rush—which drew shiploads of adventurers from virtually every country in Christendom—that made early San Francisco the most cosmopolitan of American cities—a distinction that, in the opinion of many, it continues to occupy today. Because for well over a century residents of widely different racial and cultural backgrounds have lived side by side in peace and reasonable harmony, there has grown up among these various groups a spirit of tolerance and mutual respect rarely encountered elsewhere.

Many have tried to put into words that intangible but not-to-be-mistaken aspect of the city's communal life. One of their number was Clarence E. Edwords, member of a numerous group of gourmets, winebibbers, and connoisseurs of the "good life," who flourished around the turn of the century.

In his book, *Bohemian San Francisco,* published in 1914, Edwords wrote:

San Francisco's cosmopolitanism is peculiar to itself. Here are represented the nations of earth in such distinctive colonies that one might well imagine himself possessed of the magic carpet told of in Arabian Nights tales, as he is transported in a twinkling of an eye from country to country. It is but a step across the street from America to Japan, then another step into China. Cross another street and you are in Mexico, close neighbor to France. Around the corner lies

Italy, and from Italy you pass to Lombardy, and on to Greece. So it goes until one feels that he has been around the world in an afternoon.

But the stepping across the street and one passes from one land to the other, finding all the peculiar characteristics of the various countries as indelibly fixed as if they were thousands of miles away. Speech, manners, customs, costumes and religions change with startling rapidity, and as you enter into the life of the nation you find that each has brought the best of its gastronomy for your delectation. . . .

Those to whom only the surface of things is visible are prone to express wonder at the love and enthusiasm of the San Franciscan for his home city. The casual visitor cannot understand the enchantment, the mystery, the witchery that holds one; they do not know that we steal the hours from the night to lengthen our days because the gray, whispering wraiths of fog hold for us the very breath of life; they do not know that the call of the wind, and of the sea, and of the air, is the inspiration that makes San Francisco the pleasure-ground of the world.

It is this that makes San Francisco the home of Bohemia, and whether it be in the early morning hours as one rises to greet the first gray streaks of dawn, or as the sun drops through the Golden Gate to its ocean bed, so slowly that it seems loath to leave; whether it be in the broad glare of the noon-day sun, or under the dazzling blaze of midnight lights, San Francisco ever holds out her arms wide and welcome, to those who see more in life than the dull routine of working each day in order that they may gain sufficient to enable them to work again on the morrow.

Despite a prose replete with such purple patches as this, Edwords had much of interest to say of the open-handed hospitality that had been characteristic of the Californians from the beginning. Of the Spanish-Mexican period he wrote:

Courtesy unfailing, good-fellowship always in tune, and lavish hospitality, marked the days of the Dons—those wonderfully considerate hosts who always placed a pile of gold and silver coins on the table of the guest chamber, in order that none might go away in need. Their feasts were events of careful consideration and long preparation, and those whose memories carry them back to the early days recall bounteous loading of the table when festal occasion called for display. . . .

But it was not in the grand fiestas that the finest and most palatable dishes were to found. In the family of each of these Spanish grandees were culinary secrets known to none except the "Señora de la Casa," and transmitted by her to her sons and daughters.

Then follow instructions for preparing, in the manner of the Spanish-Californians, dishes made of their three staple foods: eggs, beef, and rice.

During the first months of the gold rush the meals served in the town's restaurants were, naturally enough, of indifferent quality, hastily prepared and carelessly served. However, according to Edwords, that situation lasted only a short time.

With the immediately succeeding years the horde of gold hunters was augmented by those who brought necessities and luxuries to exchange for the yellow metal. . . . With them came also cooks to prepare delectable dishes for those who had passed the flap-jack stage, and desired the good things of life to repay them for the hardships and privations and dearth of woman's companionship. . . .

It was only natural that the early San Franciscans should foregather where good cheer was to be found, and the old El Dorado House, at Portsmouth Square, was really what may be called the first Bohemian restaurant of the city. So well was this place patronized and so exorbitant the prices charged that twenty-five thousand dollars a month was not considered an impossible rental.

Next in importance was the most fashionable restaurant of early days, the Iron Horse. It was built of heavy sheet iron that had been brought around the Horn in a sailing vessel, and catered well, becoming for several years the most famed restaurant of the city. Here, on Montgomery Street, between Jackson and Pacific, was the rendezvous of pioneers, and here the Society of California Pioneers has its inception. . . . Here also was first served Chicken in the Shell, the dish from which so many later restaurants gained fame.

This dish—which derives its name from the fact that portions are served in cockleshells—is still on the menus of certain old-time San Francisco restaurants; it is made from diced breast of young chicken cooked in a sauce compounded of cream, eggs, mushrooms, truffles and a dash of sherry.

Of the beginnings of two types of restaurants that still enjoy high favor among local diners-out—Italian and French—Edwords wrote:

Almost coincident with the opening of the Iron Horse an Italian named Bazzuro took possession of one of the stranded sailing vessels encumbering the bay, and anchored it out

in the water at the point where Davis and Pacific streets
now intersect. He opened a restaurant which immediately
attracted attention and gained good reputation for its service and its cooking. Later, when the land was filled in, Bazzuro built a house at almost the same spot and opened his
restaurant there, continuing it up to the time of the great
fire in 1906. . . .

The French peasant style came in a little earlier, beginning in a small dining room opened in Washington Street,
just above Kearny, by a French woman whose name was a
carefully guarded secret. She was known far and wide as
"Ma Tanta." Her cooking was considered the best of all the
city, and her patrons sat at a long common table, neat and
clean to the last degree. The peasant style of serving was
followed. First appeared Ma Tanta with a great bowl of
salad which she passed around, each patron helping himself. This was followed by an immense tureen of soup, held
aloft in the hands of Ma Tanta, and again each was his own
waiter. Fish, entree, roast, and dessert were served in the
same manner, and with the black coffee Ma Tanta changed
from servitor to hostess and sat with her guests and discussed
the topics of the day. . . .

In California Street, just below Dupont, the California
House boasted a great chef in the person of John Somali,
who in later years opened the Maison Riche, a fabulous restaurant that went out of existence in 1906. Gourmets soon
discovered that the California House offered something unusual and it became a famed resort. Somali's specialties were
roast turkey, Châteaubriand steak and coffee frappé. It is
said of his turkeys that their flavor was of such excellence
that one of the gourmands of the day, Michael Reese, would
always order two when he gave a dinner—one for his guests
and one for himself. . . .

Most famous of the old oyster houses was Mannings, at the corner of Pine and Webb streets. He specialized in oysters and many of his dishes have survived to the present day. It is said that the style now called "Oysters Kirkpatrick" is but a variant of Manning's "Oyster Salt Roast."

To San Franciscans, a mention of Oysters Kirkpatrick inevitably brings to mind the old Palace Hotel, which for thirty years not only dominated the city architecturally but, in the elegance of its appointments and services, represented the apex of luxury. Long a favorite with local gourmets, Oysters Kirkpatrick was the creation of an early Palace chef, and was named for John C. Kirkpatrick, one of the hotel's early managers.

San Francisco and the Palace Hotel [wrote Edwords] were almost synonymous all over the world, and it was conceded by travelers that nowhere else was there a hostelry to equal this great hotel. . . . To the bon vivant the Palace contained more to enhance the joys of living than anywhere else, and here the chefs prided themselves with providing the best in the land, prepared in such perfect ways as to make a meal the perfection of gastronomic art.

There are three distinct eras in the history of the Palace Hotel, the first being from 1876 to 1890, the second from 1890 to 1906, and the third from 1906 to the present. In the earlier days the grills, both that for gentlemen and that for ladies, were noted for their magnificent service and their wonderful cooking. A breakfast in the Ladies' Grill, with an omelet of California oysters, toast and coffee, was a meal long to be remembered. Possibly the most famous dish of the old Palace was this omelet . . . the receipt of Ernest Arbogast, the chef for many years. The slightly coppery taste of the California oysters gives a piquancy to the flavor of the omelet that can be obtained in no other way, and those who once ate of Arbogast's California oyster omelet invariably called for it again and again.

During the final decades of the century the city boasted a number of establishments—some of them handsomely fitted up—which offered patrons not only excellent food and wines but (what was of at least equal importance) facilities for dining in complete privacy. Known by the collective name of "French Restaurants," their public dining rooms—when they existed at all—were small, most of the space both on the ground floor and above being divided into small cubicles, usually with doors that could be locked from the inside. Of such resorts Edwords wrote:

French impression came strongly about this time [that is, the 1880's], and the Poodle Dog, of Paris, had its prototype at Bush and Dupont streets. This was one of the earliest of the type . . . aud numerous convivial parties of men and women found its private rooms convenient for rendezvous. . . .

In O'Farrell Street the Delmonico was one of the most famous of the French Restaurants until the fire. It was several stories high, and each story contained private rooms. Carriages drove directly into the building from the street and the occupants went by elevator to sound-proof rooms above, where they were served by discreet waiters.

No survey of food and cooking during pre-fire days would be complete without mention of that long-established local institution, the free lunch. Although the custom of providing tipplers with a tray or two of thirst-producing snacks as a means of stimulating the consumption of drinks had long been standard practice in other American cities, nowhere else were the customers served food of such quality and in so great a variety. In the seventies and eighties these repasts were, as we have seen, bountiful enough to gain the admiration—and patronage—of many visitors; however, it was the final years of the century that marked the real heyday of the free lunch.

Of that period Edwords wrote:

For the price of a beer or two the San Franciscan could, and many did, dine sumptuously. Heavy eaters with light thirsts were balanced by heavy drinkers with light appetites; and a few orders for champagne put welcome dollars into the till. Food was cheap, and it was beautifully prepared by cooks who put their hearts into the cooking. It is not surprising that the establishments which provided the best free lunches became veritable, and exclusive, clubs.

One such resort, said to have been typical of half a dozen others, was the Palace of Fine Arts, located at 16 Post Street, on the ground floor of the Lick House. The spot derived its name from a collection of paintings that adorned its walls; however, the chief attraction to its discriminating clientele lay in what its owners termed "Our Free Lunch," which was "Served with All Drinks from 4 to 11 P.M."

One of the menus of this resort fortunately survives.

Below is the "Free Lunch" offered patrons on that particular day:

Radishes     Crab Salad     Celery
Clam Juice
Pigs Head     Bolinas Bay Clams     Head Cheese
Saucisses à la Famille     Beef à la Chile Colorado
Chile Con Carne     Honolulu Beans
Chicken Croquette     Veal Croquette     Terrapin Stew
Fried Clams     Sardines     Boiled Ham
Saratoga Chips     Corned Beef
Cold Tongue     Beef Stew     Pork and Beans
Chipped Beef     Smoked Salmon
Cheese     Crackers
Cracked Crab     Holland Herring
Almonds     Pop Corn     Apples

# Part Six

# 1906

# i

As the old century ended San Franciscans looked toward the city's future with confidence and pride—and, it must be confessed, with a degree of complacency. They had, they felt, ample reason for such sentiments. For by then the stresses and strife of the city's beginnings and youth seemed safely past, and there was no reason to doubt that the period ahead would be one of quiet and orderly growth that over the years would maintain and consolidate its position as the commercial, financial, and cultural center of the entire West Coast.

During the first few years of the new century nothing took place to change that concept. Businesses and industries expanded steadily. In the downtown area multistory buildings of steel and concrete were replacing the outmoded wood and brick structures put up a generation earlier. Population drew ever closer to the 400,000 mark, and to accommodate the newcomers lines of small cottages spread steadily out over the sand hills of the city's perimeter. San Francisco at last had put aside its youthful exuberance and settled down contentedly to what promised to be a long period of uninterrupted progress.

This state of affairs held until mid-April of 1906. How

261

it was brought to a violent and catastrophic end was thus described by a local business leader, James B. Stetson:

On the morning of April 18, at 5:15, I was awakened by a very severe shock of earthquake. The shaking was so violent that it nearly threw me out of bed. It threw down a large bookcase in my chamber and broke the glass front; another bookcase fell across the floor. The bric-a-brac was thrown from the mantel and tables and strewed the floor with broken china and glass. . . .

As soon as it was over I got up and went to the window, and saw the street filled with white dust, which was caused by the falling of the St. Luke stone church on the diagonal corner from my room. [The Stetson residence was on Van Ness Avenue, at the corner of Clay.] I waited for the dust to settle, and then I saw the damage which had been done to the Claus Spreckels house and the church. The chimneys of the Spreckels mansion were gone, the stone balustrade and carved work wrecked. The roof and the points of the gables and ornamental stonework of the church had fallen, covering the sidewalk and lying piled up against the sides of the buildings to the depth of eight or ten feet.

The above is quoted from one of a number of accounts in which San Franciscans described their experiences from the time of the initial shocks until the last of the fires burned themselves out more than seventy-two hours later.

A great deal was written about the disaster, both while the fires were still raging and during the weeks that followed. First in the field were, as might be expected, the town's newspapers. These overcame all but insuperable handicaps to provide the townspeople with news of the extent of the catastrophe and of measures being taken by the civilian and military authorities to maintain order and prevent further losses of life and property.

Earliest of the local journals to appear was the *Evening Daily News,* a little four-page sheet published at 408 Fourth Street. Because its plant was several blocks from the earliest fires, and because its mechanical equipment, though damaged by the earthquake, was found to be in working order, the staff managed to get out a single sheet—printed on one side—on the afternoon of the 18th. Its headline read, "Hundreds Dead! Fire Follows Earthquake, Laying Downtown Section in Ruins—City Seems Doomed for Lack of Water." A major part of the single page was occupied by a list of the known dead and injured. Of the disaster itself, it stated:

San Francisco was practically demolished and totally paralyzed by the earthquake, which commenced at 5:11 A.M. today and continued with terrific vigor for four minutes.

Great loss of life was caused by the collapse of buildings, and many people met a more cruel death by fire. Flames broke out in all portions of the city.

The monetary loss caused by the earthquake, the fires which followed it and the depreciation of values that will result will amount to hundreds of millions of dollars.

The progress of San Francisco has received a check from which it will probably take many years to recover.

Thousands of men who went to bed wealthy last night awoke this morning practically bankrupt.

The fury of the temblor was greater than any that has been known in the history of the city.

The people are appalled, terror-stricken. Thousands, fearing a recurrence of the dreadful disaster, with results still more dire, are hastening out of San Francisco.

Many heart-rending scenes have been enacted. Families are moving their belongings helter-skelter, and moving aimlessly about, keeping in the open.

The City Hall is a complete wreck. The walls surrounding the grand dome have fallen, leaving only the skeleton frame work and the top of the dome intact. Around all sides of the building the walls have crumbled, like so many cards. The Receiving Hospital is buried.

The surgeons moved to the Mechanics' Pavilion, which today is a combined hospital and morgue. Dead and dying are brought in by autos, ambulances, and even garbage carts.

Insane patients were taken from the Emergency Hospital to the Mechanics' Pavilion. Many of them were hurt. Some broke loose and ran among the dying, adding horror to the scene.

At 8:15 a second sharp quake occurred, accentuating the terror.

The fire scenes following the earthquake were and are fearful to behold. Had the earthquake occurred an hour later, the entire city would have burst into flame.

At least forty buildings were aflame within ten minutes after the temblor passed. Among the first to go were the big buildings on Market, Battery, Sansome, First, Second, Third, Fourth, Fifth and Sixth streets, followed by a general conflagration on Seventh and Eighth streets, while in the Western Addition many fires were started.

By eight o'clock it seemed that a large part of the city was doomed.

Preparations for a second extra were under way in the *News* office when, in midafternoon, a squad of soldiers appeared, drove the staff into the street, and dynamited the building in a fruitless effort to check the advancing fires.

## ii

WHEN the earthquake struck, the regular editions of the town's three morning papers had already been printed, and their distribution was just getting under way. Although none of their plants was badly damaged, those of the *Examiner* and the *Call* were among the first threatened by the flames. The *Chronicle*, on the north side of Market Street and across from the other two, for a time appeared to be safe, and its facilities were offered its two competitors for the printing of extras. By mid-morning, however, the failure of the city water supply and the near approach of the fire caused these projects to be abandoned, and the owners of the Oakland *Tribune* were asked to make its facilities available. The *Tribune's* plant was placed at the disposal of the burned-out San Francisco papers, and the following morning, April 19, thousands of copies of a consolidated journal, the *Call-Chronicle-Examiner*, were run off. These were hurried across the bay by launch and distributed free of charge to news-hungry residents of the stricken city.

This little paper—like the *Daily News* of the previous

day—is now one of the major curiosities of American journalism: a four-page, seven-column sheet, devoted entirely to news of the disaster. Considering the difficulties under which it was produced, it covered the subject with thoroughness and reasonable accuracy. Under the headline "Earthquake and Fire; San Francisco in Ruins" the lead story began:

Death and destruction have been the fate of San Francisco.

Shaken by a temblor at 5:13 o'clock yesterday, the shock lasting 48 seconds, and scourged by flames that raged diametrically in all directions, the city is a mass of smouldering ruins. At six o'clock last evening the flames, seemingly playing with increased vigour, threatened to destroy such sections as their fury had spared during the earlier portion of the day. Building their path in a triangular circuit from the start in the early morning, they jockeyed as the day waned, left the business section, which they had entirely devastated, and skipped in a dozen directions to the residence portions. As night fell they had made their way over into the north beach section and springing anew to the south they reached out along the shipping section down the bay shore, over the hills and across toward Third and Townsend streets. Warehouses, wholesale houses and manufacturing concerns fell in their path. This completed the destruction of the entire district known as the "South of Market Street.". . .

After darkness, thousands of the homeless were making their way with their blankets and scant provisions to Golden Gate Park and the beach to find shelter. Those in the homes on the hills just north of the Hayes Valley wrecked section piled their belongings in the street and express wagons and automobiles were hauling the things away to the sparsely settled regions. Everybody in San Francisco is preparing to leave the city, for the belief is firm that San Francisco will be totally destroyed.

Downtown everything is ruin. Not a business house stands. Theaters are crumbled into heaps. Factories and commission houses lie smouldering on their former sites. All the newspaper plants have been rendered useless, the "Call" and "Examiner" buildings, excluding the "Call's" editorial rooms on Stevenson Street, being entirely destroyed. . . .

On every side there was death and destruction yesterday. Hundreds were injured, either burned, crushed or struck by falling pieces from the buildings, and some died on the operating table at Mechanics' Pavilion, improvised as a hospital for the comfort and care of 300 of the injured. The number of dead is not known but it is estimated that at least 500 met their death in the horror.

At nine o'clock, under a special message from President Roosevelt, the city was placed under martial law. Hundreds of troops patrolled the streets and drove the crowds back, while hundreds more were set to work assisting the fire and police departments. The strictest orders were issued, and in true military spirit the soldiers obeyed. During the afternoon three thieves met their death by rifle bullets while at work in the ruins. . . .

The water supply was entirely cut off, and maybe it was just as well, for the lines of fire department would have been absolutely useless at any stage. Assistant Chief Dougherty supervised the work of his men and early in the morning it was seen that the only possible chance to save the city lay in an effort to check the flames by the use of dynamite. During the day a blast could be heard in any section at intervals of only a few minutes, and buildings not destroyed by fire were blown to atoms. But through the gaps made,

the flames jumped and although the failures of the heroic
efforts of the police, firemen and soldiers were at times sick-
ening, the work was continued with a desperation that will
live as one of the features of the terrible disaster. Men
worked like fiends to combat the laughing, roaring, onrush-
ing fire demon.

### iii

SUCH newspaper accounts, committed to paper while
the city was still burning furiously, convey to present-day readers something of the impact the disaster
had on those who found themselves in the midst of it,
giving their stories a reality and sense of immediacy
lacking in the more restrained accounts of later writers.
This same feeling of participation in the events described
is to be found in the narrative quoted from earlier—that
of James B. Stetson. Stetson's account continues in these
words:

All my chimneys had been thrown down, and one was
laying in the front yard sixteen feet from the building. There
were some cracks visible in the library, but none in my room,
and only very few in the parlor and dining-room. . . . A
water-pipe broke in the ceiling of the spare room and the
water did some damage.

I then started on foot downtown; no cars were running
on any line. The sidewalks in many places were heaved up,
the chimneys thrown down, and walls cracked. I went on

California Street, over Nob Hill, and as I got in sight of the
business part of the city, I saw as many as ten or twelve fires.
When I arrived at California and Montgomery streets, the
lower part of both sides of California Street seemed to be
on fire. I went along Sansome Street to Pine and down Pine
towards Market, and when I arrived at Front Street I saw
that the Commercial Block, on the southeast corner of Front
and California streets (on the fifth floor of which was my
office), was not on fire. So I started to go toward the building. The fire was then burning fiercely at California and Battery. I went to the entrance at 123 California Street and met
the janitor coming out, who said I could not go upstairs as
the building was on fire on the fifth floor. However, I started
up. The sparks were coming down into the open area in a
shower, but there was no smoke in the building, so I was
sure it was not on fire. I got up to my room on the fifth floor
and found the door would not come open. I tried the door
of the adjoining office and found it open. From that room I
got into mine. I raised my shades, and the fire was burning
at Battery Street, fully fifty feet high. I looked through the
hall and rooms and found no smoke, and was sure that I was
safe for a few minutes. As I turned the combination of my
safe and opened it another slight shock of earthquake came.
I had a quantity of souvenirs and presents that had been
given me in years past. These I gathered up and soon had
my arms full. . . . I took my books and papers in my arms,
closed the safe, turned on the combination, and started down
the stairs to the street.

When I got on to California Street the air was a mass of
sparks and smoke blown down the street toward the ferry.
As I had to go against it to get to Front Street, I was afraid
that my papers would take fire in my arms; so I buttoned up
my coat to protect them, pulled my hat over my eyes, and

dived through, up California Street and out Front towards Pine. There I found it clear of smoke and fire. As I passed along I saw a typewriter-cover in the street. Finding it empty, I stopped and, dropping my bundle into it, started for Front and Market streets. There was no fire within a block of that corner at the time. This was about 8 A.M.— perhaps 8:30. I sat down on an empty box in the middle of Market Street for a rest, when W. R. Whittier came along and helped me with my load. We took it to the door of the Union Trust Company, and they would not let me in. I went upstairs and found Dr. Deering, who took it, and we went down and put it into the vault. (Twenty-two days afterward I received it back in as good condition as when I had left it there.)

I next went up to Third Street and found the fire raging strong at the corner of Third and Mission. My son was passing in his automobile and I got in with him. He said he was going to the Mechanics Pavilion, where he could do some work at the temporary hospital there. When we reached the Pavilion they said there were two hundred wounded inside. We went around to drug stores and hardware stores and got hot-water bags and alcohol stoves and surgeons' appliances. We took with us Miss Sarah Fry, an ex-Salvation Army woman, who was energetic and enthusiastic. When we arrived at the drug store under the St. Nicholas Hotel she jumped out and, finding the door locked, seized a chair and smashed the glass door and helped herself to hot-water bags, bandages and anything else that would be useful. . . .

On one of our trips we went out to the Park Emergency Hospital, and at 11 o'clock I found myself in the Pacific Union Club with a cup of coffee and a sandwich. I went out from the club and saw the fire raging on Market Street below Sansome. . . . By 3 o'clock it had got to the Palace

Hotel on the Mission Street side, and by 3:30 it was well on fire.

I then walked home, and at that time the streets leading to Lafayette Square and the Presidio were filled with people dragging trunks and valises along, trying to find a place of safety. As night came on the fire made it as light as day, and I could read without other light in any part of the house. . . . I felt tired and went to bed at 11 P.M. and slept until 2:40 A.M. I got up then and went downtown again to see what the situation was. From Pine and Leavenworth I could see that the fire was burning along O'Farrell from Jones to Mason and on the east side of Mason Street. The St. Francis Hotel was on fire. From California and Mason I could see that Old St. Mary's Church and Grace Cathedral were on fire. I returned home along California Street and Van Ness Avenue. Both streets were thronged with men, women, and children—some with bundles, packages, and baby-carriages; but the usual method was to drag a trunk, which made a harsh, scraping noise on the sidewalk. I overtook a man dragging a trunk with a valise on top which kept falling off. As I approached him I took the valise in one hand and with the other helped him drag the heavy trunk. As we were strangers, I am sure that he at first took me for a thief, but from his manner later on I think he changed his mind, for when I left him after a few blocks he was hearty in his thanks.

While passing the Knickerbocker Hotel on Van Ness Avenue, I saw a party of ladies and elderly gentlemen. They were very much excited and were hesitating about returning to their rooms for their personal effects. I stopped and assured them that they had plenty of time to go and return. I think I succeeded in quieting them, at least for a time. . . .

At 11 A.M. on Thursday [April 19] from my window I

could see blazes on Jones Street at Clay, and southerly as far as Sutter and Leavenworth. At noon the flames were continuous from Clay, on Jones, to California. At 2:30 it was approaching Van Ness at Hyde and Washington and reaching south as far as Sutter and Van Ness. I was in my front room watching with my field-glass as house after house took fire. . . . I saw many pigeons flying wildly about, seeking some place of safety.

At 3 o'clock the soldiers drove the people north on Van Ness and west up Franklin Street, saying they were going to dynamite the east side of Van Ness. From my window I watched the movements of the fire-fighters and dynamiters. They first set fire to every house on the east side of Van Ness Avenue between Washington and Bush streets, and by 3:30 nearly every one was on fire. Their method was this: A soldier would, with a vessel like a fruit-dish in his hand containing some inflammable stuff, enter the house, climb to the second floor, go to the front window, open it, pull down the shade and curtain, and set fire to the contents of his dish. In a short time the shades and curtain would be in a blaze. When the fire started slowly, to give it a draught they would throw bricks and stones up to the windows to break the glass. From 4 to 4:30 St. Luke's and the Presbyterian churches and all the houses from Bush to Washington were on fire. At about this time they began dynamiting. This was called back-firing, and as the line of fire was at Polk Street, the idea was to meet the flames and not allow them to cross Van Ness Avenue.

The explosions of dynamite were felt fearfully in my house; those within two blocks would jar and shake the house violently, breaking the windows, and at the same time setting off the burglar alarm. As the windows would break they tore the shades and curtains, covering the floor with glass, and cracking the walls.

For two full days the fire raged uncontrolled. In his memoir, Stetson stated that his house was several times in imminent danger of destruction both by the flames and at the hands of the dynamiters. Eventually, however, the fire burned itself out, and on the morning of the 21st he again visited the downtown area.

The streets in many places [his account continues] were filled with debris—in some places on Kearny and Montgomery streets to the depth of four feet in the middle of the street and much greater depth on the sidewalks. I found it then, and ever since, very difficult to locate myself when wandering in the ruins, as all the old landmarks were gone and the only guide often was a prominent ruin in the distance.

The water supply in our house was gone, as was also the gas and electric light. The only light we could use was candle-light, and that only until 9 P.M. The city authorities issued an order that no fires could be built in any house until the chimneys were fully rebuilt and inspected by an officer. The water we used was brought by my son in a washboiler in his automobile. He got it out near the Park. People all cooked in improvised kitchens made in the street. Our door-bell was rung several evenings, and we were ordered to "put out that light." . . .

The afternoon after the fire had exhausted itself the atmosphere was hot, the great beds of coals gave heat and glowed brightly at night. The front of my house was blistered and blackened by the intense heat. The paint melted in a peculiar way, and over two of the windows it hung like drapery. The telegraph and telephone wires made a network on every street, and for more than two weeks I carried in my pocket a pair of wire cutters, which I had often occasion to use.

On May 3rd we were able to buy food. Up to that time we obtained what we needed from the Relief Committee, such as canned meats, potatoes, coffee, crackers, etc. On May 1 I found my safe in the ruins and everything in it that was inflammable was burned to a coal. . . .

Being busy in the work of restoration, I forgot what a terrible calamity had befallen the city and the people, but I sometimes realize it, and it comes like a shock. I find that people lost the power of keeping time and dates, and if I had not made notes at the time I would be unable to recollect the events of these three days with any degree of accuracy.

The feeding of 300,000 people suddenly made destitute is a matter of great difficulty, but it has been done. . . . We got water in the house on the 1st of May, gas on the 5th of June, and cooked in the street until the 8th of May.


## iv

THE 1906 catastrophe profoundly shocked the nation and brought forth many tributes to the beauty and charm of the city that fire and earthquake had reduced to rubble. In the nature of things, nearly all that was written on the subject has long since been forgotten and today remains buried in the files of the newspapers and magazines where it appeared. There are, however, two exceptions to that rule. Both were the work of journalists who, writing under pressure while the fires were still burning, evoked the spirit of the old city with so much eloquence and discernment that San Franciscans have remembered them—and frequently quoted from them— ever since.

These are "The City That Was" and "The City That Has Fallen." The first is by Will Irwin, a San Franciscan then on the staff of the New York *Sun;* the second by William Marion Reedy, owner and editor of the then well-known St. Louis weekly, *Reedy's Mirror.*

Reedy's story, which appeared in the issue of April 26, 1906, has one point of uncommon interest: at the time he wrote it, the author had never seen the city he described so eloquently. Not until fourteen years later, during the Democratic National Convention of 1920, did Reedy first visit San Francisco, and it was there, on January 28, of that year, that he died. When copies of his 1906 tribute reached the city, the citizens—already busy with plans to rebuild on a new and grander scale—took it to their hearts. So well did it express their own feelings that they forgave him even having referred to their city not by its true name but as "Frisco."

Something of the nature of Reedy's tribute may be gained from these passages:

It was a little of Paris, of Rome, of Pekin. It was a town of temperament in which lightsomeness blent with a native beauty sense winds of the sea came in and met with winds of the desert. The fog, mostly pearl-gray but often sun-tinged to opaline, hung over the town and gave it rare values to the esuriently artistic eye. . . . The climate made for love making. The wine and fruits and flowers, and the mysterious sea mists and the wonderful odors of the East and West made life a picture, a poem. The world turned to Frisco, to California, as it turned in earlier years to Rome and Florence and Italy. There the singer, the sculptor, the painter, the novelist, sought the sky and air that freshened heart and fecundated mind. It chained the sensitive of soul, and it immuted the merely sensual lovers of luxury. Always and ever about one was the conjugating of the verb "enjoy"—not always conjugally.

It was opulent and of a mighty oriency of brightness, but with darkness to heighten the picture. The slums were the most impenetrable "in all the lands of Christensie." Its crimes surpassed, in quality of shudder, the crimes of other places. Its citizens gave to the city more gracefully than other citizens of other towns gave to them. . . .

A strong sense of beauty somehow clung to the mental image of the town, even to one who, as I, had never seen the place, its glamour always had a sort of hidden foreboding in it. There was ever the same suggestion of lethal malefic genius behind all the story that was told of its curiously *morbidezza*, amorousness of the day, and its childlike desire to forget the night. It was too far, as it sometimes seemed, and in the glory in which it lay and in which it lingered in thought, there seemed something of a light that held a pale tone of bale black for all its bliss. Its people loved it with that intensity with which we love what we are likely to lose.

There was a great gap in the history of American life, letters and character and achievement with Frisco's story omitted. . . .

Will Frisco stay fallen? A new Frisco shall up—rear itself and laugh at the sea, and when old Atlas again shifts the globe a little on his shoulders—it will laugh and dance and fight and drink and make love as before and be proud that among its other claims to greatness is that of having met and conquered a calamity that stilled and chilled the whole world's heart for a day. Before the crash and flame, Frisco was beginning to protest at being called anything but San Francisco. Yet Frisco clung, it held some winking, sly hint of frisky. Even the great black headlines over the evil news used the diminutive abbreviation like a touch of light in the cloud, a sort of fresh, smiling rose on the pall, speaking of resurrection. . . .

Vale et Ave Frisco the beautiful, the glad, the strong, the stricken, the invincible. Down with her went our hearts. Up with her go our souls. The country's hope and faith and love are more fired than the shuddering earth and all these that in the tear brightened eyes of Frisco looking out from the wreck over the Pacific where lies the future big with mighty fates for her beyond all prophecy.

## V

WILL IRWIN's memoir was written, as was that of the St. Louis editor, while the nation was still shocked at the suddenness and magnitude of the disaster. Unlike his fellow journalist, however, Irwin wrote from personal knowledge of the old San Francisco, a knowledge gained while he was a student at Stanford University and during several years as a reporter for the *Evening Bulletin*, Fremont Older's crusading newspaper. Later he had moved to New York and joined the staff of the *Sun*, and it was in that paper that his story appeared, in the issue for April 21. Later that year an expanded version was published in a little book called *The City That Was*.

Irwin's tribute opens with a quotation from Willie Britt, a California boxer of the day, who was then in New York:

"I'd rather," said Britt, "be a busted lamp post on Battery Street, San Francisco, than the Waldorf-Astoria."

The old San Francisco [wrote Irwin] is dead. The gayest, lightest hearted, and most pleasure loving city of the western continent, and in many ways the most interesting and romantic, is a horde of refugees living among ruins. It may rebuild; it probably will; but those who have known that peculiar city by the Golden Gate, have caught its flavor of the Arabian Nights, feel it can never be the same. It is as though a pretty, frivolous woman has passed through a great tragedy. She survives, but she is sobered and different. If it rises out of the ashes it must be a modern city, much like other cities and without its old atmosphere.

Having told something of the wrecked town's physical setting and of its fogs and bracing winds and brilliant sunsets, he continued:

So much for the strange climate, which invites out of doors and which has played its part in making the character of the people. The externals of the city are . . . just as curious. One usually entered San Francisco by way of the bay. Across its yellow flood, covered with the fleets from the strange seas of the Pacific, San Francisco presented itself in a hill panorama. Probably no other city of the world, excepting perhaps Naples, could be so viewed at first sight. It rose above the passenger, as he reached dockage, in a succession of hill terraces. At one side was Telegraph Hill, the end of the peninsula, a height so abrupt that it had a one hundred and fifty foot sheer cliff on its seaward side. Further along lay Nob Hill, crowned with the Mark Hopkins mansion, which had the effect of a citadel, and in later years by the great, white Fairmont. Further along was Russian Hill, the highest point. Below was the business district, whose low site caused all the trouble.

Except for the modern buildings, the fruit of the last ten years, the town presented at first sight a disreputable appearance. Most of the buildings were low and of wood. In the middle period of the '70's, when a great part of San Francisco was building, the newly-rich perpetrated some atrocious architecture. In that time too everyone put bow windows on his house to catch all the morning sunlight that was coming through the fog; and those little houses, with bow windows and fancy work all down their fronts, were characteristic of the middle class residence districts.

Then the Italians, who tumbled over Telegraph Hill, had built as they listed and with little regard for streets, and their houses hung crazily on the side hill which was little less than a precipice. The Chinese, although they occupied an abandoned business district, had remade their dwellings Chinese fashion, and the Mexicans and Spaniards had added to their houses those little balconies without which life is not life to a Spaniard.

Yet the most characteristic thing after all was the coloring. The sea fog had a trick of painting every exposed object a sea gray which had a tinge of dull green in it. This, under the leaden sky of a San Francisco morning, had a depressing effect on first sight and afterwards became a delight to the eye. For the color was soft, gentle and infinitely attractive in mass.

The hills were steep beyond conception. Where Vallejo Street ran up Russian Hill it progressed for four blocks by regular steps like a flight of stairs. It is unnecessary to say that no teams ever came up this street or any other like it, and the grass grew long among the paving stones until the Italians who live thereabouts took advantage of this herbage to pasture a cow or two. At the end of four blocks, the pavers had given it up and the last stage to the summit was a winding path. On the very top a colony of artists lived in little villas of houses whose windows got the whole panorama of the bay. Luckily for these people, a cable car scaled the hill on the other side, so that it was not much of a climb to home.

With these hills, and with the strangeness of the architecture and with the green-gray tinge over everything, the city fell always into vistas and pictures, a setting for the romance which hung over everything, which had always hung over life in San Francisco since the padres came and gathered the Indians about Mission Dolores.

And it was a city of romance and a gateway to adventure. It opened out on the mysterious Pacific, the untamed ocean; and through the Golden Gate entered China, Japan, the South Sea Islands, Lower California, the west coast of South America, Australia. There was a sprinkling, too, of Alaska and Siberia. From his windows on Russian Hill one saw always something strange and suggestive creeping through the mists of the bay. It would be a South Sea Island brig, bringing in copra, to take out cottons and idols; a Chinese junk after shark's livers; an old whaler, which seemed to drip oil, home from a year of cruising in the Arctic. Even the

tramp windjammers were deep-chested craft, capable of
rounding the Horn or of circumnavigating the globe; and
they came in streaked and picturesque from their long
voyaging.

In the orange colored dawn which always comes through
the mists of that bay, the fishing fleet would crawl in under
triangular lateen sails; for the fishermen of San Francisco
Bay are all Neapolitans who have brought their customs and
sail their lateen rigs stained an orange brown and shaped,
when the wind fills them, like the ear of a horse.

Along the waterfront the people of these craft met. "The
melting pot of the races," Stevenson called it; and this was
always the city of his soul. There were black Gilbert
Islanders, almost indistinguishable from negroes; lighter
Kanakas from Hawaii and Samoa; Lascars in turbans; thick-
set Russian sailors; wild Chinese with unbraided hair; Italian
fishermen in tam o'shanters, loud shirts and blue sashes;
Greeks, Alaska Indians, little bay Spanish-Americans, together with men of all the European races. They came in and
out among the queer craft, to lose themselves in the disreputable, tumble-down, but always mysterious shanties and
small saloons. In the back rooms of these saloons South Sea
Island traders and captains, fresh from the lands of romance,
whaling masters, people who were trying to get up treasure
expeditions, filibusters, Alaskan miners, used to meet and
trade adventures.

There was another element, less picturesque and equally
characteristic, along the waterfront. San Francisco was the
back eddy of European civilization—one end of the world.
The drifters came here and stopped, lingered a while to live
by their wits in a country where living after a fashion has
always been marvellously cheap. These people haunted the

waterfront and the Barbary Coast by night, and lay by day
on the grass on Portsmouth Square. . . .

The Barbary Coast was a loud bit of hell. No one knows
who coined the name. The place was simply three blocks of
solid dance halls, there for the delight of the sailors of the
world. On a fine busy night every door blared loud music
from orchestras, steam pianos and gramaphones, and the
cumulative effect of the sound which reached the street was
chaos and pandemonium. Almost anything might be happen-
ing behind the swinging doors. For a fine and picturesque
bundle of names characteristic of the place, a police story of
three or four years ago is typical. Hell broke out in the Eye
Wink Dance Hall. The trouble was started by a sailor known
as Kanaka Pete, who lived in the What Cheer House, over a
woman known as Iodoform Kate. Kanaka Pete chased the
man he had marked to the Little Silver Dollar, where he
halted and punctured him. The by-product of his gun made
some holes in the front of the Wink Eye, which were proudly
kept as souvenirs, and were probably there until it went out
in the fire. . . .

Until the last decade almost anything except the common-
place and the expected might happen to a man on the waterfront. The cheerful industry of shanghaiing was reduced to a
science. A citizen taking a drink in one of the saloons which
hung out over the water might be dropped through the floor
into a boat, or he might drink with a stranger and wake up in
the forecastle of a whaler bound for the Arctic. . . . Kearny
Street, a wilder and stranger Bowery, was the main thorough-
fare of these people. An exiled Californian, mourning over
the city of his heart, has said:

In half an hour of Kearny Street I could raise a dozen men
for any wild adventure, from pulling down a statue to searching for the Cocos Island treasure." This is hardly an exag-

geration. It was the Rialto of the desperate, Street of the Adventurers. . . .

The foreign quarters are worth an article in themselves. Chief of these was, of course, Chinatown, of which everyone has heard who ever heard of San Francisco. A district six blocks long and two wide, housed 30,000 Chinese when the quarter was full. The dwellings were old business blocks of the early days; but the Chinese had added to them, had rebuilt them, had run out their own balconies and entrances, and had given the quarter that feeling of huddled irregularity which makes all Chinese-built dwellings fall naturally into pictures. Not only this; they had burrowed to the depth of a story or two under the ground, and through this ran passages in which the Chinese transacted their dark and devious affairs—as the smuggling of opium, the traffic in slave girls and the settlement of their difficulties. . . .

On the slopes of Telegraph Hill dwelt the Mexicans and Spanish, in low houses, which they transformed by balconies into a semblance of Spain. Above, and streaming over the hill, were the Italians. The tenement quarter of San Francisco shone by contrast with those of Chicago and New York, for while these people lived in old and humble houses they had room to breathe and an eminence for light and air. Their shanties clung to the side of the hill or hung on the very edge of the precipice overlooking the bay, on the verge of which a wall kept their babies from falling. The effect was picturesque, and this hill was the delight of painters. It was more like Italy than anything in the Italian quarter of New York and Chicago—the very climate and surroundings, the wine country close at hand, the bay for their lateen boats, helped them. . . .

Many years ago someone set up at the summit of this peak [Lone Mountain] a sixty foot cross of timber. . . . It has risen for fifty years above the gay, luxuriant and lovable city, in full view from every valley. It stands tonight, above the desolation of ruins.

The bonny, merry city—the good, gray city—O that one who has mingled the wine of her bounding life with the wine of his youth should live to write the obituary of Old San Francisco!

Will Irwin ended his paean with these words, and they seem a fitting note on which to bring to a close this gathering of tributes by many hands and over many years to the capricious, volatile, sometimes obstreperous but ever fascinating City by the Golden Gate.

# Acknowledgments and Bibliography

To compile an anthology of writings about a city having a history as varied and colorful as that of San Francisco could hardly fail to be a congenial task under any circumstances, but in this instance it has been made much easier by the interest and cooperation of a numerous group of individuals and institutions. For suggestions as to what to include, or for help in locating certain hard-to-find items, thanks are due to James deT. Abajian, Terry Bender, Richard H. Dillon, Bernice Dittli, Mervyn Eidenmuller, Helen Giffen, George P. Hammond, Robert Haynes, Harold Holmes, Warren Howell, John A. Hussey, David Magee, and Irene Simpson; among institutions, to the Bancroft Library, Berkeley, the San Francisco Public Library, The California Historical Society, The Society of California Pioneers, The Book Club of California, the Wells Fargo Museum, all of San Francisco.

For permission to use excerpts from books still in copyright grateful acknowledgment is made to the following: Columbia University Press (J. Goldsborough Bruff's *Journals and Drawings*); B. W. Huebsch (Will Irwin's *The City That Was*); Doubleday & Company, Inc. (Harriet Lane Levy's *920 O'Farrell Street;* from *920 O'Farrell Street* by Harriet Lane Levy. Copyright 1947 by Harriet Lane Levy. Reprinted by permission of Doubleday & Company, Inc.) Houghton Mifflin Company (Amelia Ransome Neville's *The Fantastic City*), and Paul Elder (Clarence E. Edwords' *Bohemian San Francisco*).

# 286 THIS WAS SAN FRANCISCO

Following is a list of the books, pamphlets, newspapers and magazines from which material has been quoted:

*Alta California* (newspaper), San Francisco.

Anon. *The Voyage of the Racoon: A "Secret" Journal of a Visit to Oregon, California and Hawaii, 1813–1814.* San Francisco: The Book Club of California, 1958.

Anon. *The Laws of San Francisco, 1847.* San Marino: The Huntington Library, 1947.

Anon. "Filings from an Old Saw," *The Golden Era* (weekly), San Francisco, 1852.

BANCROFT, HUBERT H. *A History of California.* San Francisco: The History Company, 1886–1890.

———. *California Inter Pocula.* San Francisco: The History Company, 1888.

BEECHEY, FREDERICK WILLIAM. *Narrative of a Voyage to the Pacific . . .* London: Sampson Low & Son, 1856.

BIERCE, AMBROSE. *Selections from Prattle.* San Francisco: The Book Club of California, 1936.

BROWN, JOHN HENRY. *Reminiscences and Incidents of Early Days of San Francisco.* San Francisco: The Grabhorn Press, 1933.

BRUFF, J. GOLDSBOROUGH. *The Journals and Drawings of J. Goldsborough Bruff.* New York: Columbia University Press, 1944.

BURGESS, GELETT. *Bayside Bohemia.* San Francisco: The Book Club of California, 1954.

*Californian* (newspaper), Monterey and San Francisco.

*Call-Chronicle-Examiner* (newspaper), San Francisco, April 19, 1906.

CHAMISSO, ADELBERT VON. *A Sojourn at San Francisco Bay in 1816.* San Francisco: The Book Club of California, 1936.

COFFIN, GEORGE B.. *Pioneer Voyage to California and around the World, 1849–1852.* Chicago: Gorham B. Coffin, 1908.

COLEMAN, WILLIAM T. "San Francisco Vigilance Committees," *The Century Magazine,* New York, November, 1891.

*Daily News* (newspaper), San Francisco, April 18, 1906.

DANA, RICHARD HENRY. *Two Years before the Mast*. New York: Harper & Brothers, 1840.

DERBY, GEORGE H. *Phoenixiana*. New York: D. Appleton & Company, 1856.

EDWARDS, PHILIP LEGET. *The Diary of Philip Leget Edwards* . . . San Francisco: The Grabhorn Press, 1932.

EDWORDS, CLARENCE E. *Bohemian San Francisco*. San Francisco: Paul Elder & Company, 1914.

*Evening Bulletin* (newspaper), San Francisco.

FARNHAM, ELIZA W. *California, In-doors and Out*. New York: Dix, Edwards & Company, 1856.

FRÉMONT, JESSIE BENTON. *A Year of American Travel*. San Francisco: The Book Club of California, 1960.

GREGORY, JOSEPH W. *Gregory's Guide for California Travellers* . . . New York: Nefis & Cornish, 1850.

HITTELL, JOHN S. *A History of the City of San Francisco*. San Francisco: A. L. Bancroft & Company, 1878.

IRWIN, WILL. *The City That Was*. New York: W. B. Huebsch, 1906.

KIPLING, RUDYARD. *Rudyard Kipling's Letters from San Francisco*. San Francisco: The Colt Press, 1949.

KOTZEBUE, OTTO VON. *A Voyage of Discovery into the South Seas and Beering's Straits* . . . London, 1831.

LETTS, J. M. *California Illustrated*. New York: R. T. Young, 1853.

LEVISON, J. B. *Memories for My Family*. San Francisco: Privately printed, 1933.

LEVY, HARRIET LANE. *920 O'Farrell Street*. New York: Doubleday & Company, 1947.

MARRYAT, FRANK. *Mountains and Molehills*. New York: Harper & Brothers, 1855.

MEYERS, WILLIAM H. *Journal of a Cruise to California and the Sandwich Islands* . . . San Francisco: The Book Club of California, 1955.

NEVILLE, AMELIA RANSOME. *The Fantastic City*. Boston: Houghton Mifflin Company, 1932.

PALOU, FRANCISCO. *Historical Memoirs of New California in 1776.* San Francisco: The California Historical Society, 1874.

PRIETO, GUILLERMO. *San Francisco in the Seventies.* San Francisco: John Henry Nash, 1938.

RAE, W. F. *Westward by Rail.* London: Longmans, Green & Company, 1871.

REEDY, WILLIAM MARION. *The City That Has Fallen.* San Francisco: The Book Club of California, 1933.

ROSALES, VICENTE PÉREZ. *California Adventure.* San Francisco: The Book Club of California, 1947.

RUSSAILH, ALBERT BENARD DE. *Last Adventure.* San Francisco: The Westgate Press, 1931.

SOULE, FRANK; GIHON, JOHN H., and NESBET, JAMES. *The Annals of San Francisco.* New York: D. Appleton & Company, 1855.

STETSON, JAMES B. *San Francisco during the Eventful Days of April, 1906.* San Francisco: Privately printed, 1906.

STODDARD, CHARLES WARREN. *In the Footprints of the Padres.* San Francisco: A. M. Robertson, 1902.

TAYLOR, BAYARD. *Eldorado; or, Adventures in the Path of Empire.* London: Richard Bentley, 1850.

TROLLOPE, ANTHONY. *A Letter from Anthony Trollope Describing a Visit to California in 1875.* San Francisco: The Colt Press, 1956.

WIERZBICKI, F. P. *California as It Is and as It May Be.* San Francisco: The Grabhorn Press, 1933.

WILLIAMS, SAMUEL. "The City of the Golden Gate," *Scribner's Monthly,* New York, July, 1875.

# Index

289